W9-AQP-791

Breeds
And
Half-Breeds

E
71
.S67
1969

Breeds And Half-Breeds

GORDON SPECK

Clarkson N. Potter, Inc./Publisher **NEW YORK**

DISTRIBUTED BY CROWN PUBLISHERS, INC.

193822

For

LILLIAN

Copyright © 1969, by Gordon Speck
Library of Congress Catalog Card Number: 69-11686
Printed in the United States of America
Published simultaneously in Canada by
General Publishing Company Limited
First Edition

ACKNOWLEDGMENTS

MY very great debt to the scholars who have written the standard works on frontier America is acknowledged, but not repaid, by the citations to their works.

There remain the many persons on both sides of the Atlantic who granted access to or themselves searched their archives and libraries for items of interest or verification of details; who drew upon their reserves of knowledge to suggest other possible sources of information; who knew where copies of old maps could be found and studied, and where detailed modern ones could be bought at nominal prices; who looked for evidence which is not extant, and by their diligence established its nonexistence.

For all this I am in debt. In addition, I wish to thank the Misses Phoebe Harris, Olga Gatz, and Wanda Brockman and their staffs of the Seattle Public Library; and Mesdames William De Munbrum, Betty Ballasch, and Estrella Hill; and Mr. John Ott, Sno-Isle Regional Library, Edmonds, for their interest in this volume and for facilitating the interlibrary loans which saved me much expensive travel.

GORDON SPECK

Edmonds, Washington

CONTENTS

PART III. RIVER TRADERS AND MOUNTAIN MEN 149

PART IV. MOUNTAIN MAN STORYTELLER 245

PROLOGUE

THE stories that follow tell of the obscure men and (sometimes) women whose knowledge, bravery, and devotion to their masters made possible the history-book heroes of the New World frontier: a frontier which would have been infinitely more difficult to conquer, given that time and those men, had the American natives been uniformly hostile and used their superb woodcraft and ability for deceit to push the invaders back into the sea.

For make no mistake; it would have taken more than a few Spanish dons, adventurous Frenchmen, or stubborn Englishmen herding their half-starved, diseased, and often terrified conscripts into the fever swamps of the Everglades or the ice of Hudson Bay to seize this land. This realm was not to be taken by untrained, superstition-plagued "soldiers" shanghied on the quays of London and Lisbon. The conquerors could succeed only if helped by the breeds and, later, the half-breeds whose destiny caused them to further the eventual destruction of their own way of life.

And if some of the expeditions failed because storm and disease and ignorance outfought the lust for gold, others crossed the swamps, found the passes, paddled the beaver streams, and created an empire with the help of a friendly Indian or half-breed.

It is obvious that expeditions into unknown lands, if they are to be successful, must have three types of leaders: the dreamers; the field generals who execute the dream; and the guides and interpreters who know the sources of food, fire, and water, know the local dangers and how to avoid them, know friend from enemy and how to cultivate the one and appease the other, know when to acquiesce to the whims of the generals and when to assert the authority bred of superior knowledge. Every North American expedition tried to have such individuals attached to it.

And if the commanders sometimes rejected the advice of their interpreters and these in turn sometimes made foolish mistakes that endangered the major objectives, that did not diminish their importance.

American Indians were generally unpredictable and no white man ever knew what to expect from them, except that it would be illogical from his point of view. As the years went by and the white man moved deeper and deeper into the continent, the interpreter-guides became more important. Often part-Indian, always longtime associates with the natives, and generally married to one or more tribeswomen, they could think in terms of Indian psychology. Thus, they were constantly called upon to make contact with the tribes and assess their temper, and they rarely refused. About their only concession to the dangers involved was the caution with which they approached their tasks.

These wilderness familiars were cast in many molds: they were escaped Negro slaves, Indian chiefs, half-breeds, or white expatriates who found civilization too dull or hoped the frontier would shield them from the consequences of illegal acts.

Those who were Indian were distinguished only by their friendship for the interloping white man. They retained the mores and philosophies of their birth and merely added a new loyalty, an outright betrayal of which was so rare that commanders seldom bothered to consider its possibility.

Those who were half-breeds were devoted, basically, to both their progenitors, a fact which sometimes compelled them to make difficult choices. But here, too, betrayal of the white man never went beyond a diversion of his goods to a market he had not intended. He did not need to fear for his life.

The expatriates were less predictable. It would be the rankest hypocrisy to pretend they were, in general, respectable and God-fearing men; to the contrary, they were often well outside the pale and rarely feared anything—certainly not God. As a visual token of their disdain for the society they had abandoned, they often adopted Indian dress, almost invariably took Indian wives, and within a few short years became more Indian than white. But even these were seldom accused of complete betrayal of their employer's interests.

Whatever their origin or diet or mode of dress or thought, the interpreter-guides were a lusty and mighty breed. And looming as a proud and commanding backdrop before which they could perform their feats of tongue and trail were eventually some 1,200 to 1,500 French-Indian voyageurs, *[1] or boatmen, and a smaller number of mountain men trappers—both peculiar to the American scene, unique in the history of man. "They had no forerunners, and their like can never again appear on earth."[2]

There was no impassable barrier between the interpreter-guide and his more lowly companions, the voyageur and the mountain man. Ability and character could raise one up. Sloth or bad faith could push one down. Every voyageur or mountain man was a potential interpreter-guide.

But whatever their station, they were the mavericks, the heretics, of their time. They hated the very smell of. civilization, save for the one night when they whooped into its glitter and vice to squander a year's earnings in a single orgy.

At the same time there were differences between the voyageur and the mountain man. Four-fifths of the voyageurs were French-Indian Creoles, whereas the mountain men were much less frequently of mixed blood. Each laughed at the mores and taboos of organized society but each had an inflexible code of his own.

Voyageurs, in general, were hated or feared by both Church and State. The Church was antagonistic toward them because a simple ritual at some shrine dedicated to Saint Anne, patron saint of the boatmen, satisfied their spiritual desires—a ritual invariably followed by a drunken debauch that put to shame the sins of Rome; and because "Our missions are reduced to such extremity that we can no longer maintain them against the infinity of disorder, brutality, violence, injustice, impiety, impurity, insolence, scorn and insult which the deplorable and infamous traffic in brandy has spread universally among the indians of these parts."[3]

---

* The source notes will be found on pages 321–349.

The voyageurs were feared by the State because, for all their supposed timidity, they defied the death penalty for trading without a license, and by their illegal commerce upset the "licensed monopoly" system which was universal on the frontier. Their ability to smuggle into or out of a restricted zone could be matched only by the Laffite pirates at New Orleans.

Furthermore, they gloried in flaunting the law as such—any law, all law, it mattered not. Sometimes this disrespect led to collusion with a venal colonial officer for their mutual profit; other times it led to armed revolt. In either case it interfered with the laws of "divinely ordained kings."

The voyageur was essentially an adventurer who had no real hope of material ease. He knew that a chunk of dog salted with ashes or a bowl of corn mush laced with lard, followed by a pipe of cheap tobacco for dessert, might be his sole fare for a thousand miles, and that his only shelter would be the sky or his canoe tipped sideways against sun or blizzard; he expected that someday a knife would flash or a tomahawk scream and write finis to his little world.[4]

Few voyageurs slept under headstones.

The voyageur, generally a Canadian, was a contrary aggregate. His specialty was the river, but he could cover twenty-five or thirty miles a day on snowshoes. He seldom knew how to swim but usually chose the risk of white water to the safety of portaging around it. He often carried no gun, despite constant danger, and fighting was his favorite sport. He was forever boasting, "I am a man of the North," to distinguish himself from his warm-climate, "bread-eating" brother of the southern rivers. Yet he passively accepted a wage scale, hours of labor, and a diet commonly associated with peonage.

He sang while he paddled or poled, danced with his fellows, was kind-hearted to those he knew—and savagely brutal to dumb animals.

The voyageur traveled light. Moccasins and rough leggings, a blanket coat, a woolen cap, a plaid cotton shirt, and cloth or leather trousers, all held together with a fabric belt from which hung a murderous knife, a tobacco pouch, firing materials, and such odd-ments as his fancy dictated—these plus a blanket or animal hide and a crude packsack to hold his spare shirt constituted his worldly goods. With them he challenged a continent.

James P. Beckwourth, the mulatto Crow chief, said, "When

Canadians are fairly broken in and have become familiar with Indian character, they make the best of Indian fighters, especially when put to it in defense of their own lives. They become superior trappers too, . . . with a capacity to endure the extremest hardships and privations, and to endure starvation for an incredibly long period."[5] When worse came to worst and positive death by starvation loomed, the voyageur would barter his woman or clothes for a handful of dried meat.[6]

But "Jean Baptiste will not think, he is not paid for it; when he has a minute's respite he smokes his pipe, his constant companion and all goes well; he will go through hardships, but requires a full belly, at least once a day, good Tobacco to smoke, a warm Blanket, and a kind Master who will take his share of hard times and be the first in danger . . . ," said David Thompson.[7]

And if the journalists differ about the voyageur, they but emphasize his contrary nature.

He was ignorant as well as illiterate; often, as an individual, faint-hearted, but as one of a group he was willing to assume staggering risks; profane and lewd, he was scorned as a coward and "pork-eater," yet was unsurpassed on river or portage.

Ten voyageurs could paddle a 500-pound 36-foot freight canoe capable of carrying five tons of cargo for twenty hours on a scant breakfast, no lunch, and a mush-and-lard supper.[8] Two could carry a 30-foot craft across a portage that "six Americans could not. . . ."[9] They could cordelle a 50-foot pirogue against the Missouri current and average twenty miles a day on hardtack and "high wine," the raw grain alcohol of the Indian trade.[10]

Tomorrow there might be a fat dog or a buffalo hump. Then they could squat on their haunches and gorge. A carpenter, working on the first post on the Minnesota River, said, "there was not one of us who did not eat more than ten pounds of it [buffalo] daily and drink four bowls of the broth."[11]

In theory, the voyageur was rationed eight pounds of meat per day —but often only in theory. Most days he had to settle for mush and lard. However, given the chance, he could manage twice the supposed ration. There was an old saying that two voyageurs could eat a whole side of buffalo at one time,[12] and if that amount was distorted to provide a more colorful tale, nevertheless a voyageur or mountain man could—and often did—eat at a single sitting several times the amount served an entire family in our day.

But then, they did several times the work.

"A man in the Canadian Service* who cannot carry two packs of eighty Lbs. each one & an half Leagues [four to five miles] Losses his trip that is his wages. But time & Practice would make it easy. . . ."[13]

Actually, river freight was more commonly packed in ninety-pound "pieces," and a voyageur had to portage his minimum of two pieces to remain on the payroll. But he considered it no hardship. A really good man could handle six pieces, a total of 540 pounds.[14]

And then there was the case of the young voyageur who asked permission of the commander one morning up on the Red River to spend the day in the latter's private quarters because of illness. This was a most unusual request, and questioning disclosed a "helpless, abandoned wretch, who was not of the sex I had supposed, but an . . . Orkney girl, pregnant, and actually in child birth . . . she opened her jacket, and displayed a pair of beautiful round, white breasts. . . ."

Before the day was done the young lady gave birth to a strapping boy. She had masqueraded so well she had served without question (except to the father of her child) as a boy at James Bay, at Bandon House on the Assiniboine River, and at Pembina, north of the Dakotas.[15]

There was just no predicting what a voyageur would do next!

Not all voyageurs were half-breeds, malcontents, or rebels against established order. There were notable exceptions,† but the story the orthodox belongs in another place.

As suggested, the voyageur and mountain man belonged to different clans. They had the same loves and hates and wore the same clothes, with due allowance for local supplies and personal tastes, but where the voyageur was preponderantly half-breed the mountain man, of whom there were never more than one or two hundred really important ones, was more likely to be an expatriate. While the voyageur was happiest in close association with his fellows on the river or charging joyously into town in search of fun, the mountain man was

---

* "Canadian Service" has no significance. Voyageurs worked the rivers from New Orleans to Great Slave Lake and beyond.

† Jean Nicolet came to Canada with Champlain, explored westward into the Wisconsin area, and laid the groundwork for Nicholas Perrot, who in turn became an authority on Wisconsin Indians, French commandant at Green Bay, and, on retirement to lower Canada, a great interpreter for a long list of important clients.

an individualist who thrived on solitude and preferred to risk life and fortune largely unassisted.

The voyageur was an efficient explorer when accompanied by his companions and led by a good commander, but the mountain man needed no such support. He had no particular objections to companions or commanders within what he thought to be reasonable limits. He just didn't care. Completely fearless, with a gigantic ego, he would go off day or night, winter or summer, as long as the excursion promised wealth.

Onto the belt holding *his* nondescript garments together the mountain man hooked a box of beaver bait, a tobacco pouch, flint and tinder, and his hatchet—a blade not always used to split kindling, for a mountain man could scalp as well as any Sioux.

Except when bankrupt in both cash and credit, the mountain man owned an animal, usually a horse, sometimes a mule or burro, and on rare occasions a draft dog. His animal was a many-purpose beast. It was ridden when possible, and it carried a saddle, half a dozen beaver traps, trade goods, a change of clothes, a rifle boot, and the pelts. If Indians attacked, the animal was invariably used as a breastwork, alive or dead. Or if the choice became necessary, the load was cached and the beast was killed for food, and the mountain man proceeded on foot.

And so it was the Indians, the half-breed voyageurs, and the mountain men who as interpreter-guides led the history book heroes across America for three exciting centuries.

Long before government and law got around to such official "exploring" parties as Zebulon Pike's, John C. Frémont's, or Charles Wilkes's, the interpreter-guides had solved the major mysteries of the New World. They spoke the Indian tongues, were masters of their sign language,* could read their smokes, had hunted their valleys, crossed their passes, and had at least one tribal wife somewhere between the Missouri and California, between New Orleans and Hudson Bay.

---

* Indian members of the fraternity could "hold conferences for several hours, upon different subjects, during the whole of which time not a single word is pronounced upon either side, and still they appear to comprehend each other perfectly well . . . ," said Alexander Henry the younger (Elliot Coues, *New Light on the Early History of the Greater Northwest*, New York, Francis P. Harper, 1897, I, p. 335).

The interpreter-guides, whether breeds or half-breeds, Christian or savage, were a proud and puissant clique, any discussion of which must bear the onus of repetition. They were a small, highly mobile group not infrequently in the service of more than one master at the same time, and it is often impossible to relate a given episode without encountering an interpreter we have just buried at another scene.

And yet most of them must remain anonymous, for their tribal or baptismal names were often unpronounceable by the men they served, and these in turn were equally often too illiterate to leave a record or too thoughtless to give credit where due.

Who they are, whence they come or whither they go, their names even, except such as they choose to adopt or which may be given them, are all questions which none but themselves can answer. As their usefulness . . . depends not upon the unravelling of either of these mysteries, but little thought is bestowed upon them. Do you know the country thoroughly, and can you speak any of the Indian languages, constitute the only examination. . . .

They are almost invariably men of very superior judgement or common sense, with education better than that of the average frontiersman. Their most striking characteristics are love of adventure, a natural and cultivated knowledge of the country without recourse to maps . . . and an intimate acquaintance with all the habits and customs of the [Indians].

So wrote General Custer of his Army guides and scouts during the Indian wars in which he lost his life.[16]

Perhaps it is as well that their like, master and servant, cannot come again, for any attempt to re-create their sort could result only in a fleshless travesty. Possibly we can, with some tribute to them, retell their story.

Some few were accorded a measure of journalistic notice.

There was Doña Marina, interpreter-secretary and accomplished mistress of Hernando Cortés.[17] There was Tupia, Tahitian chief priest, who served Captain James Cook as infallible interpreter-guide over thousands of South Pacific miles.[18] There was California Joe, of unrecorded ancestry, who tended General Custer in Western Indian land and then one day, years later, barged into a session of the California legislature thinking it was a meeting of "indian peace commissioners" because most "of them had bald heads."[19] There was Manoah, a French Canadian, who cast aside his civilization, adopted Indian life, married a Mandan girl, lived many "years with these people," and then one day forgot his role and taunted his Indian friends as a lesser breed, and died—from a Mandan bullet.[20] There was Friday, the Arapaho waif who was rescued from the desert by Tom Fitzpatrick, was schooled in St. Louis, and when he was rejected by a pretty white girl, returned to his people and wandered a full lifetime over Arapaho trails as friend and interpreter to any man who asked.[21]

And there were many more—obscure, unnamed, forgotten—but without whose services there could have been no New World frontier as we know it.

It is the purpose of these pages, however, to offer tribute to a selected few who rose above the mainstream and left a legible mark. Few if any of them were better guides, more accomplished interpreters, or sincerer friends of the white man than the Chipewyan chief who opens our book: Matonabbee, who helped Samuel Hearne prove that no waterway bisects our continent and thus laid to rest one of the two or three greatest myths in history.

Breeds
And
Half-Breeds

Breeds
And
Half-Breeds

PART I

MATONABBEE
AND THE MYTH OF ANIAN

ONE school of novelists and historians maintains that early New World heroes were gross entrepreneurs bent on gouging a fortune from Eldorado without respect for God or fear of man. Another school would have us believe that religious liberty and personal freedom were the mainsprings of our genesis. Such interpretations may be true within their limits, but they leave out of account a third driving force which has shaped our destiny: myths and "such stuff as dreams are made on"—the Gilded Man, the Seven Cities of Cibola, and the Strait of Anian. And the greatest breed associated with such myths was the Chipewyan chief Matonabbee.

THE SEARCH
FOR THE STRAIT OF ANIAN

1500–1772

COLUMBUS had barely returned from his first voyage before there was hatched the myth of the Strait of Anian, or the Northwest Passage, a supposed waterway connecting the Atlantic and Pacific through our continent.

Historians have argued for generations over how the story of Anian got started but have never produced a positive answer. We do not really care. All that matters is the fact that even before Columbus' death there was an almost universal belief that he had done two things: that he had discovered an unknown bit of land jutting off from India, which in those days was more or less a synonym for Asia; and that he and his immediate followers had missed the strait which would bypass this bit of earth and allow an approach to the known parts of the East.

Some of the more eager advocates of this latter belief even dug into Marco Polo's reminiscences and spread the story that the doughty Venetian had mentioned a strait between China and India.

As might be expected, with the lapse of time the Strait of Anian, as the passage was commonly called, did a good deal of changing of place. As long as Europe was convinced that Columbus had landed on an unknown part of India, Anian was associated with the mainland of Asia: it was a province in northeast China; it was a bay off Kamchatka; it separated some islands from the mainland; it separated Columbus' "India" from the mainland. It was, in fact, a geographic term scattered anywhere in northeast Asia where nothing else was located.

However, there were exceptions. Juan de la Cosa's map of the New World in 1500 had a strait below the equator in Central America. But when Balboa crossed Panama in 1513 and arrogantly claimed for Spain all the lands marked by the "South Sea," he forced a new approach to the Anian story. If the land and sea area Columbus had discovered was as narrow as Balboa had just found it to be, it was argued that such a narrow land mass must end shortly and that Anian was almost at hand, even if Balboa had not found it.

And so, men and ships fought farther and farther south until, thirty years after Columbus, Magellan clawed his way between Tierra del Fuego and the mainland. In so doing he proved that South America was of continental size; the "South Sea" was a body of water larger than any ever before known to man; and, what at the moment was more important, there was no strait between Balboa's point of exit on the Pacific and Tierra del Fuego.

That information had cost a staggering price. Magellan left home with five ships and 237 men. A single ship and 18 men returned, of which Magellan was not one.

If Anian was not south of Balboa's route, it must be north; and as the maps poured from the cartographers' pens, more sovereigns gave their millions and more men offered their lives in the fruitless search.

The fate of John Cabot and his crew is moot; Cortés sent two of his captains and went himself; Jacques Cartier thought the St. Lawrence might well be the "Passage to Cataia"; Cabrillo and Ferrelo searched from Mexico to California, and Cabrillo died on the return trip in 1542; the swaggering Sir Francis Drake kept a sharp eye out for Anian as he pillaged the Pacific in 1577; Sir Humphrey Gilbert lost his ship, his men, and his own life on his second search for Anian in 1583.

Sebastián Vizcaíno fighting Pacific storms in 1603, John Smith rescued by Pocahontas, Henry Hudson set adrift by a mutinous crew, Jens Munk discovering the mouth of the Churchill River in Hudson Bay, Marquette and Jolliet paddling softly down the Mississippi, Radisson and Groseilliers laying the foundations for the Hudson's Bay Company—all these believed in and were searching for the Strait of Anian.

Samuel Pepys took great pride in his library of "voyages" describing the strait, and even the redoubtable Ben Franklin helped Charles

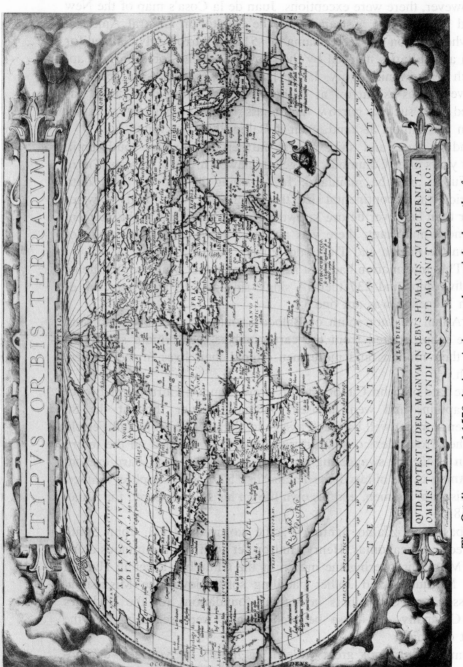

The Ortelius map of 1570 depicts Anian on the mainland south of a mythical strait and four polar islands. *Courtesy Library of Congress.*

Swaine raise £1,300, get a license from Governor Ogle of Maryland, outfit the *Argo,* and see it "gone for the northwest passage" in 1753.

Of all the voyagers who risked and lost their lives in the search for Anian, few were more tragic than the expeditions of Jens Munk and Henry Hudson. Munk's story is relevant to our present tale because he discovered the mouth of the Churchill River in Hudson Bay and was the first white man to attempt to open the frozen doors leading to the great Barren Grounds.

Jens Munk was a Dane who had seen extensive service throughout northern European waters. He had visited Iceland, had tried twice to reach Novaya Zemlya, and had attempted the Northeast Passage; he had fought the Swedes and North Sea pirates, and had been foreign representative for his government. Munk was about to sail for India when his orders were changed and he was sent to Hudson Bay with two ships and sixty-four men to seek Anian.

Without mishap Munk discovered the mouth of the Churchill River and elected to winter there. It was December of 1619. The ice was four feet thick by the time the boats were pulled ashore and shored against the winter. Out in the Bay, the gales were already jamming the ice into gigantic piles forty fathoms thick,[1] but Munk had seen many an iceberg and gave the weather no thought. Firewood could be cut a little way up the river, he had plenty of wine and salt meat, and the winter promised to be no more exciting than many he had spent in his home waters.

Then Jens Munk learned what the Hudson Bay North could do. A week after Christmas, "we suffered . . . severely from that terrible frost . . . [and the] illness which . . . was very peculiar. . . . all the limbs and joints were drawn together, with great pains in the loins, as if a thousand knives were thrust through them. The body was . . . blue and brown, . . . [and] quite powerless. . . . all the teeth were loose, so that we could not eat any victuals."[2]

Scurvy—the killer which stalked every expedition until men learned that almost any meat was better than salt meat. It was to be a long time before the white man learned what the natives of the North seemed to know by instinct, that raw red meat, uncooked fish, and marrow sucked from a cracked bone would prevent scurvy almost as well as orange juice.

But it was 1619, and up on the Churchill River brave men died;

a shallow grave was chiseled from the frozen earth; and a gunner touched his match to his powder as a final salute to an officer and saw his cannon burst from the frost. Two weeks later Munk begged the ships' surgeon to do something, and that worthy replied that if prayer and God could not help, neither could he.

By mid-February twenty men were dead. A fortnight later there were scarcely enough able-bodied to carry the dead ashore. By the first of April, the corpses lay where they fell, lack of strength and the fearful cold having put an end to burials. The wine lay untouched because no one had the strength to crawl into the holds after it; ship's fittings stoked meager fires; and men died.

Mid-April, and only Munk and four others could sit up.

May 10, eleven men were alive, and all the dead but the two who died on the eleventh and twelfth rotted where they lay.

June: Munk scratched out a simple request that should another sailor one day find his bones, they be given a Christian burial, and "Herewith, goodnight to all the world; and my soul into the hand of God, etc Jens Munk."[3]

June 8: sixty-one men were dead. "As I could not now any more stand the . . . stench from the dead bodies . . . I managed . . . to get out of the berth . . . considering it would not matter where . . . I died. I spent that night on the deck, using the clothes of the dead" for covering.[4]

Then Munk and the last two seamen literally crawled ashore and ate a few spears of grass. Enough life returned for them to catch one small fish, and then enough more to fire one shot at one wild goose.

Six weeks later Jens Munk and two sailors, all who were left of the sixty-four, rigged their sloop and sailed for home.[5]

And if all these had not found Anian, neither had they proved it did not exist. Just as the search entered its last quarter-century, the English Parliament set up a prize of £20,000 for its discovery. Such a fortune added impetus and once more changed the focal point for the search. By 1750 every foot of the Atlantic coast from Tierra del Fuego to Hudson Bay and from the Strait of Magellan to California on the Pacific had been searched.

There was no passage.

Men had tramped laboriously from the Atlantic to the Great Lakes and crossed no strait; they had paddled from Lake Superior to the

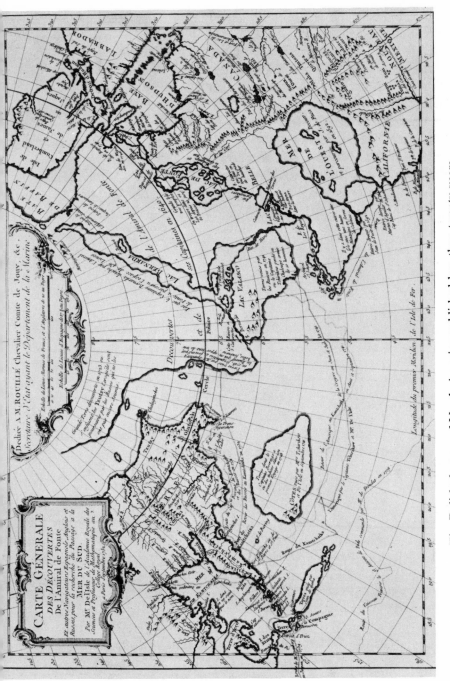

The Delisle fantasy of North America published less than twenty years before the Hearne-Matonabbee expedition. *Courtesy Library of Congress.*

Gulf of Mexico and found no Anian; they had dodged Indians from Lake Superior to Hudson Bay overland and found no Northwest Passage.

Only one segment of the New World could possibly hide the great myth—that quarter of North America west of Hudson Bay to the Pacific and north to the Arctic. If no Anian existed there, then there was no passage through either continent of the New World.

It is one of the mockeries of history that libraries are crammed with the lives of those who failed to find Anian, while the two men who proved its non-existence remain virtually unknown—Samuel Hearne and the Chipewyan chief Matonabbee.

2

THE HUDSON'S BAY COMPANY

1670–1770

THE story of Matonabbee, the Chipewyan, must consider a stone with many sides: the century 1670–1770, the Hudson's Bay Company and Fort Prince of Wales, the Myth of Anian just reviewed, the Coppermine River, and the relationship of Samuel Hearne and Matonabbee.

A full century before these men became historical figures, the English people had rebelled against the sanctimonious laws of Cromwell and had invited Charles II to resume the throne of the Stuarts. Years of Cavalier corruption, royal intrigue, exploitation of natural and human resources, and moral decay followed.

Despite that, the century brought great historic events, good and ill: a Cavalier Parliament passed severe restrictive laws against all "dissenters"; Charles II was succeeded by his ardent Catholic brother, James II; and England plunged into the Revolution of 1688 and wrote the Bill of Rights.

But Britain was more than that. The century made her the leader of world culture. Dr. Samuel Johnson in *belles lettres,* Jeremiah Horrocks in astronomy, Dr. James Lind in medicine, Alexander Dalrymple in hydrography, Dr. Daniel Solander in botany, Thomas Pennant in zoology—the work of these and many more was admittedly world pre-eminent. And "Among the men of science the rule of Sir Joseph Banks was as absolute and undisputed as was that of his friend, Dr. Johnson, among the men of letters."[1]

Across the Channel, Louis XIV made the Court of Versailles the envy of every crowned head in the world, and by his and his successors' extravagance planted the seeds which inevitably flowered on the day of the Bastille.

Given the Bourbons and the Stuarts, inevitable too was the deadly game between them for world power, a game which ended only when the Netherlands, Austria, Spain, Sweden, and others were pushed aside, France driven from North America, and the Treaty of Paris in 1763 had seated England as the first power in the world, her flag flying from Africa to the Ganges to Hudson Bay.

But her empire existed sometimes more on paper than in reality, and was more an exercise in oratory than in financial profit. No part of her domain illustrated this more clearly than the immense land west and north of Hudson Bay.

Ten years after Charles II reestablished the Stuarts, he gave to his cousin, Prince Rupert, and seventeen favorites a charter for the "Gentlemen Adventurers Trading into Hudson Bay," and in so doing set up the greatest monument to autocracy ever in force on this continent.

The Charter gave the Hudson's Bay Company sovereign power over almost one-third of North America. In that vast domain it had a monopoly of trade, domestic and foreign; it could issue currency; it could make and enforce laws, and even had rights of life and death; it could raise an army and declare war and peace.

The charter said, too, that Prince Rupert and his seventeen friends "Have . . . undertaken an expedition for Hudson's Bay, . . . for the discovery of a new passage into the South Sea, and for . . . trade for furs, minerals and other considerable commodities."

Gradually, throughout its first century, the Company established a few coastal trading posts on Hudson Bay: Fort Rupert, Moose Factory, Fort Albany, York Factory, Severn, and Fort Prince of Wales. But of inland exploration there was almost none. Two employees, Henry Kelsey and Anthony Hendry (also spelled Henday), did go into the West, but they were harshly deterred from any attempt to repeat their work, partly because of the Company's skepticism about their reports and partly because the western Indians, content in their relationships with the French, saw no reason to travel all the way to Hudson Bay to sell their pelts.

The Company was content to operate a feudal, semislave economy devoted solely to profit. Fort commanders were paid £100 per year, and common servants £8 to £25 depending on ability and the whim of the home office. A part of even these meager wages was held back to enforce secrecy about business, forfeitable if the employee was caught discussing Company affairs with outsiders. No one was trusted. Men were searched as they entered or left the forts lest a handful of beads be exchanged for private profit—a policy which resulted in smuggling.

Under such a system Company employees tended to be "insular minded tradesmen set down in a strange and forbidding land, [with] no desire or incentive to get away from salt water or risk their lives among savages."[2]

But it was a virgin land, and Company profits equaled twice the original capital in the first decade, and on two occasions the net annual income was 50 percent of the capital stock. Profits were so great it seemed politic to split the stock two or three times to disguise the rate of income.[3]

Naturally, such wealth was fought over, despite treaties and supposed boundaries. This came about, first, because the land north and west of Hudson Bay had never been explored, and international agreements either disregarded it entirely or referred to it in such terms as to be wholly valueless in practice, and second, because world affairs had little effect on the independent French and English traders with their voyageurs who roamed the far places of the North in open defiance of the Company charter. These darlings of "private enterprise" held scant respect for any law, and none at all for a charter designed to curb their profits.

Their inroads, plus the constant wars, at one time cut the theoretical monopoly of one-third of North America to actual control of one trading post, the upkeep of which was straining Company credit. Indeed, the governor and committee in London suggested they would give up all claims to the south end of Hudson Bay if only they were guaranteed a working monopoly on the west shore.[4]

More and more the Company had to build their posts with force and hold them with fortifications. Until the very end of the century, 1670–1770, France was legally entitled to live, trade, and make war someplace in North America.

And she did so.

During this century, too, there were increasing complaints against the Company for failure to fulfill the obligations of its charter. Twelve years after the founding of the Company, none of the charterees had ever set foot on their holdings. The "Gentlemen Adventurers" were more interested in adventures in boudoirs than on Hudson Bay. Fifty years after the charter, the Company did not even claim to have searched for Anian in a serious fashion.

Now, it is obvious that the country which found and controlled Anian would be in a position to rule both the Atlantic and the Pacific. Also, the discovery would be to the disadvantage of someone, in this case Spain. She was still mistress in the Pacific from South America northward into the unexplored wilderness. She *did not* want Anian found, since if it existed at all it now had to be within the boundaries of the Company charter, and would thereby challenge her control of the Pacific.

At the same time there were growing numbers of Englishmen who believed one of two things: Anian had been found and kept secret for selfish commercial reasons, or it had not been found because the Company had not tried hard enough to do so.

The latter belief was brought to a head by Arthur Dobbs, Ulsterman, member of the Irish House of Commons, politician, statesman, and in later life governor of North Carolina. Dobbs believed that the existence of Anian had not been disproved and that the search should be resumed—with the Hudson's Bay Company footing the bill. The Company refused to do so on the grounds that its regular coastwise traders had found no sign of it and that it had sent James Knight on a special search, one from which ships and men had never returned. The Company had done enough.

Dobbs, being a suspicious man, demanded to see the Company charter, was refused, forced the issue, and compelled Sir Bibye Lake, governor of the Company, to admit that the charter charged the Company with searching for Anian. Nevertheless, Sir Bibye demurred to try again, saying that war with France was imminent. Dobbs's pressure, however, was so great that Governor Lake hurriedly sent James Napper in 1736 into the Bay as far north as Rankin Inlet to make a preliminary survey for a more extensive search to follow.

Hoping to appease Dobbs, Sir Bibye publicly reported that the Napper voyage had found no Anian, "nor any the least Appearance of a Passage."[5] This only convinced Dobbs that the Company was withholding information, and in 1741 he pushed through an order for a former captain of the Company, Christopher Middleton, to command a Crown expedition to the Bay to look for the passage.

Although the Company formally agreed to cooperate, it resented this invasion of its sovereign territory, and when Middleton arrived off the mouth of the Churchill on the west side of Hudson Bay, he was greeted by cannon shots from Fort Prince of Wales. He ran up the white flag and made contact with James Isham, governor of the fort

and an old friend, who placed the blame for the gunfire on an underling who had been giving orders during Isham's temporary absence.

Since it was too late to explore that season, the two friends passed
the winter without too much friction of purposes. On July 1, 1742,
Middleton sailed north to Wager River, Roe's Welcome, Repulse Bay,
and Frozen Strait. "Undoubtedly there is no Hope of a Passage to
encourage any further Trial between Churchill and so far as we have
gone," said he.[6]

Dobbs was not satisfied. He accused Middleton of selling out to
the Company; initiated a Court of Inquiry which vindicated Middleton; got a Parliamentary investigation; wrote and lectured constantly;
persuaded Parliament to offer a £20,000 prize for the discovery of
the strait; and sponsored a public subscription to send the *Dobbs
Galley* and the *California* into Hudson Bay on still another expedition,
one which returned with conflicting reports: If the Bay were carefully
explored it would "shew such a passage,"[7] and it "would be in vain to
push it any further that way."[8]

But it was too late now. The Company must prove Anian one way
or the other or admit to default on its charter obligations.

Such, then, were the conditions existing in England and on Hudson
Bay in 1733–1771, while Fort Prince of Wales was building.

It was after the Treaty of Utrecht, 1713, that the Company had
first decided to build a fort at the mouth of the Churchill River on
the only natural harbor on the west side of Hudson Bay. It was
ordered about 1715 on the recommendation of James Knight, Company governor in America, who only four years later was to lead two
ships into the north seeking trade and Anian, from which journey no
one ever returned.

Fort Prince of Wales,* as the new post was named, was to serve
the Company as its northern trade outlet and as a bastion against
foreign invasion. Little faith was put in the latest French-English
accord, the Treaty of Utrecht, and even less in international peace.

Knight's temporary wooden structure was obviously inadequate
for defensive purposes, and in 1733 construction began on what was
intended to be one of the most impregnable forts in North America.
Even today its ruins present a formidable pile of dressed stone more
than three hundred feet square with walls thirty to forty feet thick.
Behind the parapets forty cannon pointed out to sea, and inside the

* Early works often use the form "Prince of Wales's Fort."

Exterior of Fort Prince of Wales, largely unchanged from the time of Matonabbee and Samuel Hearne. *Canadian National. Copyright reserved. Made in Canada.*

walls were all the usual houses, shops, and supply units necessary to maintain trade and a staff of half a hundred.

Outside the walls lived the resident Indians, of whom two tribes lived in and around the fort: the nomadic Chipewyans, of Athapascan linguistic stock (not to be confused with the Chippewas), and a tribe of Crees, commonly called the Southern or Home Guard Indians.

The Chipewyans were a proud and peaceful people who served the Company as guides and go-betweens with the tribes farther inland. They were a moral, sober lot who drank little, ate much, and stole and lied less than most. Their social and moral codes were not much formalized, but they believed in good and evil spirits and had their own version of the creation.

The Southern Indians, who acted as hunters and common laborers, were almost the opposite. They had a religious ritual but were virtually devoid of moral standards as we know them. They lied; they stole; they were equally treacherous with friends or foes; they cohabited with their own mothers, daughters, or sisters. In short, they were a very unpleasant tribe. But they were not stupid, and their penchant for deviltry caused the Chipewyans and the Company a notable amount of trouble.

Only one man was ever able to hold these diverse cultures in peaceful contact with civilization and retain the affection and respect of all three elements—Matonabbee the Chipewyan chief.

Gun placements atop the walls of Fort Prince of Wales. *Canadian National. Copyright reserved. Made in Canada.*

Interior of Fort Prince of Wales. Fires set by La Pérouse destroyed only the upper wooden portions of the buildings inside the walls of the fort. *Canadian National. Copyright reserved. Made in Canada.*

3

MATONABBEE AND SAMUEL HEARNE

1736?–1770

MATONABBEE, probably the greatest of all the Indian interpreter-guides, was born into this Company society about 1736. His father was a Chipewyan, and his mother a slave girl bought from the Southern Indians on one of their trading trips to Fort Prince of Wales.

The romanticists claim that Richard Norton, Company governor at the Fort, arranged the match, but since the Chipewyans had no marriage ceremony it is difficult to see how the legend got started.

Matonabbee's mother remained close to the Fort, and the little fellow became a favorite at the "Big House," as the home of the governor was called. When Matonabbee's father died, soon after the baby was born, Norton adopted the boy. Later, when Norton went to England, Chipewyan relatives came to the Fort and took Matonabbee away with them to roam the Barren Grounds.

On these mighty Barren Grounds, Matonabbee learned how to survive in the midst of 400,000 square miles of permafrost extending hundreds of feet into the earth, yet with the greatest recorded temperature range of any place on the continent: −87 degrees in winter and 100 degrees in summer. During the hot season the earth may thaw out enough to support a few spears of stunted grass, a thin sod of edible moss, or some scrubby willows surrounded by mile after mile of bare rocks across which howl and slash the northern gales.

It is a dismal and forbidding land, but one with its own charm, nevertheless: a land where for a few days each year ptarmigan by the thousands nest their young, where the white Arctic fox pads up and down hunting his prey, where an old snowy owl blinks in the sun and pounces on a mouse, where herds of caribou cross on their annual migrations, where shaggy musk-oxen stand silently and stare stupidly at an approaching hunter, where hordes of stinging insects challenge one's sanity; a land where a solitary wolf stalks the crippled or old, where golden eagles soar but have never been known to nest, where uncounted geese gossip and raise their kind, and where still pass, in minute flocks, the whooping cranes.

But for all this, it was, and still is, the Barren Grounds, a place essentially unfit for human habitation where both man and beast must know the law, a place to avoid if possible and endure if need be.

Matonabbee stayed with his people until he was sixteen. By then he was almost six feet tall, well in excess of other Chipewyans, and this gave him a social position which he exploited to its fullest extent. But he was neither braggart nor bully. His modesty and kindly disposition were often remarked upon, and by the time he reached maturity he was probably the best-known and most popular Indian between the Churchill River and the Arctic. And this favorable position was as solid with the whites as with the natives.

About this time Ferdinand Jacobs became governor at Fort Prince of Wales, and he hired Matonabbee as a hunter. For the next several years, the big Chipewyan served in and about the Fort. He worked under Moses Norton, Richard Norton's half-breed son, who in time was to become the Fort's most notorious governor; he sailed under Magnus Johnston on trading trips up and down the western coast of Hudson Bay; he mastered the language of the Southern Indians and picked up a working knowledge of English and a smattering of Christianity, although this last did not impress Matonabbee greatly. He was, he said, an unbeliever and would leave this world as he came into it, without religion.

But his acts belied his words, and he gave respect to all religions, Christian and pagan. Years later, Samuel Hearne said that

Notwithstanding his aversion for religion, I have met with few Christians who possessed more good moral qualities, or fewer bad ones. Matonabbee ... could tell a better story of our Savior's birth and life, than one half of those who call themselves Christian; yet he always declared to me, that neither he, nor any of his countrymen, had an idea of a future state. . . . I have seen him several times assist at some of the sacred rites performed by the Southern Indians, apparently with as much zeal, as if he had given as much credit to them as they did: and . . . I am persuaded [he would] have assisted at the altar of a Christian church, or Jewish synagogue; not

. . . to reap any advantage to himself, but . . . to assist others who believed in such ceremonies. [1]

Matonabbee was strictly honest, due allowance being made for the mores of his people. He loved Spanish wines but seldom drank to excess. His table manners were exceptionally good, and the story is told that he would set one of his wives to rounding up the vermin which always infested their hairy undergarments and that he would "receive them with both hands, and lick them in as fast and with as good grace as any European epicure would the mites in a cheese." [2]

Of course Matonabbee was not perfect. He could and did commit acts of jealous rage that should shame any human. And he had a well-developed sense of acquisitiveness which led him to exploit his friends and foes with equally gay imperturbability.

By the time Matonabbee reached manhood, intertribal warfare and the English-French struggles were seriously interfering with Hudson's Bay Company business. Governor Jacobs took advantage of Matonabbee's knowledge and popularity, and sent him inland to straighten out several quarrels between the Chipewyans and their neighbors.

On the first of these expeditions, Matonabbee was in danger of suffering the torture-death routine common to American Indians. These ceremonies always involved a long-drawn-out foreplay on the part of the captors, boasting all sorts of past and future acts with emphasis on how they were going to make the present captive squirm. Matonabbee put up with this procedure for what he considered a reasonable length of time and then roared his tormentors down. He was tired of this nonsense, he said. If they were going to kill him, they should either get about it or keep still.

This was most unorthodox. Captives were supposed to remain stoically quiet, and stoically accept the torch and spear. A tongue-lashing from the victim was unheard of. He must indeed have powerful medicine! It so astounded the braves around the fire they set Matonabbee free, and he went about his business of adjusting intertribal troubles.

The following year almost the identical experience took place with another band, and again Matonabbee said that if that was the way it was to be, they should get at it. From that day on, Matonabbee was never personally in danger from the interior tribes. He remained their friend and master through many years and over thousands of miles of their nomadic domain.

The land was always incredible and often frightening, but the factors at the Company posts hoped to make a fortune from it for the "Gentlemen Adventurers" of London. And contrary to the popular opinion of our day, both sides of the Atlantic were willing to achieve that affluence in ways other than fur trading if such a policy offered more profit.

The Great Company on Hudson Bay bought and sold many things, ranging from furs and whale oil to wild goose quills for London secretaries. And for many years it had been interested in tales brought by the Chipewyans of fabulous copper deposits to be found on a water far to the north and west. Samples of the ore made it almost impossible not to equate these stories with the Myth of Anian. What could be grander than to find the Northwest Passage surrounded by copper?

In time these tales of Anian and copper became so intermixed it was impossible to separate them. The Indians, wishing to curry favor and not in the least understanding the vision of a Northwest Passage, readily admitted that the mines were on a great waterway or river; wishful thinking made the white man believe that the mines were located on Anian; and so the search for copper somehow became the search for the Coppermine River, the Coppermine River became Anian, and it was left for time, Samuel Hearne, and Matonabbee to set it all straight.

In the meantime, Samuel Hearne reached manhood. He was born in London in 1745. His father was supervisor of the London water-works close by London Bridge on the Thames. On the death of the elder Hearne, Samuel's mother moved to her girlhood home, Beamin-ster, where she put young Samuel and his sister in school. But Samuel was not very happy. He begged to leave school, and was finally ap-prenticed at age eleven to the great Captain Hood of the Royal British Navy.

Samuel saw service in the Seven Years' War, sailed widely in European waters, and seemed on the way to becoming a well-liked, sturdy English naval man when he suddenly resigned and hired out to the Hudson's Bay Company on February 12, 1766. He was sent to Fort Prince of Wales and assigned duty on the sloop *Churchill* at a salary of £25 per annum.

Hearne was a tall, handsome Englishman with a desire to make a name for himself and "benefit mankind," as he put it. He was slow in maturing and was often considered indolent and without ambition. He was neither, but he was too soft-hearted for his own good and was generally imposed upon by others.

Nevertheless, he had a way with him. By the time he arrived on the Churchill River, Moses Norton, able, half-breed, debauchee son of Richard Norton who had adopted Matonabbee, was governor of Fort Prince of Wales. It was not long before Hearne had induced Norton to recommend that since the interior northwest of the Fort had never been explored and no white man had ever reached the American Arctic by land, Hearne should be allowed to enter that region and seek Anian and the copper mines, for the purposes of improving Company finances and perhaps allaying the criticisms fostered by Arthur Dobbs.

The Company agreed, providing the expense was limited to two or three men who were to travel with the Indians and live off the country. Hearne accepted these restrictions, and the First Coppermine Expedition got under way the beginning of the winter of 1769.

Hearne had the usual instructions: send reports; take samples of the flora, fauna, and soil; make peace with the Indians; establish commercial intercourse; and find Anian and the mines.

The inadequacy of Hearne's personal preparations are almost un-believable: "I took only the clothes I then had on, one spare coat, a pair of drawers, and as much cloth as would make me two or three pairs of Indian stockings, which, together with a blanket for bedding, composed the whole of my stock of clothing."[3] And Samuel Hearne was heading into the sub-Arctic at the beginning of winter!

He and two white companions managed to get a few days away from the Churchill before they were robbed of their goods and deserted by the Indians. They trudged back to the Fort.

Norton agreed to a second trip, and Hearne started west alone, except for his Indian companions, on the morning of February 23, 1770. This time he got as far as the southern edge of Aberdeen Lake before an accident to his quadrant plus another pillaging by his Indians caused him to turn about once more, defeated.

Hearne started home with a band of semifriendly Indians, but he was in sore straits. It was winter. Temperatures were often far below the limits safe for human survival, and he had neither clothes nor

Samuel Hearne. From a portrait published after his death. *Champlain Society*.

snowshoes and was using a single blanket thrown around three poles for a tent.

There were many Indian women in the band with which Hearne was now traveling, but they would not work without pay and he had no goods with which to hire them. He was therefore alone for all practical purposes. He could have died from exposure, starved to death, or been killed by accident, and no Indian would have turned a hand to rescue him. It was the code.

It is difficult to see how Hearne could have survived longer without help. His present companions' sole interest was collecting hides for their winter wardrobe, and they were not going to share anything with a stranger. Copper mines could wait, and the Strait of Anian was far beyond their simple understanding.

There is a storybook tinge to the fact that just when one more night without adequate shelter might have ended the life of Samuel Hearne, the Chipewyan Matonabbee drifted into camp on September 20, 1770. He greeted Hearne, whom he had seen at Fort Prince of Wales many times, and his old Indian friends, and immediately took charge of the whole situation. He ordered his own women to make clothes, prepare food, and arrange for a tent for Hearne at once. That done, the two men sat down to compare notes.

Hearne told of his two failures, and Matonabbee agreed that the trouble was a lack of women to do the work.

"Women," said he, "were made for labour. They ... pitch our tents, make and mend our clothing, keep us warm at night; and, in fact, there is no such thing as travelling any considerable distance, or for any length of time, in this country, without their assistance. Women ... are maintained at trifling expense; for as they always stand cook, the very licking of their fingers ... is sufficient for their subsistence."[4]

After further talk, Matonabbee asked Hearne what he proposed to do. Did he intend to make a third trip?

Hearne was now suffering the truth of the threadbare axiom that experience brings maturity. The obvious disdain of the Indians and his two failures had brought him up sharply against his own weaknesses. He knew that if he was ever going to "make a name for himself," he must be about it; he must lay aside some of his philosophy of gentle persuasion and permit the stubborn determination of which he was capable to take over the direction of his career.

This change of emphasis appears to have been somewhat sudden. So far in his life Hearne had plodded along in the shadow of whatever event was leading him, content to take success or failure without elation or complaint. Now he donned a new coat and boasted that he would forfeit his life rather than give up the search for Anian. This was the kind of talk the big Chipewyan understood, and the upshot of the evening's powwow was a lifelong friendship between the native and the polished Englishman.

Matonabbee had traversed most of the region west and north of Fort Prince of Wales as far as the continental divide and the Arctic; he had been to the copper mines with I-dat-le-aza, another Indian leader, in 1769, the year of Hearne's first trip; he had reported this trip to Norton, and was still at the post when Hearne left on his initial journey. Why Norton did not send Matonabbee on that first expedition will probably never be known.

In any event, Matonabbee now offered to help Hearne return to the Churchill River, appease Norton if necessary, and organize a third expedition, and to go with him to seek copper and Anian once more.

Willows for snowshoes and sleds were the first essentials, however, and Matonabbee told Hearne where they could be found. Then the two men coasted along toward the Fort, sometimes together, sometimes apart. Hearne was able to travel faster than the Indians with families, and when weather conditions worsened Matonabbee urged him to hurry ahead, make his peace with Norton, and say that Matonabbee would arrive in a few days.

Such was the juncture of the fortunes of Matonabbee, Samuel Hearne, and the myth of the Strait of Anian.

4

THE THIRD
COPPERMINE EXPEDITION

1770

GOVERNOR Norton is said to have told London that Hearne was not fit to lead an expedition,[1] but that version is hard to reconcile with the facts. As soon as Matonabbee arrived, Norton permitted the Indian and Hearne to collect goods and organize the Third Coppermine Expedition; and the Company soon raised Hearne's wages to £130 a year, a decided increase over his beginning wage of £25. Such acts are not compatible with dissatisfaction with a man's work.

Some dispute did develop over the personnel Matonabbee and Hearne were to take. Norton wanted his Southern Indian relatives in key positions, but Matonabbee refused to have them and Norton acquiesced—a tribute to the Chipewyan's position, since it was not the custom of Company governors to take orders from Indians. Furthermore, Matonabbee got his way about having women assigned to the Third Expedition. Moses Norton gave in gracefully and even concluded his instructions to Hearne with "my best wishes for health and happiness, together with a successful journey, and a quick return to safety. Amen. Moses Norton."[2]

It has been a favorite sport of historians to haggle over the exact relationship of Matonabbee and Samuel Hearne, and some have concluded that Matonabbee was the actual leader of the expedition and Hearne only a figurehead. The fact is that neither man ever encroached on the prerogatives of the other, each limiting himself to expressing an opinion when he believed it right to do so. We do not know exactly how or when they resolved their spheres of authority. We do know that even by the time they got to Fort Prince of Wales

24

from the second expedition, Hearne had agreed that Matonabbee was to have his way in the day-by-day preparations and orders for travel, while Hearne was to be responsible for the objectives of the expedition: to make charts of their routes, study and record every possible item of natural history, make friends and business contacts for the Company, locate the copper mines and chart them so they could be returned to with relative ease, and find Anian.

And so in all the months they risked their lives together, never once did Hearne challenge the Chipewyan in the field where he knew the Indian to be pre-eminent. But neither did he allow Matonabbee to forget the rights and duties of the commander.

The relationship of Hearne and Matonabbee was unique. England was very near her apex as a world power, and every Englishman felt the pride and thrust of that position. Samuel Hearne was no exception, and yet he willingly shared his authority with an illiterate Indian. It is doubtful whether one could find another expedition on which there was such rapport between a commander and a servant, or where an interpreter-guide began his duties by collecting supplies, laying out routes, and arranging personnel, started with the expedition on the first day, and returned with it months later with the mission accomplished.

Hearne's personal and technical accoutrements were little if any better on his third trip than on his first. Again he made no pretense of taking enough clothes to last the time he expected to be gone, and he must either kill his food or die. This gamble on starvation was an ingredient of every early exploration in North America, but no other commander voluntarily took the solitary risk assumed by Hearne. Other expeditions either were not heading toward the Arctic or included white companions to share the risks. Hearne put his life in the hands of the Chipewyan, knowing that even Matonabbee could not kill caribou where there were no caribou.

Matonabbee's organization of personnel was entirely different from that used by such explorers as Lewis and Clark, whose soldier-volunteers were military-trained and army-equipped and signed on for the round trip. Matonabbee had a small number (we do not know how many) of resident Indians assigned to him by Norton; but the main body of his support was to be Indian families who would give a rough promise to obey his instructions, move in a generally north and west direction, and allow the expedition to share in their collective protection. The number on any one day was very fluid. Families not attached to Fort Prince of Wales were expected to come and go at will, obeying Matonabbee only as long as they were attached to the expedition, and even then only to the extent that he could impose his will on them by superior strength of mind. Matonabbee was expected to recruit new families as others dropped out. Sometimes he would have an excess in the company and at other times a shortage.

What few trade goods they carried were packed either on the backs of squaws or on the rude but effective Indian sleds. They consisted of nothing but two poles bent upward and backward at the front to serve as runners with rough-hewn boards lashed across them at right angles to serve as a bed for the load. If they were crude, they had the merit of ease of manufacture, and the raw materials could be obtained from almost any scrub brush.

Collecting and recording scientific data was Hearne's duty. He would keep field notes and record his daily trek on small outline maps, and from time to time he would transfer these data to a master sheet on which he had already placed such information as was available at Fort Prince of Wales. Unfortunately, his field notes were missing from the archives of the Hudson's Bay Company as early as 1819. Only the corrected journal which he prepared after his return is known.

Hearne made his observations with a thirty-year-old Elton quadrant in the use of which he was but tolerably efficient, a fact which laid him open to much criticism when the armchair explorers discovered some errors in his computations.

The early route of the Third Coppermine Expedition was to be along the west shore of Hudson Bay northward toward Egg and Seal rivers, but the journey got off to a ragged start. One of Matonabbee's wives was ill the day of the departure, and he ordered her hauled on a sled, a most uncommon consideration. But then, Matonabbee was a most uncommon Indian. Many of his countrymen secretly laughed at such softness toward a woman, but they knew better than to taunt him about it.

It was mid-December. Game was scarce. A food cache had been robbed, and already the expedition must go hungry for three days until an old campsite gave stale leftovers for one meal.

With no food supplies at all, they moved out onto the Barren

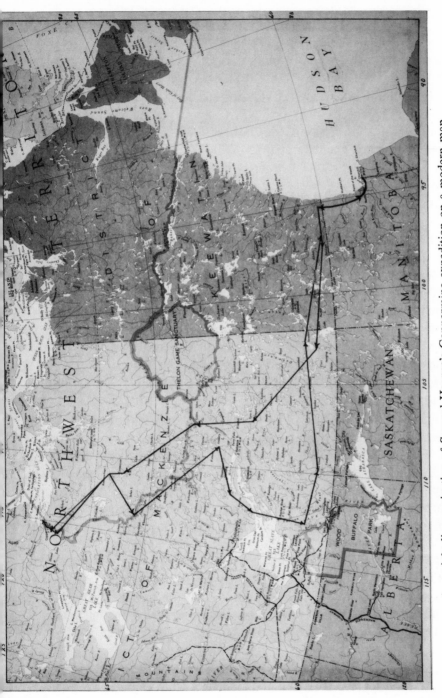

A straight-line projection of Samuel Hearne's Coppermine expedition on a modern map of the Canadian North. *Courtesy of the Canadian Permanent Committee on Geographic Names, Department of Mines and Technical Surveys, Ottawa.*

Grounds, where for nine days they "traversed nothing but entire barren ground with empty bellies" and "for the last three days had not tasted a morsel of anything," * said Hearne.

Even the Chipewyans could not go forever without food, and when the Barren Grounds gave way to a tiny patch of timber in which four caribou were grazing, the Indians killed all four and, pretending their equipment needed repairs, pitched a camp and began to eat. "I . . . think that the want of food was the chief thing that detained them, as they never ceased eating the whole day," said Hearne.[3]

It was December 25, 1770.

"I must confess I never spent so dull a Christmas," wrote Hearne.[4]

Back on the Churchill River, the fires roared high, the cups were full, and for a moment Samuel Hearne hated Matonabbee and wished he were back with his own kind. He had already failed twice; he was very young, only twenty-five; he was a long way from home; he was very, very much alone; and if today there were caribou, he knew that tomorrow he would again face a very real and present danger of starvation—in short, he had the blues. Today he was willing to leave Anian and a name for himself to other men.

Matonabbee felt no such dejection. It was always a feast or a famine, and once you got used to it. . . .

A week later, on New Year's Eve, 1770, Matonabbee and Hearne reached the ice of Nueltin Lake, a slender, indefinite mass of water a hundred miles long, bedded firmly across the intersection of 60 degrees north and 100 degrees west and 900 feet above the level of Hudson Bay. Hearne had possibly touched the northern end of the lake as he returned from his second expedition, and lesser Company men may perhaps have crossed its ice on one of their rare entrances into the interior, but Hearne's New Year's Eve arrival marked the effective discovery of the lake. Hearne Bay, on the east shore, honors the event.

On Nueltin, Matonabbee bagged more caribou and gorged until he was so ill he had to be hauled across the ice for fourteen miles by one of his already overburdened wives. Hearne chided him that it served him right for being a glutton.

---

* The apparent discrepancy in the number of days without food may perhaps be explained by noting that the Indians often staved off starvation by eating parts of their leathern clothing or the Barren Grounds moss, both of which still left them with "empty bellies" for all practical purposes.

"Nonsense," said Matonabbee; he knew when he had had enough the same as any wild animal did.

Hearne countered that even a bear regurgitated when it ate too many berries.

These retorts carried no fire. Matonabbee and Hearne were only showing their affection in the inverse manner of men who understood each other. Each man knew he could not change the ways of the other —indeed, it is doubtful whether either wanted to.

The Chipewyans often went several days without food, and considered it mildly amusing provided it was not carried too far. During such enforced fasts, a tribal saying ran, "Do you have any inclination for an intrigue with a strange woman?" They were a brave and earthy people, and took their pleasures where and when they found them.

Matonabbee had extra wives here and there all over the Northland, and on the other side of Nueltin he met a band of his people among whom was one of these spares. For some strange reason Matonabbee called all of his wives Martin. * If this led to confusion for his friends, it simplified things for the big chief. He had only to shout one name and service was at hand.

Throughout January of 1771, Matonabbee and Hearne moved west and a little north at a slow eight or nine miles per day. Food was relatively abundant for the moment, but they faced starvation whenever they ventured on the Barren Grounds this time of year. Hearne wrote, "very extensive tracts . . . in those parts . . . are incapable of affording support to any number of the human race even during the short time they are passing through them . . . [and] many hundreds . . . [consequently] starved to death."

The Third Coppermine Expedition was to experience that tragedy months later.

Matonabbee was leading westward now, keeping inside the tree line where game might be found. Northward was the modern Windy Lake; in their line of march was Poorfish Lake; and ninety miles from Nueltin and 400 feet higher was Kasba Lake, sprawling crablike

---

* Or Marten, according to some sources. Perhaps they were so named because of the popularity among the Indians of either the swallowlike bird or the valuable fur animal, depending on which variation of the spelling we assume as correct.

across 102 degrees west and just north of 60 degrees. It was bitter cold when the expedition arrived there the first week in February.

Several of the Indians were much frozen, but none of them more disagreeably so than one of Matonabbee's wives, whose thighs and buttocks were in a manner incrusted with frost; and when thawed, several blisters arose, nearly as large as sheep's bladders. The pain the poor woman suffered on this occasion was greatly aggravated by the laughter and jeering of her companions, who said that she was rightly served for belting her clothes so high. I must acknowledge that I was not in the number of those who pitied her, as I thought she took too much pains to shew a clean heel and a good leg; her garters being always in sight, which, though by no means considered here as bordering on indecency, is by far too airy to withstand the rigourous cold of a severe winter in a high Northern latitude.[5]

Thus wrote Hearne with a trace of British stuffiness.

More often now the Northland winds piled the snow into deeper and deeper drifts; daylight came tardily, but the sub-Arctic was not to interfere just yet with the slow, steady search for Anian. It might be anywhere. Hearne was impatient, and so they tramped on until the end of February when they came to Snowbird Lake, where Matonabbee said they would remain the rest of the winter. Hearne was disappointed at the delay, but he knew it would be suicide to challenge the far reaches of the Barrens without food, and there were no caribou there now. Around Snowbird and inside the tree line, however, they were so numerous the Chipewyans drove them into hastily built pounds and clubbed or speared them to death.

Now was the time to eat! Make up for past hungers, gorge against the future. And what eating—raw or cooked!

"I have frequently . . . sat around a freshly killed deer, and . . . I thought that raw brains and many other parts were exceedingly good," said Hearne.[6] Or fat from a newly killed animal was cut into bite-sized pieces and given to certain selected men and boys, whose mouths and teeth had passed rather rigid standards of cleanliness, to be chewed. These morsels were then mixed with unchewed bits of meat and stirred into the animal's blood and the half-digested contents of its stomach. Water was added to make a porridge, and the whole was returned to the stomach and hung in the smoke from the fires to await fermentation. "It might be eaten by those who have the nicest palates. . . . I . . . thought it exceedingly good," observed Hearne.[7]

Unborn calves, fawns, and tiny beaver were good too. "I am not the only European who . . . joins in pronouncing them the greatest dainties that can be eaten. Whoever wishes to know what is good must live with the Indians."[8]

Maybe.

However, Hearne's judgment was shared, at least in principle, by Vilhjalmur Stefansson, the great Arctic explorer of our own time, who took heartily to task those Northern explorers who cooked their meat, threw away the bones and marrow, and in general wasted or spoiled their limited supplies by trying to use them according to civilized standards. Stefansson would have smiled knowingly had he heard Matonabbee coaxing Hearne to try the vermin which crawled so happily rampant through the hairy garments of the Indians, and Hearne replying that it was not really worthwhile learning to like them since there would be no supply to draw from when he returned to Fort Prince of Wales.

Hearne was a diplomat too.

MATONABBEE AND HIS WIVES

AND SO Hearne, Matonabbee, and the Chipewyans ate and loafed through the winter, and took the northward trail again when spring came.

A wild March storm upset tents, broke poles, and forced them all to huddle in what natural shelter they could find and wait it out; they crossed a band of Indians going to the Churchill sometime during the coming summer, and Hearne reported his present position to Norton as 61 degrees north and 19 degrees west of the Fort; they made new tent poles for present use on the Barren Grounds which would later be converted into snowshoes; they cut exact parts for knockdown canoes to be set up whenever the ice left the lakes and rivers; and they gained ten new tents with seventy men, women, and children.

Then it was mid-April, and Matonabbee had spring fever. Every new squaw in sight raised his pulse, and a few days later he obtained his seventh wife.

Probably the assumptive position of women on the Barren Grounds was little different from anywhere else among New World natives, but the exigencies of their lives exacted concessions from the norm. It is no secret that modern American culture is greatly influenced by an unvoiced matriarchy, but it might surprise some to know of the power of Chipewyan women—not that they held any recognized status, except of semislavery. Their forte was the skills which have always baffled and sometimes infuriated men from the age of ooze to the age of jet propulsion. The women held the reservoir of knowledge without which life was impossible for any length of time in the North. They were the only ones who knew how to make a caribou stomach palatable, stretch the sub-Arctic moss into a meal, coax fire in wet tundra herbage, repair worn-out clothes—in fact, the only ones who could keep Chipewyan culture afloat.

And they used that power to alleviate their drudgery as often as they could. Their lives were short. They were old women at thirty; few lived beyond forty years. Their first marriages, often before puberty, were arranged by their elders and were generally to men many years older who were chosen for their financial position.

Pregnancies among these child brides were apparently rare, partly because the girls were often delivered to their husbands years after the agreement was closed, and also because it is believed that native women of both Americas knew how to prevent pregnancies or produce abortions by means of local herbs.[1]

This is partially supported by the indirect evidence that families of more than six children were uncommon, and that although Chipewyan women were more reticent than some others, they lost no time. James Isham put it more bluntly. "Maidens are Very rare to be found at 13 or 14 Years, and I believe m'y Safely say none at 15 Years. . . . the Grey mair is the best horse most on End with them as well as other Nations that is more polite." And he added that half-breed youngsters were "straight Lim'd active . . . [and] are pretty Numerous."[2]

It has been said repeatedly that life among primitive peoples tends to be earthy, and it might be added that it often has a delightfully sly twist as well. Now and again Chipewyan women got tired of being half-animal and half-slave, and at the appropriate times moved away from the family fire to spend a few days *thun-nardy*, in their private tent. Oddly, however, *thun-nardy* had a way of coinciding with marital quarrels. Wives were known to live alone for several weeks while the husband did nothing more than keep an eye on the situation to make sure his spouse *was* alone, for Chipewyan men were jealous of their women, though custom provided for an exchange of beds with a favored friend, and the offer of a wife to a guest was standard protocol.

Matonabbee preferred big, hulking women who for size would have "made good grenadiers," said Hearne. But then Matonabbee was a practical man. Chipewyan women did prodigious labors. Packs of 140 pounds were common during the summer wanderings, and they hauled very much greater loads on their sleds. "Grenadiers" were valuable.

Nevertheless, Chipewyans had a standard of beauty, and Matonabbee was very much a Chipewyan: ". . . a broad flat face, small eyes, high cheek bones, three or four broad black lines across each cheek, a low forehead, a large broad chin, a clumsy hook nose, a tawny hide and breasts hanging down to the belt."[3] These were the criteria of northern beauty.

By the time Matonabbee took on his seventh wife, the whole tundra world was on the move, birds, beasts, and man, for the Indians were as nomadic as the lesser breeds. Toward the end of April, Matonabbee sent one of his brothers ahead to what Hearne called Clowey Lake, not now identifiable,[4] to set up the precut canoes, as the ice was becoming unsafe for large parties. The expedition itself arrived at the lake on May 3, 1771, and found 200 other Indians also setting up their canoes. This aggregate of potential thieves might well have wrecked the Third Coppermine Expedition as similar ones had the second, but Matonabbee came from a different die. He was a powerful man, and his authority in the North was very near absolute. He put the new neighbors in their place with finality.

Hearne had been gone from Fort Prince of Wales for six months. He had suffered great hunger and cold and it is safe to say that for every air mile covered, the expedition had walked two miles by trail. He had therefore tramped not less than 1,200 to 1,500 miles, but he had found neither Anian nor the copper mines.

Inasmuch as lakes are the outstanding topographical feature of the domain of Hearne's route, it is best followed in relation to them. Westward from Fort Prince of Wales he had discovered Nueltin, Kasba, and Snowbird lakes and had crossed or bypassed literally hundreds of others, unnamed even now. At the moment he was moving almost due northwest, and the next day, May 27, 1771, he would discover Clinton-Colden Lake, 64 degrees north and 100 degrees 30 minutes west of Greenwich.

It was the farthest north any white man had been in the interior of North America. Hearne and Matonabbee were cutting steadily into the last segment of the continent in which a Northwest Passage could possibly exist.

But if Anian or the copper mines had not been found, nevertheless, the shores which Hearne sketched on his daily maps represented far from idle accomplishments: Nueltin is almost twice the size of Lake Champlain, Kasba is three and a half times the size of Yellowstone, and Clinton-Colden equals Lake Pontchartrain at New Orleans. Even Snowbird is larger than Tahoe in area if not in tourist registrations.

Meanwhile, Matonabbee had acquired an eighth "Martin." Wives enhanced his prestige and he loved women. But the more he had, the more trouble they caused him.

Chipewyan wives (not including the child brides contracted for delivery years later) were obtained in one of three ways: by purchase, force, or wrestling.

The wrestling matches were community sporting events, and it was sometimes difficult to tell whether the woman or the game was the main attraction. There were rules. A small man was permitted to cut off his hair, grease his ears, and rush from his tent and throw a larger opponent before the latter was aware. But the man who currently held the woman was permitted to keep spies posted to prevent such trickery.

It was all great fun. For the men. No one cared how the girls felt. Naturally, they were sometimes glad to go to a new tent, but "Custom, or delicacy if you please, has taught them to think it necessary to whimper a little, let the change be ever so much to their inclination," said Hearne.

Often the girls objected. "On those occasions their grief and reluctance to follow their new lord has been so great, that the business has often ended in the greatest brutality: for, in the struggle, I have seen the poor girls stripped quite naked, and carried by main force to their new lodgings."[5]

Matonabbee's newest wife was one of these. She objected haughtily to entering his tent, saying she would rather be the only wife of a poor man than "have the seventh or eighth share of the greatest man in the country."[6] Added to this insult was a derogatory remark made by the defeated spouse. Matonabbee's jealousy flared out of control on the instant. Stiff with rage, he seized a knife and attacked the ex-husband. "Without any preface whatever, he took him by the collar and began his horrible design," said Hearne.[7]

Matonabbee's intention was murder.

He stabbed again and again until his fury was drained, after which he wiped the blood from the knife, tossed it back to one of his Martins, calmly washed his hands, and said to Hearne, "Did I not do right?"

Now, murder was not condoned by the Chipewyans, and they had a very effective punishment: complete ostracism from any human association and the cry, "There goes the murderer," whenever the wretch was sighted by chance.

Matonabbee was spared this fate, for by luck every one of his savage knife thrusts had missed a vital organ, and the young man eventually recovered.

Later this wife ran away from Matonabbee and rejoined her previous husband. We shall meet them again.

Poor Matonabbee! He had considerably more wife trouble at Clinton-Colden. While his attempt at murder was still local gossip, another Chipewyan, even more physically powerful than Matonabbee, insisted on wrestling for still another Martin.

Matonabbee had one of three choices: wrestle and lose the girl; refuse to wrestle and lose face; or take advantage of another delightful, if roguish, custom of his people and buy back his own wife before he lost her. Matonabbee chose the last, and it cost him a Chipewyan fortune: ammunition, iron goods, and a kettle. Good wives came high on the Barren Grounds.

And to make the day entirely miserable, Matonabbee lost yet another wife through some scheme of his own which backfired. He was so disgusted that he announced his intention of leaving Hearne to join a band which would show him the respect he deserved.

Obviously, such a turn of affairs would wreck the Third Coppermine Expedition. Hearne exercised his leadership. He flattered Matonabbee until the chief became so excited with his own importance and the greatness of Hearne's mission that he roused the whole camp and ordered an immediate advance to the north, although it was already late in the day. This was not quite what Hearne had expected, but he was too wise to protest, and dawdled along with the others for seven miles before Matonabbee allowed the women to set camp again.

Many hundreds of Indians were attached to Matonabbee's banner now, and on the last day of May he stopped the expedition, called the numerous subleaders together, and ordered them to detach the families in preparation for a push to the mines and return. Only the squaws necessary to the work were to remain with the expedition, although Matonabbee decided it would take two of his youngest wives to serve him!

The chief designated a rendezvous, and amid much wailing and many tears he led the reduced party out of camp at 9:30 P.M. on May 31, 1771, still moving north and west. It was daylight almost around the clock now, and little attention was paid to which part of the clock was in use.

It would be easy to conclude that long before this time Hearne had lost sight of the reasons for his weary miles, and was floundering about the Barren Grounds lost in the trivia of the day. Nothing could be less true. Whatever his other faults, Hearne could keep things in focus without harping. While Anian obviously was not caught in a Chipewyan caribou snare, nor were the copper mines located in the middle of Clinton-Colden Lake, why not still enjoy these for what they were, an adjunct to today's feast and a pleasant place to camp?

Anian might be found tomorrow.

6

THE COPPERMINE RIVER

1771

SAMUEL HEARNE had watched, doubtless with amusement, the wiles of Matonabbee and his wives. Nevertheless, he had not been insensible to certain bits of behavior on the part of Matonabbee and the Indians which seemed incompatible with exploration. There had been an unusual influx of small bands without any apparent reason; as far back as Clowey Lake, the men had been making shields decorated with rude symbols—objects which manifestly had nothing to do with hunting; there had been long, half-secret conferences about Eskimos to which Hearne pointedly had not been invited; and now Matonabbee had separated the main body of the women and children and assigned them to a rear guard.

Somewhat tardily, Hearne concluded that the real purpose of Matonabbee's cooperation had been to lead a mass murder party against the Eskimos while on the Company payroll rather than to help the white man find Anian or the copper mines.

Matonabbee denied this and implied that he was compelled to agree to the wishes of his companions, but the evidence is against him on that particular score. First, there is little indication that he could be coerced into any action against his will, his whole life being a negation of that idea. Second, the Chipewyans believed that whenever one of their number died under the least unusual circumstances, it was the fault of an Eskimo hex. For this and other reasons long ago forgotten by both sides, the Chipewyans and the Eskimos were inveterate enemies, and murdered each other at every opportunity. And Matonabbee was first and always a Chipewyan.

Anyway, all pretense was laid aside, and preparations for an attack on a nearby Eskimo camp were accelerated.

Hearne was in a delicate position. His first order of instruction was to find Anian and the copper mines, and he could not perform these duties if his expedition was to founder on the rock of tribal war. More than that, Hearne himself was the gentlest of men, and he had a deep aversion to any such attack. But he must not protest too much and be thought a coward, and it took very little to convince a Chipewyan of that. So he made what defense of the Eskimos he dared; received quietly the go-back-with-the-women-and-children-if-you-are-afraid taunts; did a little boasting of his own; and then aided in the preparations for the attack.

"When I came to consider seriously, I saw . . . it was the highest folly for an individual like me, and in my situation, to attempt to turn the current of a national prejudice. . . ." With this thought he said to Matonabbee that "I did not care if they rendered the name and race of Esquimaux extinct."[1]

The lie was received "with great satisfaction" by the Indians.

While all this was happening, Matonabbee worked his bloodthirsty command to within eighty miles of Contwoyto Lake, just below the Arctic Circle at 110 degrees west; but summer rain driven by hurricane winds had cut the tents, broken poles, soaked everything, and made travel both difficult and hazardous.

Time was running out. The Eskimos must be found and killed; aid to Hearne must be resumed; and there was the long trek back to Fort Prince of Wales before sub-Arctic winter closed in again and stopped all safe movement on the Barren Grounds.

When the winds slackened and a rift appeared in the clouds, the Indians burst into a dither of speed. Scarcely gulping a morning meal they rushed off, north and west: past Lake Aylmer, just at the shoulder of Clinton-Colden; east of Lac de Gras and Lac du Sauvage; across Pellatt Lake and on to Contwoyto—eighty miles in four days over a plateau 1,200 to 1,500 feet high and studded with spring potholes and major lakes.

Every mile tramped, every lake crossed reduced the area in which the Northwest Passage might be hidden. The myth of Anian would soon be resolved—provided Samuel Hearne survived the raid against the Eskimos.

Hearne was now seventy miles farther north and 300 miles farther west than any white man had ever been inland in North America.

From 1492 to 1771, almost three centuries since the discovery of the New World, and thousands of its inhabitants were not yet aware of that discovery and had not seen their new neighbors. The exploration of this hemisphere was, indeed still is, a slow and incredibly heroic pageant in which Matonabbee and Samuel Hearne played significant parts.

Sometime during the last four days, a band of Red Knives, or Copper Indians, joined Matonabbee, and their presence offered a welcome break in Hearne's dour thoughts about the coming battle. Hearne was the first white man the Coppers had seen, and they went over him with embarrassing detail. They finally agreed he was a man, albeit a very poor specimen: his hair was bleached out, his eyes were too light, and his skin reminded them of caribou meat soaked in water too long.

Hearne found the Coppers disappointing, too. Regarding Anian, they gave only vague replies to the effect that the ice never melted, an obvious bit of knowledge in those latitudes. And their information regarding mines was even less satisfactory.

The expedition–war party was now at or near the modern Kathawachaga, a small lake just off the northeast corner of Contwoyto. Here Matonabbee finally brought himself to forego his beloved squaws. From now on, no women!

July 1, 1771: The warriors and Hearne tucked a few bites of dried caribou into their trail sacks and headed for the Arctic coast. A summer sleet storm carried into the second morning, and July 3 broke leaden-skied. Before they could get into motion, their world turned into a screaming, drifting whiteness in which it was impossible to see, speak to one another, or move.

Hour piled on hour, and each man could only huddle in the lee of a boulder and wait—wait for twenty-four hours while the cold seeped into his marrow and the snow piled into frozen drifts.

It is a lonesome track that great men walk, and Samuel Hearne was never more lonely than during the hours he lay hunched behind a rock somewhere beyond Contwoyto, profoundly disturbed by the part he was playing in a war he was powerless to stop and rightly concerned for his own future.

Keenly aware of his deficiency in the science of observation, he knew he was always partly lost. No civilized man had even an inkling of where he was in that vast land behind Hudson Bay.

Perhaps no one really cared.

To go on meant the screams of hate and war and lust; to turn back meant a third defeat and certain death, wandering alone, slower and slower in ever dimmer circles until. . . . No, no, he could not do that. He would not be denied now! He must keep faith and face with Matonabbee; yet it was not right that babes at breast should die because of an ancient hate; but Anian must be found or proved a myth. Was there a "name for himself" just beyond the swirling white? Was there a compromise between Anian and massacre?

Perhaps. But Samuel Hearne never found it.

And still the snow came down, came for five days and nights. Came while Matonabbee and his warriors crawled "on hands and knees" across the "Stony Mountains"; came while some of the warriors deserted, saying the fun of killing Eskimos would not compensate for this difficulty of travel; came until July 8, when the sun suddenly broke through and it became as sweltering hot as it had been cold, and the giant northern mosquitoes landed with "stings almost insufferable."

Hourly, now, the hope for Anian was waning. Was Matonabbee really seeking it and the copper mines, or was he only stalking Eskimos? Could he be trusted in the final trial, or was the Third Coppermine Expedition to be but an extended version of two previous failures?

Samuel Hearne could not know how close he was to the ore or how near the end of the many-centuries' search for a Northwest Passage through North America. He must wait a little while. Wait until they killed a caribou and feasted on roast stomach; wait until the naked warriors walked to a tiny stream bubbling westward toward a fringe of trees.

Was it the Coppermine River, as Matonabbee said?

Could it be Anian?

The journals of great explorers rarely dramatize their moment of high success. Alexander Mackenzie buried the first east-west crossing of our continent in a discussion of the debris under Indian houses; Cortés submerged the discovery of ancient Mexico in a mass of military trivia.

And Samuel Hearne ate roast stomach, tramped ten miles, and "came to that long wished for spot, the Coppermine River."[2]

Perhaps such reticence is why Hearne has been neglected as a great explorer. He is always just out of sight behind his own accomplishments. He passes over his feats as if to mention them were bad manners. And historians have somehow bowed to that humility, noting the modesty and missing the deeds.

Hearne reached the Coppermine River at Sandstone Rapids. It took only one glance to know it was not Anian, a waterway he had been led to believe would accommodate Company ships; this stream would barely float an Indian canoe, and was blocked by falls impossible to navigate.

Nevertheless, the river must be charted and described, and Hearne set to work as he and Matonabbee walked swiftly toward the Arctic, each keeping his own counsel. It would not do to let the Indian know how insignificant was his boasted river. It would not do to let the Englishman know that any further exploration must wait on war.

Each man was goaded by his own thoughts—a civilization apart. Where was Anian? Where were the Eskimos? Here on the banks of the Coppermine, neither man was sympathetic to the dreams of the other. Matonabbee was tracking an immemorial foe. Samuel Hearne was laying the Myth of Anian.

BUT THERE IS NO ANIAN

1771

JULY 15, 1771: The last starved tree gave way to the cold, and only bare rock and tundra led on to the sea. Matonabbee's scouts returned saying there were five tents of Eskimos close by some falls only twelve miles downstream and so placed as to be easily surprised.

The Eskimos were on the west side of the Coppermine, so Matonabbee's warriors crossed over. They got out their wooden shields, mixed rude black and red paint from the only natural colors at hand, and daubed the shields with "images of imaginary beings, which, according to their silly notions, are the inhabitants of the different elements, Earth, Sea, Air, etc. . . ."[1]

With these simple preparations, they began their stealthy approach. No talking now; take the back way even if it means slithering knee-deep through icy marshes; military law, orders silently obeyed, and Matonabbee is king. There is no way to stop the massacre now. Only God can save the sleeping Eskimos.

Hearne fights off the anguish and plods along, as helpless to stop his little war as millions like him, before and after, have been helpless to stop theirs, and like him, hating every minute of it.

Only 200 yards; breathing almost suspended; no crunching a lingering piece of ice; down now, on bellies; be sure; take no chances; they must not be permitted to escape or even fight back.

Hearne had once been invited to drop behind and keep out of the way of the Chipewyan fun, but he had refused to risk thus being caught alone on a battlefield. Then he was offered a bayonet and a spear for his "protection." "At this time I could not be provided with a target [shield]; nor did I want to be encumbered with such an unnecessary piece of lumber," said he.

Time now for the last-minute rites: paint the faces black and red;

strip naked so as to be swift and sure; tie up the hair or cut it so as to offer no leverage.

"Fearing I might have occasion to run with the rest, I thought it advisable to pull off my stockings and cap, and tie my hair as close as possible."[2]

Quietly, quietly: a few more yards. It is one hour past midnight, July 17, 1771.

Now!

In a few seconds the horrible scene commenced; it was shocking beyond description; the poor unhappy victims were surprised in the midst of their sleep; and had neither time nor power to make any resistance; men, women, and children, in all upward of twenty, ran out of their tents stark naked, and endeavored to make their escape; but the Indians having possession of all the landside, to no place could they fly for shelter.[3]

Three spears pinned a young woman at Hearne's feet where she was "twining round like an eel." Hearne asked for her life, and when denied issued an ultimatum: kill quickly or he would. A bloody spear was yanked out and "thrust through her breast near the heart."

The Indians were, said Hearne, ". . . particularly [brutish] in their curiosity in examining, and the remarks they made, on the formation of the women; which they pretended to say differed materially from their own." But ". . . had there actually been as much difference between them as there is said to be between the Hottentots and those of Europe, it would not have been in my power to mark the distinction."[4]

All this was not the first blood Samuel Hearne had seen. Hood and the Royal Navy shed blood, too. But there was a sickening difference between grapeshot from an enemy vessel and massacre at Bloody Falls.

Across the Coppermine were seven tents, most of whose inhabitants escaped while the Indians were going for their canoes to recross the river. On the way an old woman fishing at the foot of the falls was killed, and an old man, foolish enough to try to rescue his personal treasures, failed to flee in time. "I verily believe not less than twenty had a hand in his death, as his whole body was like a cullender."[5]

After the massacre, the Indians wreaked as much havoc as they could on both Eskimo camps, "sat down [and] made a good meal of salmon," and said they were again ready to aid Hearne, with due regard for their purification rites.

These rituals consisted only in refraining from eating certain foods; smearing their faces with red and black at mealtimes; using only one pipe and one dish, both of which would be thrown into ceremonial fires at the conclusion of the period; and delegating the preparation of all food to whichever member or members had not shed blood.

In the present instance, all except two Indians offered acceptable proof of their bloodguilt, and to these two fell the task of cooking. Hearne, for once the pompous Englishman, was well pleased, since to prepare his own food "would have been no less fatiguing, . . . humiliating and vexatious."

Chipewyan and Copper warriors were not the only ones glad to find a way to avoid squaw's work!

Thus, with the smell of blood and the screams of butchered Eskimos tormenting his thoughts, Samuel Hearne resumed the search for Anian.

Eight miles more. The Arctic Sea was actually in sight. Not much hope now, but orders and good explorership demanded that Hearne go on to the end: to the end of his outgoing trail and the end of the Myth of Anian. On he must push to salt water, the first white man to reach the American Arctic by land.

Seals played on the offshore ice and a dense fog rolled in from the north as a simple board was raised to lay claim for the Great Company. The Coppermine River was obviously useless for trading purposes. It was fruitless to remain.

"At the mouth of the river the sea is full of islands and shoals . . . and it has put an end to all dispute concerning a North West Passage through Hudson's Bay."[6]

Only men ignorant of this epochal journey, or too stubborn to accept the work of a great commoner and a great Indian, would ever again waste lives and fortunes in the barren search for Anian. There were such—Cook, Vancouver, and others—but they played little part in the drama that was Samuel Hearne's and Matonabbee's.

Hearne recorded no high drama himself. There was no pageantry for another generation to ape, no writing of his own importance, not even of his disappointment—only his sense of history. He was intensely aware of his accomplishment. But there on the Arctic Sea at six o'clock on the morning of July 18, 1771, Samuel Hearne was very much alone, alone with the death of the Myth of Anian and with the problem of his own immediate future, for Matonabbee had made few promises beyond today.

If Hearne had proved there was no Northwest Passage, he had not found the copper mines. But neither had he slept since July 15. He lay down where he was.

Now, Matonabbee's mines were more than legend. They existed. Thirty miles upstream from the mouth of the Coppermine River, about where the modern Burnt Creek comes in from the west, Hearne found them. They were, said he, a "jumble of rocks and gravel, which had been rent many ways by an earthquake."[7] Hardly what he had been led to expect; and yet he should not have been too surprised. On the way up the river, he had heard the Indian legend of the lone squaw who had first found the mines and led her men to them each year. But because they took liberties which she resented, she sat down on the mines one day and vowed she would remain until the earth swallowed both her and the ore. And the next summer the men found her half buried and the year after that she had disappeared, leaving only the "jumble of rocks and gravel" which Matonabbee showed Hearne.

In truth, this was only a fraction of the vast ore beds which extend east of the Coppermine for nearly 200 miles. No complete survey has ever been made of the total accumulation of copper. Estimates of its value vary from "not worth the cost of extraction" to the belief that it equals that on Lake Superior.[8] Hundreds of claims were filed and allowed to lapse between 1912 and 1954, and in August of 1955 alone over 100 new claims were filed by a single company.

Hearne himself carried a four-pound chunk of copper, still preserved in the British Museum, back to Fort Prince of Wales, but he made no attempt to search beyond the Coppermine River. For this he has been sharply criticized, perhaps with justice.

In his defense, however, it may be said that he had no knowledge of minerology, that he had fulfilled the letter of his instructions, and that winter would have closed in before he could have looked very far.

But most important, he had to remain with Matonabbee if he were ever to regain the Churchill. And the Indians certainly had no intention of spending the winter on the Arctic coast away from their beloved women.

With these considerations, Hearne and the Chipewyans headed home, but on a route far different from the one Hearne expected.

Early snowstorms made travel spasmodic, and it was July 22 before the expedition got a hundred miles away from the Coppermine discovery point toward Kathawachaga and the women. And Maton-abbee was fretting. Two wives near and five more somewhere out under the midnight sun, perhaps roasting stomachs in campfire smokes. Time to find them.

Forty-five miles today!

One o'clock A.M., July 24, 1771: Eat, rest a bit, and hurry on; Kathawachaga is down at the horizon. Perhaps those are Chipewyan fires and not hope-phantoms!

One hundred and sixty miles and seven days from Bloody Falls. Then five hours more to go.

Kathawachaga! Anticipation turns bitter. Only one of Maton-abbee's several fathers-in-law sits by a lonely fire.

No women. No boys and girls to stand in wide-eyed hero worship.

"All our women had got set across the river. . . ."

"Our women"! They have been here. The tundra moss is smolder-ing. Hurry! We can catch them yet tonight.

Eleven P.M. They rested here, too.

Ten miles more.

Two o'clock—the first women.

Contwoyto Lake. Purification fires. Rest. Food. Love.

Indeed, it had been a race between Chipewyan passion and Hearne stamina. The "unmerciful rate" had cut footgear to shreds; numb, swollen feet bumped blindly against rocks; nails festered and loosened; raw flesh absorbed sharp sand, and a bloody trail marked the insensate dash from the Coppermine to Contwoyto and the families.

But Chipewyan feet were not "the twentieth part in so bad a state as mine, . . . quite honeycombed by the dirt and gravel eating into raw flesh," said Hearne.[9]

THE RETURN TO THE CHURCHILL

1772

Two weeks after Bloody Falls, the last rendezvous with the families took place somewhere between Contwoyto and Point Lake, 113 degrees west and 65 degrees 30 minutes north. To this camp advance scouts brought the last straggling units of Matonabbee's command, including several of his wives and the man whom he had so savagely stabbed on the outward journey. With the latter, too, was the wife who had run away from Matonabbee shortly after the stabbing.

To avoid further trouble, the woman was immediately delivered to Matonabbee, where she sat moaning, *"See'd dinne, see'd dinne"*— "My husband, my husband."

Matonabbee pretended he was unaware of her presence until her wailing got on his nerves, when he suddenly snapped that if she thought that much of her man, she should never have left him in the first place and must go back to him.

As if she had had any choice in any of it! But it was the big Chipewyan's way of publicly atoning for the sin of attempted murder.

At Point Lake, Matonabbee turned almost at right angles and traveled southwest until he reached the trees again early in September. This time they passed west of Lac de Gras, discovered MacKay Lake, crossed or bypassed Margaret and scores of lesser lakes, entered the trees again at 109 degrees west and 63 degrees 30 minutes north, and arrived at the modern Cook Lake, where Matonabbee changed courses again without warning and headed away from home, almost due west.

Hearne was not too unhappy. He was doing what he wanted to do, explore. Modestly but with surprising efficiency, considering his training, he was drawing the first maps of the northern hinterland, an accomplishment for which he has seldom received his due.

The Indians traded among themselves, stole where and when they could, ate and starved and feasted. Matonabbee imagined another insult and threatened to leave, and Hearne told him to go ahead, although such action was unworthy of a Chipewyan chief. The Indians abandoned an old woman because she could no longer keep up, and Hearne suffered with her as she staggered to her feet and fought the soft snow three times before she fell behind to die alone— as she had always known one day she must.

It was their law.

And so they slogged on, west and a little south, and on Christmas Eve, 1771, they discovered Great Slave Lake, the tenth largest in the world: 2,000 feet deep, 300 miles long, 11,000 square miles of inland sea, its southern shores green with forest, its northern arms reaching for the tundra.

Once more a great geographical discovery is so buried in a modest journal that it can easily be missed: "we shaped our course more to the Southward, and on the twenty-fourth, arrived at the North side of the great Athapuscow Lake."[1]

The Matonabbee Point and Hearne Channel of modern maps are paltry tributes.

Hearne celebrated a lonesome Christmas on the northwest shore of Great Slave Lake, and then crossed over by way of the Simpson Islands to enter buffalo country for the first time.

One day he and Matonabbee followed a strange snowshoe track to a little hut in which a young Dogrib girl sat alone. During the summer of 1770 she had been taken prisoner and made a slave. She had escaped, got lost, and built her hut. She snared small game and birds and made clothes from their skin and feathers, and when Matonabbee and Hearne found her, she had actually stored a small surplus of food.

She was, said Hearne, "one of the finest women . . . I have seen in any part of North America."[2]

What a night followed!

She was won and lost a dozen times. Matonabbee was all for getting into the fun and would have done so except that one of his wives taunted him that he already had more women then he "could properly attend." For which affront to his manhood he beat her until she eventually died from the effects. It was murder under English law but not under Chipewyan; wives should be quiet, especially on delicate subjects.

All such digressions were exciting enough, but they did not further exploration. The Third Coppermine Expedition was almost at a standstill 500 airline miles south of Bloody Falls and just below Great Slave Lake. Fort Prince of Wales was almost 700 miles due east.

Long ago Hearne had found that Matonabbee was making no pretense of retracing their outgoing trail. Whether the chief knew exactly where they were may be debated, and Hearne certainly had only a general idea. His quadrant was gone, his watch ruined by the rain and snow, and his only means of navigation were the sun, the polestar, and rule of thumb. Using these, it was apparent they were moving straight south, which if continued long enough would land them in the Gulf of Mexico, not Hudson Bay. Thus, as the pace of the expedition became slower and slower, Hearne, for the only time on the whole journey, interfered with Matonabbee's trail orders and called a general council to discuss their position.

At this council the several lesser chiefs and Matonabbee agreed, apparently without ill feeling, to set trap lines, collect pelts, and be at Fort Prince of Wales in time for the annual ship for London.

All we know of the following month is that Hearne was going home. Without quadrant or watch, it was impossible for him to take observations, and it is impossible for us to do more than recognize an occasional landmark mentioned in his journal.

Regardless of where they were, Matonabbee coaxed as many bands as possible to join his command, since the more customers he took to Fort Prince of Wales, the greater his prestige.

And it was a busy time: tending traps and scraping pelts; collecting birch rind for canoes and tent poles for the Barren Grounds; fishing in Hill Island Lake, 150 miles east of Great Slave Lake; robbing strangers and assaulting their women; wading knee-deep through spring ice and slush; fighting tremendous gales when it was impossible to walk upright in the open and dangerous to do so even in the shelter of trees.

May Day was "exceedingly fine and pleasant," but a following northern storm caught them "on top of a high barren hill." It knocked them off their feet and held them in a prostrate position through a long night in "a puddle of water, occasioned by the heat of our bodies melting the snow," said Hearne.[3]

Then, just as they approached Wholdaia Lake, only seventy miles west of Kasba, the lake discovered on the outward journey, the expedition faced total disaster.

For ten days the 200 Indians had killed no caribou. On the eleventh day four small animals furnished only a taste for each person. In desperation, small groups broke hither and yon seeking food, but they always returned as hungry as they left.

Death was very present.

Starved bellies swelled. Eyes deepened in their sockets and lost their luster. Women and children stumbled along, numbly waiting.

"It is a melancholy truth," wrote Hearne, "and a disgrace to the little humanity of which these people are possessed, . . . that in times of want the poor women always come off short; and when real distress approaches, many of them are allowed to starve. . . ."

Ten days later, "Our numbers are greatly lessened," and three caribou "served us for two or three meals."[4]

How many had starved?

No one knows. A few old folks and children had been sent to the Barren Grounds. Some had drifted off in small bands. A few remained.

The pity of these deaths was that the Third Coppermine Expedition was almost home. On June 18 they were at Egg River, then a few days later at the Seal River crossing, and finally at Fort Prince of Wales on June 30, 1772.

I arrived in good health at Prince of Wales' Fort, after having been absent eighteen months and twenty three days. Though my discoveries are not likely to prove of any material advantage to the Nation at large, or indeed to the Hudson's Bay Company, yet I have the pleasure to think that I have fully complied with the orders of my Masters, and that it has put a final end to all disputes concerning a North West Passage through Hudson's Bay.[5]

SUICIDE

1782

IT was an uneasy time, those years when Matonabbee and Samuel Hearne tramped the vast reaches of the Barren Grounds—an era which Hearne could have understood only imperfectly and which was entirely outside the ken of Matonabbee. Nevertheless, neither could escape it. It clouded one man's reputation. It cost the other his life.

Theirs was a century of heroic deeds and perplexing questions. Perhaps the mobs of Paris would not explode into the bloodiest revolution of history; perhaps the beleaguered outposts of empire on the China Seas and across the African veld would hold firm against the hates of exploited peoples; perhaps the Little Corsican would stop dreaming of his sweep across Europe to the Volga and beyond, and after that across the Atlantic to wipe out the memory of the Plains of Abraham high above the river at Quebec; perhaps the irate farmers of Vermont and the scheming traders of Boston would not demand their human rights; perhaps Sam Adams and Thomas Paine and Voltaire and Rousseau could be hushed; perhaps democracy and republics could be exorcised, and gentlemen and chivalry could again flash down the freshly sanded courses of the jousts.

Perhaps it was only an idle tale that the French trappers stranded in the interior of North America by the Treaty of Paris of 1763 were usurping furs and markets reserved in perpetuity to the Hudson's Bay Company; perhaps the bookkeepers had made a ghastly mistake, and Company profits had not collapsed from a rousing 10 percent on stock split twice at three for one to no dividends at all for some years.

Perhaps if one closed one's eyes, the breakup of feudalism would go away, and Fort Prince of Wales and York Factory could again buy a prime pelt for a pound of cheap tobacco; or exchange a "looking glass" and a comb for two beaver hides; or sell a cheap gun, likely to burst on the first shot, for as many pelts as it took, one flat on top of the other, to reach the muzzle when the butt was set on the earthen floor.

Perhaps that turbulent century could be stopped.

But somehow it didn't work out that way. The pamphleteers expounded; the great unwashed rioted and sneered at kings; Napoleon and the intellectuals with fire and words upset the smug contentment of a thousand years; and the abandoned French trappers and independent English traders from Montreal continued their brand of private enterprise by expanding into the Company's theoretical monopoly.

In a belated attempt to neutralize or even stop these invaders, the Company ordered Samuel Hearne to build Cumberland House at The Pas. He went beyond his instructions and established the factory on the Saskatchewan River at Sturgeon Lake. The post was barely in its second season and still much too new for its effect on Company finances to be determined when Hearne was hastily recalled to assume command of Fort Prince of Wales following the death of Moses Norton.

For the moment England and France were technically at peace, and the Company hoped to be on the way to some stability. This prospect was shattered by the outbreak of the American Revolution. There was no danger that the "rabble from Boston" would seize the stone fort at the mouth of the Churchill, but George III and his ministers knew that France would not long forego trying to retrieve her American empire which she had so lately lost by the Treaty of Paris of 1763. Nor did she. Very soon French money was paying for Colonial arms, and French officers were helping Washington whip the "rabble" into an army.

When the time was ripe, secrecy was thrown aside and the French-American alliance was announced.

In the meantime, London officials blamed Hearne for their declining profits and salved their corporate consciences by sending 150 copies of *The Country Clergyman's Advice to Parishioners* to be distributed at Hudson Bay!

In the meantime too, Matonabbee came and went at Fort Prince of Wales as usual, ignorant of and uninterested in the unfolding drama which would soon end his personal world. Loafing around the storehouses at the Fort, he used his friendship with Hearne to gouge preposterous "gifts" of anything that took his fancy. One such tribute totaled seven lieutenants' coats, fifteen common coats, eight guns, eighteen hats, 140 pounds of powder and shot, a few ice chisels, files, knives, mirrors, hatchets, stockings, and 400 "beaver worth" of other goods—the price of his abstaining from trade with Company competitors. Hearne recorded his annoyance, but an affection as deep as theirs could be disturbed only on the surface by a game each man knew was a game, were it ever so expensive. And one day the Chipewyan would prove his fealty to Hearne with the ultimate gift, his life.

But first Samuel Hearne and his men, and one gentle Indian girl, must undergo defeat and death.

In February of 1778 France signed two treaties with the rebelling American colonies, providing that she was to use her might openly against England and in aid of the colonies. Pursuant to that end, Jean François de Galaup, Count de La Pérouse, was ordered in 1782 to seize British forts in Hudson Bay, with special attention to York Factory and Fort Prince of Wales.

La Pérouse had three ships carrying almost 150 guns, as well as four fieldpieces, two mortars, and 300 bombshells—items to be remembered in the events that followed.

On arriving in Hudson Bay, La Pérouse anchored a few miles north of Fort Prince of Wales and sent a party to sound the Churchill River. When that act brought no opposition from Hearne, the Frenchman landed 400 troops and marched against the Fort.

Samuel Hearne opened the gates and surrendered.

Not a shot was fired. La Pérouse partially dismantled the bastion, loaded his booty and prisoners aboard his ships, and sailed for York Factory and home.

Partisans have argued ever since about the reasons for Hearne's surrender. Only a few years later, David Thompson, perhaps the greatest of all Canadian surveyors, said, "The men in the fort begged ... Hearne to ... mow ... the French with ... grape [but] he refused; [and] surrendered at discretion. ... Mr. Hearne was ... looked upon with compt by the french ... [and was] dismissed for cowardice."[1]

A century later an authority on the Canadian North characterized Hearne as "panic stricken" and "craven."[2] But we must disagree. It is an absurdity to follow Hearne on his first two abortive expeditions into the North, across the Barren Grounds to Bloody Falls and the Arctic, and back to Great Slave Lake and Cumberland House and the Churchill River, and then to accuse him of cowardice. He was no more a coward than Matonabbee, perchance less if their respective cultures are considered.

Why, then, did Hearne surrender Fort Prince of Wales and by so doing initiate the deaths of innocent persons? Perhaps the general public will never know. If the Company knew, it studiously avoided sharing its knowledge. Yet several items deserve consideration.

Samuel Hearne was a student of the French intellectuals, and he once held Voltaire's *Dictionary* before David Thompson's shocked eyes and remarked, "here is my belief, and I have no other."[3] La Pérouse had 150 guns and more than 400 men. Samuel Hearne had one-third as many guns and thirty-nine men. Perhaps he thought men's souls outweighed bundles of fur.

"Resistance would have made good reading today, and would have been folly at the time."[4]

Furthermore, La Pérouse treated Hearne as an honored guest abroad his flagship. Once away from the Bay, the Frenchman read the journal from which we have quoted, and extracted a promise from Hearne to publish it as soon as peace would permit.[5] And when Fort Prince of Wales was returned to the Company at the end of the war, Hearne was sent back to build a new and better trading post. The actions of La Pérouse and the Company are not consistent with opinions of contempt and cowardice. But that controversy lay in the future.

La Pérouse had sailed away from the Churchill giving no thought to the Indians living about the Fort, who had depended on the Company for every item of their existence from food and shelter to clothes and simple medicines. In one day La Pérouse had destroyed their relative security. But most of them could and did revert to their ancient paths, for the Indians of the North did not inhabit their domain; they wandered across it following the caribou and the ptarmigan or seeking edible moss.

But one victim of La Pérouse's raid could not go back: Mary

Norton, daughter of the half-breed Governor Moses Norton of Fort Prince of Wales. Mary did not like Indians, and had an intense aversion to the crudities of native culture, particularly those of the squaws. While she was still an adorable black-eyed moppet, she had pouted and coaxed until her doting father permitted her to loiter about the officers' mess at the "big house," where every childish whim was pampered. Had Mary been the scion of a society away from the Bay, she might have grown into an insufferable adult; but American tribes have always pampered their children, so that the indulgences were not too far beyond those she might have received had she grown up in a caribou tent on the Barren Grounds. But her upbringing had one fatal difference from the Indian. Mary Norton never learned any of the skills essential to nomadic life in the North. She did not know the barest rudiments of trail housewifery.

In view of the overall absence of moral restraints on the frontier, one might expect that Mary would have passed the age of innocence by the time La Pérouse arrived. In fact, she was twenty years old, gentle, shy, and afraid of any man except those who had made her life so happy thus far. When the red and white Company flag came down and Hearne and his men were taken away as prisoners of war, she took one look at the sex-hungry French soldiers and bolted for the hinterland.

It was September. Down along the Hudson and St. Lawrence rivers, nature was about to stage her annual color pageant. But behind the Bay, it was the first of winter. Ice had been forming in cold pockets for several weeks, and the warm September sun was constantly interrupted by snowfalls.

Mary Norton was helpless. Even the most skilled Chipewyan could have done little more than survive until he found a band of friends. The caribou had moved to their winter feeding grounds, and only ptarmigan and a few snowshoe rabbits offered a chance of survival. But Mary did not know how to find or catch either.

And so, running from the terror of the French soldiers, she plunged into the terror of starvation. How long she stumbled among the scrubby trees and boulders behind the Fort none can say. The indescribably beautiful but inexorable North does not grant a second chance. Then as now, one had to obey the rules and make no mistakes. Whitening bones from the days of Jens Munk to those of the bush pilot bear testimony to that truth.

Mary Norton's lie there, too.

The last act in the tragedy on the Churchill was about to begin. Matonabbee did not see the surrender of the Fort, and there is no record of whether Hearne thought of him and tried to leave him a message. No one knows why the native information system which the white man found mysterious and often embarrassing failed to inform Matonabbee of events on the Churchill River. No one has explained why the Chipewyan felt the way he did when one day, after La Pérouse had gone and Mary Norton had starved, he came and stood outside the stone walls and let the acid floods of disillusionment wash across his soul.

Where was the impregnability of the Fort? Where was the infallibility of the white hero who had tramped to the Arctic and back and shared with him the snow and the sun, and the deaths of Bloody Falls, and the feasts and gossip and loves of winter camps, the chase of the caribou, and the earthy humor around a thousand fires? Why had the white man's smallpox so recently come and killed eight or nine of every ten Chipewyans? Did the defeat of Fort Prince of Wales and the death of his people mirror the end of his rule on the Barren Grounds?

No man can ever know the final workings of another mind. But whatever Matonabbee's thoughts, there were no answers. He could not foresee that Hearne would be back to rule again, able to give him extravagant tribute and talk about old trails and plan for new ones. He could not tell that the fort on the river would still be standing three centuries later, even if eclipsed by grain ships loading for the docks of the world; or that the Company store on the north side of Great Slave Lake, not too far from where he and Hearne had crossed it that Christmastime, would be selling knives and mirrors and ribbons to his descendants' Martins—along with canned milk and baby food; or that Yellowknife mothers would be carrying their babies on their backs as the old Chipewyans had done, and their young girls would be giggling at the queer ways of white men even as the Red Knives had laughed at Samuel Hearne.

He could not foresee the wide street called Matonabbee Avenue and the working shafts of gold mines, or forehear the drone of planes bringing Eskimo boys from the farthest islands of the Arctic Circle to learn the white man's letters and machines and in their turn face the eternal problem of the clash of cultures.

And perhaps because Matonabbee could neither get answers to his questions nor see the future, he threw a rope around his neck and hanged himself,[6] leaving six Martins and four children to starve to death and lay their bones beside those of Mary Norton.

It was a bitter end to a full life. But Matonabbee made his own rules for living; and if life would not obey those rules, he had no use for it.

He had never been afraid to live. He was not afraid to die.

PART II

THE LEWIS AND CLARK MEN:
JUSSEAUME, DROUILLARD,
AND CHARBONNEAU

THE demise of the Anian myth did not end the exploration and subjugation of a continent. All that vast region west of the Mississippi to the Cascades and Sierra Nevadas and from Taos north to the Klondike was yet to be conquered. It is in this mighty land that we find the great mountain man and voyageur interpreters, of whom those attached to the Lewis and Clark Expedition were but the first to achieve fame.

EXTRA-EXPEDITIONARY
PURSUITS

Circa 1800

IT has been the custom of historians and novelists alike to picture the Lewis and Clark Expedition as a great scientific adventure, which it was; the commanders as well-bred gentlemen, which they were; and the men as volunteers devoted to a dream of service and empire, which they were not.

And because the whole truth might keep the story from certain staid libraries and Christmas bookshelves, the scribes have managed to create an expedition of men quite as unreal as those to be found in a Horatio Alger story.

They have become plain stodgy.

Only one of them could approach that dismal state in truth. Captain Meriwether Lewis was indeed almost too respectable, too wellborn. Thirty years old, private secretary to the President, educated, and socially prominent, he had drunk deep from the spring of Jefferson's enthusiasm for trans-Mississippi exploration, but despite that, he was perhaps just a bit prosy.

Lieutenant William Clark, to give him his actual military rank, was three years older than Lewis and came from a long line of eminent Clarks, but his heart was on the frontier, not the Potomac. He was nearing "middle life" on the mortality tables of his day, but he cared not a whit. Both before and after the great expedition, he was generally fighting Indians or wooing their friendship as circumstances dictated, for Clark was a just man and understood the cry of the red Indian as well as any white missionary ever did.

William Clark had a smattering of formal education but he spoke the language of the frontier, succinctly demonstrated when he scrib-

Map of the Trans-Mississippi Territory of the United States during the period of the American fur trade, 1807–1843. *Courtesy Library of Congress.*

bled in his daybook that he had doctored a "sulky Bitch . . . efflicted with pains in her back."[1]

He was a red-haired, red-blooded adventurer—and very much a ladies' man, be they single or married. Calling on "Mr Ducett [Duquet] . . . who has a charming wife"[2] was most enjoyable. But they must be young. No thirtyish spinsters for William Clark. And when he finally married, it was the fifteen-year-old Judith (Julia) Hancock who tamed him.

Altogether, the Lewis and Clark Expedition was a trek of young men. They were out for adventure and, excepting the commanders, had little understanding of or interest in the significance of their venture. George Shannon was only seventeen, and between him and his oldest companion was a lusty, earthy crew of unmarried soldiers of fortune far more attracted to the fleshpots of the Mandan Indians than to the community life of prairie dogs. If the commanders wished to collect plants, describe coyotes, and stuff "Oregon robins," very well, but they would investigate the price of local sin.

It was a time when democracy was a magic word, and frontier military units generally elected some or all of their officers. It followed that the common soldier seldom had more than a tongue-in-cheek respect for his officers. That Lewis and Clark had not been so elected mattered not at all, and only days after the commanders set up camp on the American side across from St. Louis, their exuberant charges began to chafe under orders. By spring they had "Tried Several men for missconduct."[3] John Collins was given fifty lashes for being away without leave and "behaveing in an unbecomeing manner at the Ball last night . . . and for Speaking in a language . . . tending to bring into disrespect the orders of the Commanding officer."[4]

Early in March, 1804, Lewis was "mortifyed and disappointed at the disorderly conduct of Reuben Fields, in refusing to mount guard when in the due roteen of duty he was warned."[5] On the way up the Missouri, Collins and Hugh Hall were caught stealing whiskey and given 100 lashes and fifty respectively;[6] Alexander Willard received twenty-five stripes per day for four days for "Lying down and Sleeping on his post";[7] and J. Newman was "confined for mutinous expression," given seventy-five lashes, detached from the official party, made to serve as a common laborer, and "exposed to such drudgeries as they think proper."[8]

But if these boisterous young men had little respect for their officers, they took their punishments like men, got a sympathetic comrade to rub a soothing potion over their bleeding backs (and make no mistake, they *were* bleeding), and began dreaming of the Sodom which was Mandan.

The Mandans, the Gros Ventres of the Prairies, and the fragments of other peoples who had been accepted by the former two, adopted or enslaved, had not always lived in their present towns on the Missouri. The Mandans had been driven from the headwaters of the Red River by the Ojibways, and even after arriving on the Missouri had moved once or twice before settling at their present site some fifty miles northwest of the modern Bismarck.

It was a cosmopolitan area of 300 lodges grouped into several separate towns. The lodges were circular and domed, set partially underground. They measured as much as forty feet in diameter, and were built with a smoke hole fifteen or twenty feet above the earthen floor. The entrance, large enough to admit a man and horse with ease, was approached through a narrow stockaded semitunnel, easy to defend and very effective against Dakota blizzards. Horse stalls, raised bed sites, ritual fires, trophy poles, cooking areas, and gossip centers made up the interior geography. Furniture, as we know it, was nonexistent.

The dome of the lodge was held in place by ten- to twelve-foot poles set upright in the ground. On top of these were interlaced other logs and poles of sufficient strength to support the final covering of deep sod. With such insulation the lodges were comfortable in either extreme heat or cold. The top of the dome formed a splendid vantage point from which to watch village athletics, personal brawls, or the approach of friend or enemy.

The total population of the towns was perhaps in excess of 3,000, with a military potential of 400 to 500 warriors.[9] The latters' favorite weapon was an eight-foot spear tipped with an iron triangle nine or ten inches long and four or five inches across the base.

But on the whole the Mandans were a peaceful, agricultural people raising a variety of corn, melons, squash, and beans on the river-bottom plots allotted to each family by the tribal seers. They stirred the rich Missouri soil with fire-hardened sticks or hoes made from the shoulder blades of deer or buffalo. In good years there was a surplus of food to sell to other tribes or passing traders. And their children chased the marauding crows from the fields, even as the white boys

Mandan Town at the time of the Missouri River Fur Trade. Taken from Carl Bodmer painting. *Courtesy of State Historical Society of North Dakota.*

View of the Mandan village Mih-tutta-hang-kush, not far from Fort Clark on the Upper Missouri. The village is on the steep cape across the river, over which the Indians are crossing on the ice. Watercolor by Karl Bodmer, 1809–1893. *Northern Natural Gas Company Collection, Joslyn Art Museum, Omaha, Nebraska.*

Bird's-eye view of Mandan village. By George
Catlin. *Courtesy of Smithsonian Institution.*

A Mandan chief in state dress. *U.S. Signal Corps, Photo 111-sc-92849, The National Archives.*

and girls did around St. Louis.

The Mandans were average-sized Indians but were subject to albinoism, resulting in very light skins, hazel eyes, and often brown hair. Their features were regular, their noses prominent, their mouths good, and teeth sound.

They had horses but did not value them so highly as did the Sioux or Crows. They liked to gamble and dance, and they set up a feast on the slightest excuse. They journeyed up and down the rivers in clumsy bullboats made of buffalo hides stretched over willow poles and resembling nothing so much as huge, furry mush bowls.

In general the Mandans were neat and clean by Indian standards. They were courteous, smiled easily but seldom laughed, and treated their women with something less than customary brutality. An injured party or his relatives were permitted to avenge offenses against him or his property. Murder was considered a dangerous passion since murderer and family were both liable to vengeance, but the Mandans treated all crime with the materialistic philosophy that it could be satisfied with the proper amount of worldly goods.

Illogically, the inhabitants of the several towns often did not understand one another's language. "Very few of the Mandanes learn it [Gros Ventres]," said David Thompson.[10]

The Mandan religious system was elaborate and derived from ancient forms—worship of the sun, spring fertility, appeasement of the gods, and on through the catalogue of primitive rites.

But of all these national attributes, the voyageur and mountain man were interested primarily in the Mandans' "almost total want of chastity."[11] Rightly or otherwise, Mandan religion and Mandan sex had become inextricably woven, and the traders made full use of their opportunity.

It would not be far wrong to say that the Mandan town held the same lure for Missouri rivermen as did the Sandwich Islands for Pacific seamen, who often sailed thousands of extra miles to be where food was abundant, housing unnecessary, and sin unlimited.

If the first two inducements did not always apply to the Mandans, the last was comparable, and Lewis and Clark's young adventurers spent no time debating the probity of sin. They intended to enjoy it.

"The Rickores [Arikaras] we put off dureing the time we were at the Towns but 2 Squars were Sent by a man to follow us, they came up this evening, and pursisted in their civilities. . . . Their womin verry fond of carressing our men &c. . . . 2 young squars verry anxious to accompany us. . . ."[12]

And when Mandan patriarchs sat around a slow fire in their earthen houses with young warriors behind them, pulses racing; and every young wife, naked except for a robe loosely clasped, led an old man "to a convenient place" as a ceremony to ensure that the buffalo would come close and be plentiful—well, expedition men lost their interest

in religion. The Mandans "gave him 4 Girls,"[13] amd "Messrs Jus-
somme and McCrachan said they had often partaken of the latter
part" of this ritual.[14]

Sergeant Patrick Gass, whose lively journal is all too little known,
thought he might

give some account of the fair sex of the Missouri: and entertain . . . with
narratives of feats of love as well as arms. Though we could furnish a
sufficient number of entertaining stories . . . , we do not think it prudent
to swell our Journal with them. . . . It may be observed generally that
chastity is not very highly esteemed by these people, and that the severe and
loathsome effects of certain French principles are not uncommon among
them. . . . the women are generally considered an article of traffic and
indulgencies are sold at a very moderate price . . . for an old tobacco box,
one of our men was granted the honour of passing a night with the daughter
of the head chief of the Mandan nation.[15]

And Sergeant Gass could have added that chastity was even less
esteemed by his men, all of which resulted in the "Venerials Complaints which is verry Common amongst the natives and the men
Catch it from them."[16]

Thus, if Lewis and Clark believed they could build a rough
frontier fort, start huge fires, and sit quietly until spring, they were
to be disappointed. Long before Fort Mandan, as they naturally
called their stockade, was ready for comfortable living, annoyances
of every sort were piling in, a sizable share of which involved Indian
women.

An angry brave lost his temper and tried to murder his wife; and
Lewis and Clark interfered, not knowing that the present violence
had been bred two weeks earlier when the couple had quarreled and
the woman had deserted her husband to live with the wives of the
expedition interpreters. But since such desertion carried the death
penalty according to the Indian code, the woman had reconsidered
and returned to her bed, only to be severely beaten and stabbed.
She then ran to the American camp a second time.

The case might have been settled inside the Indian rules, but the
irate husband claimed that Sergeant John Ordway had seduced the
lady. Lewis and Clark ordered no "intercourse with this woman under
penalty of Punishment," and told Ordway to pay the husband one

horse. Then, despite this tacit acceptance of Ordway's guilt, Clark propounded the amazing fiction that since such goings-on were unknown in white society, Ordway could not be guilty!

Then a rumor began to circulate that the Americans planned to join the Sioux in one of their eternal wars against their neighbors, and the command had to try to scotch the canard. Also, one of the North West Company traders, Baptiste La France, was making derogatory remarks about American intentions in general, and F. A. Larocque had to be told either to control his men or to take the "Consequences if they do not put a stop to . . . it."[17] Lewis also heard that the North West Company was giving flags and medals to the Mandans, and extracted a ready promise from Larocque not to do so again, which promise Larocque confided to *his* journal would be easy to keep since he had neither flags nor medals with him!

Traders came and went all winter, and each must see the Americans and beg some advantage for himself.

The thermometer dropped to −22 degrees a week before Christmas and then plunged to −40, catching a man and a small boy out on the prairie with a single robe. The pair came into town next morning unharmed except for frostbite of the boy's feet. Joseph Whitehouse got frozen so severely he could not walk, and in another case, Lewis became surgeon and amputated a man's frozen toes.

René Jusseaume's squaw left him, and he became ill and received a "Dost of Salts"; a Minnetaree wife begged that her services be purchased; and Lewis discovered that the Indian women were opening the Fort gates at night to allow male visitors, so new locks had to be installed.

Tom Howard, one of the expedition soldiers, got home too late one evening and, rather than call the guard, crawled over the stockade with his Indian companion, thus largely canceling the value of the Fort in the minds of the Indians; Lewis, for the sake of diplomacy, allowed Jusseaume to prescribe the powdered rattles of the prairie rattlesnake to ease Sacajawea's labor; a hundred Sioux stole two horses from George Drouillard, and three hunting companions and Lewis failed to recruit a Mandan posse to retrieve his property.

And Larocque brazenly asked Lewis and Clark for permission to accompany them to the Pacific. He was brusquely refused.

It was a busy winter, those long months with the Mandans, waiting for spring and the opportunity to prove to Jefferson that he had not misplaced his trust in a cultured secretary and a frontier army lieutenant.

Between the Mandans and the Columbia River, wickedness had less chance; but the females on the river of Oregon "wore short skirts and a flap over their 22^{d}"[18] with a G-string "drawn tite between their legs . . . so as to barely hide those parts . . . so sacredly hid and secured by our women." Indeed, "this battery of Venus is not altogether impervious to the penetrating eye of the amorite," said William Clark.[19]

Captain Lewis didn't notice.

Sergeant Gass did. The girls, said he, wore a "kind of fringe petticoats, made of filaments or tassels of the white cedar bark wrought with a string at the upper part, which is tied round the waist. These tassels . . . are of some use . . . while the ladies are standing erect and the weather calm; but in any other position, or when the wind blows, their charms have but precarious defence."[20]

Harlotry throve mightily on the Pacific likewise. There wasn't much else to do. It rained incessantly, and sin helped assuage the monotony of boiled elk and rotted salmon.

The supply of ribbons "to bestow on their favourite Lasses" dwindled and Silas Goodrich recovered from "Louis Veneri . . . which he contracted from a Chinook damsel. I cured him as I did Gibson . . . with the uce of murcury,"[21] and the commanders prepared to return to St. Louis.

To infer from all the above that the Lewis and Clark men did nothing but carouse and break rules would be a base injustice indeed. They did a magnificent job of delineating the face of a great land, albeit in the same fashion that Sir Francis Drake's young buccaneers charted the Pacific—boldly and sinfully.

And neither exploration nor sin could have been accomplished without the aid of the company's interpreters: René Jusseaume, George Drouillard, and Toussaint Charbonneau.

RENÉ JUSSEAUME

1789?–1830?

THE "loveliest myth of all America was . . . the West. It was a poem of the sunset . . . of waste places and lonely peaks, a land of valleys and hills that drank water of the rains of heaven, a lost impossible province under far clouds, where men were not dwarfs and where adventure truly was."[1]

Yet life in this "loveliest myth" was somewhat complicated. True, men worked only when they had to, which was most of the time; ate when they could, which was generally irregularly; and relaxed when and where the fleshpots flourished. But by the same rules they had to be reasonably efficient in all manner of tasks—or they died. The frontier offered food for the killing when it could be found; and nature was unbelievably beautiful, but she was also a hard and ruthless ruler. There were no limits to the hours of work, no exclusive channels of labor. A man must do many things.

Learning to survive and learning to communicate with the natives were the prime requisites of frontier life, and it was a rare trapper or trader who could not double as an interpreter of sorts.

René Jusseaume, least of the Lewis and Clark interpreters, was such a one.

Jusseaume was a Canadian, presumably French, and had come to the Mandans perhaps as early as 1789.[2] He had a "wife and family who dress and live like the natives. He retains the outward appearance of a Christian, but his principles, as far as I can observe, are much worse than those of the Mandans: he is possessed of every superstition natural to those people, nor is he different in every mean, dirty trick they have acquired from intercourse with the set of scoundrels who visit these parts . . . some to trade and others to screen themselves from justice," said Alexander Henry the younger.[3]

Notwithstanding this reputation, René Jusseaume was on the payroll of the North West Company on the Red River a few years after his arrival in the West.

In the meantime, the great David Thompson, surveyor-explorer for both the Hudson's Bay Company and the North West Company, was rising to frontier fame. In 1797 he left the first company and joined the second; he departed from Alexander Fraser's House at the head of Reindeer River and set off for Cumberland House up near The Pas; thence he went back down to Lake Winnipeg, the Grand Portage, and Lake Superior. Here he encountered and joined forces with the greatest of the fur brigade commanders, Hugh McGillis.

In company with McGillis, he tramped over, paddled through, and surveyed hundreds of square miles of the Canadian fur country between Cumberland House and John McDonnell's House, a mile and a half above the mouth of the Souris (Mouse) River.

David Thompson was a restless, intense man. Despite the advent of winter, when he arrived at McDonnell's House he determined to go at once to the Mandans via the Souris Valley, purportedly to establish regular North West Company trade with them and other Missouri River tribes.[4] But English traders had reached the Mandans probably as early as the close of the American Revolution, and the most Thompson could do was divert business to his company and perhaps induce the Indians to abandon their recent attachment to roving Spanish traders up from the South.[5]

Thompson started for the Missouri accompanied by "Monsr Jussome who fluently spoke the Mandan Language [and] Mr Hugh McCrachan a good hearted Irishman,"[6] along with seven other men, probably voyageurs out to become "free traders."

While it was true that McCrachan and Jusseaume were familiar with the Mandans and that McCrachan had made the present journey many times, Thompson's confidence in Jusseaume's fluency was not justified. The Canadian had been on the Missouri for nearly a decade, perhaps longer, but he had not acquired real proficiency in the Indian tongues. Alexander Henry the younger said Jusseaume spoke the Mandan language only "tolerably well," and called him "that old sneaking cheat whose character was more despicable than the worst among the natives."[7] Lewis and Clark said they found him "to be assumeing and discont'd."[8]

René Jusseaume could seldom deliver the quality of services of which he constantly boasted.

Thompson was in trouble on two counts before he left the Souris River post late in November, 1797. He had a poor interpreter-guide, and he was ill equipped with animals. He had but two horses. Jusseaume had only one, and the remainder of the crew owned a total of thirty half-savage and untrained dogs on which they spent endless hours, untangling harnesses and cursing the snarling brutes.

Yet there was cause for some optimism. The rivers were frozen, and three inches of dry snow promised a fast trail. The morning of departure was crisp and bright, but as the sun climbed slowly it brought no warmth. Exhaled breath spiraled into freezing vapors; fingers uncovered to fill a pipe with biting trade tobacco were quickly numb; soft moccasins squeaked louder and louder on the crystal snow. By sundown it was zero, by eight o'clock 20 degrees below, and by morning 27 degrees below zero.

Travel was impossible, and the men waited, shot at buffalo, and damned the cold. When it moderated five days later, fierce prairie winds had whipped the dry snow into huge drifts often as impossible to cross as sheer cliffs of granite.

Thompson had intended to follow the Souris except for cutting across a bend whenever this offered a better route. But he had not reckoned with his voyageurs' fear of the compass. They wished to remain close to the river, apparently not knowing that its reverse bend would place them in Saskatchewan, not among the Mandans. McCrachan had been to the Missouri several times, but he was not a guide, and Jusseaume had become hopelessly confused by the recent storms—if indeed he had ever been otherwise.

A week after they left McDonnell's House, some chance-met Indians told Thompson the Sioux knew of their journey and intended to prevent them from reaching the Mandans. "I did not like this news," said Thompson, "but the men paid no attention."[9] Voyageurs frightened by a compass they did not understand were disdainful of the Sioux who threatened their lives.

Next morning Jusseaume suggested a shortcut, but "Mons.r Jussome could not say where we were,"[10] and Thompson declined. It was an alarming situation. The ten men were partly lost, they had no adequate shelter, and they were without either an honest guide or an efficient interpreter. They did, however, appear to have food, for Thompson's journal says he "reproved them, for what I thought Gluttony, eating full eight pounds of fresh meat p^r day . . . ," at which the men replied that eating was their greatest pleasure.[11]

Under those circumstances, Thompson, McCrachan, and one other decided to press ahead relying on the compass. The others, too frightened to trust a flickering needle, dallied behind until the leaders were a half-mile ahead, when they all scampered to catch up like schoolboys caught out after the tardy bell.

Actually Thompson had spied a grove of oaks in the distance through his telescope, but he was too wise to squander his leadership by giving away secrets.

One wonders whether René Jusseaume knew of the deception.

Thompson now deployed his frightened men in a straight line close enough together to be heard by shouting but far enough apart to maneuver the untrained dogs. By so doing he got men and dogs to the oaks, set up a tent, waited out a new storm, and then moved up the Souris until they came to a friendly Indian camp where Jusseaume was at last of some help. He bargained to exchange dogs for two horses which had become lame.

The animals were lame, said the Indians, because they were white-footed and had yellow hoofs which could not tolerate a difficult journey. Black-footed horses were the only kind to use for such work as Thompson demanded, they said, and dogs were probably better than any hoof-color of horse.

It was mid-December, and the thermometer held at 20 to 30 degrees below zero day and night. Thompson must leave the Souris if he was to reach the Mandans, but he had lost most of his faith in Jusseaume and could not hire another guide. He took his own counsel and pushed ahead, keeping his men "close in file." In spite of these precautions, one man with a single dog fell behind, got lost in the snow and early dark, became too weak to walk, and fell to his hands and knees, "bawling with all his might until we fortunately heard him," said Thompson.[12]

So, with one near-tragedy after another, Thompson outwore Jusseaume's failures; outlasted a −32-degree Christmas season; nursed McCrachan through a siege of illness; survived a prairie blizzard which he failed to recognize for the killer it can be; left the Souris near the modern Verendrye, North Dakota, and struck overland;

outwitted a band of hostile Sioux; and arrived on the Missouri only six miles above the Mandans—a neat bit of dead reckoning.

Thompson, McCrachan, Jusseaume, and the voyageurs had tramped 238 miles through one of the coldest winters in Dakota history.

David Thompson never had more than a secondary interest in the fur business. Exploring, surveying, and studying the peoples he met were his prime concerns. As soon as the routines of his present trade venture could be decently finished, he plunged into a more intriguing subject, a history of the Mandans. McCrachan and Jusseaume were urged to help, but they "were illiterate* . . . and either did not understand my questions, or the Natives had no answers to give."[13]

It was unfortunate, but Hugh McCrachan was not a linguist and René Jusseaume was not interested in history.

With no further incentive for remaining on the Missouri, Thompson left the Mandans January 10, 1798, and resumed his notable work in the Canadian West.

In the meantime, Spanish traders from the Southwest were reaping profits. It sometimes shocks the provincial-minded to find that years before Lewis and Clark ever thought of crossing the continent, small companies of Spanish traders were leaving St. Louis, Santa Fe, and Taos and fighting north to the Mandans with red wine, Spanish leather, copper pots, and all the gimcracks of Indian trade.

But René Jusseaume, the Canadian squaw man, knew these things. While Thompson was vainly trying to get a history of the Mandans, Jusseaume was going from lodge to lodge, sponging free smokes and food and urging the Indians to desert the Spaniards and buy exclusively from the North West Company, to which he seemed to have had some vague sense of loyalty.

However, it never occurred to him, being the kind of fellow he was, to do this honestly. His mind was warped into devious patterns, and in the present instance he made a deal whereby certain Indians were to enter the lodging of the latest Spanish trader, John Evans (actually

---

* René Jusseaume was not entirely illiterate. Several examples of his signature are extant, among them the promissory note from him to J. Février dated Prairie du Chien, October 10, 1790, now preserved in the P. Chouteau Maffit Collection, Missouri Historical Society, St. Louis; and an instrument of indenture between Jusseaume and Meriwether Lewis dated May 13, 1809, now in the Meriwether Lewis Collection, Missouri Historical Society, St. Louis.

a Welshman), and rob and kill him. When this detestable plot fizzled, Jusseaume tried shooting Evans in the back. Prompt action by Evans' interpreter saved him. Disgusted, Jusseaume left for the Assiniboines along the upper Souris before Evans could retaliate.

Such, then, was René Jusseaume's introduction into history. From then on he was always a part of the Missouri story. He never achieved the distinction of Matonabbee or George Drouillard because he lacked both the ability and their integrity. Instead he skulked on the fringes of great events, a sort of historical jackal—too ignoble to praise, too conspicuous to ignore.

Following Thompson's visit to the Mandans, little of moment involved Jusseaume until Lewis and Clark hired him briefly during their outgoing winter on the Missouri. He kept them posted on the activities of rival visitors, accompanied them on short excursions, and regaled them with Indian lore of varying degrees of accuracy. But the commanders must have rued their bargain many times, for Jusseaume moved inside the American quarters, where there was more to eat, more warmth, less danger—and more opportunity for general skulduggery, such as quarreling or selling the services of one's wife.

We know little more about Jusseaume's activities during that winter. The journals rarely mention the "old sneaking cheat," and when spring came and the expedition headed for the Pacific, Jusseaume was left behind, presumably off the payroll. But some kind of understanding was maintained between Jusseaume and the American commanders on implementing Lewis' conviction that if a large number of Indian chiefs could be induced to visit the President in Washington, Indian-white relations would be improved.

Lewis had been propagandizing along these lines all winter, but he had to depart for the Pacific without knowing whether his campaign would succeed. He cannot be blamed for not seeing the pitfalls of the plan, for he had had relatively little first-hand contact with the Indians. Clark, a product of the frontier and thoroughly familiar with its psychology, undoubtedly knew the problems involved but refrained from saying so, for before they had ever crossed the Missouri into the West, he had been made to understand that he was in subordinate command, despite his popular coequal title of captain. And if he never let this color his relations with Lewis, either in public or in his journals, the reader of the unexpurgated daybooks would indeed be careless not to note that Clark walked while Lewis rode the pirogue; Clark tramped off on side excursions while Lewis wrote up the journals in the relative comfort of the big leather tent; and Clark got the less efficient interpreter. Thus, it does not stretch credulity too far to suspect that Clark may have harbored reservations about sending Indians to Washington but that he was too loyal to Lewis to say anything.

In any event, the expedition left for the West and René Jusseaume remained with the Mandans with instructions to recruit a Washington delegation. That is the last we hear of him until the expedition returned from the Pacific and he was rehired to escort Chief Big White, or Sheheke, and his family to see the President.

The choice of Jusseaume for this duty was strange, because surely Drouillard or Charbonneau, the husband of Sacajawea, either of whom was better qualified, would have made the journey. Perhaps the commanders felt that since Jusseaume had helped recruit Big White, he deserved the excursion. Perhaps he was the more persuasive talker.

It is best to leave Jusseaume's journey to Washington, about which few details are known, to be interpolated where it impinges on more important events.* Suffice it to say here that in the course of the long and very unsatisfactory trip, Jusseaume was wounded—how does not appear clear—and, not being one to let an opportunity go untested, he evolved a plan to plump for what in our day are known as disability allowances.

Jusseaume petitioned "Monsieur le Président" in these terms: he was crippled for life and could never work again or support his family; he must get back to the Mandans so his wife's parents could take care of their many children; and as a bit of unasked-for advice, he added that the American flag would never be respected by the Indians until it was backed by force. [14]

René Jusseaume was about as reprehensible a character as the interpreter-guide clan ever turned up, but he was not devoid of finer points, among which was a sincere interest in the welfare of his half-breed children. On May 13, 1809, Jusseaume apprenticed a son, "Toussaint Jussome, aged about thirteen years unto . . . Meriwether Lewis" for a period of five years, Lewis to be responsible for all the expenses of raising and educating the young man. [15]

Little more is known about René Jusseaume. After arranging the

---

* We will take up Big White's adventure again in Chapters 21 and 27.

above apprenticeship, he entered the employ of Manuel Lisa and remained generally under his banner until the Spaniard died in 1820. More than a decade later, Maximilian, Prince of Wied, remarked on his visit to the frontier that Jusseaume still could not be relied upon as an interpreter. Time and practice had not perfected his abilities.

But where and when the "old sneaking cheat" ceased his sins are one with the pattern of frontier deaths: a shallow grave, a mumbled "Rest in peace," and no obituary.

GEORGE DROUILLARD

?–1810

GEORGE DROUILLARD, or Drewyer as they incorrectly called him, was the first of the famous interpreters to join Lewis and Clark on their trans-America journey.

He was a Pawnee-French half-breed—straight, powerful, and taciturn. Brown eyes dominated a face more Indian than French, and from his Pawnee mother and volatile father came an explosive temper which got him into one or two serious affairs.

Hampered by his propensity for escaping journalistic attention, Drouillard remains elusive and colorless. He did not particularly like to fight; he had no more than an average interest in frontier sin; he never made a fool of himself or sought publicity. So much of his work was done alone that he was and is more a name than a personality.[1]

Yet his service to Lewis and Clark was of prime importance, and Manuel Lisa would have been hard pressed to initiate his Missouri fur empire without the sagacity of George Drouillard.

From whom, why, and where did the half-breed receive the education which was far above his birth and station in life?

Where did "all my brothers and sisters" live, and what did they do?

Who was the "artist" who covered his blond body with barbaric tattooing from the waist down?[2]

Did George Drouillard ever take a wife, French or native?

They remain questions.

Of his life before 1803 we know only that his father, from British Detroit, had married Angélique Descamps, had sired several children, and was interpreter for the Royal Army when it was defeated by

George Rogers Clark during the American Revolution;[3] and that it was the senior Clark who recommended young Drouillard to Meriwether Lewis. Drouillard joined Lewis on December 16, 1803, at Fort Massac, eight miles below Paducah, Kentucky, on the Illinois side of the river.

Later Lewis sent a note to Clark saying that Drouillard had arrived from Tennessee with eight men, that he was not much impressed with their quality, but that no commitments had been made beyond offering Drouillard $25 per month as guide and interpreter.[4] There was "not a hunter among them," said Lewis—one of the prize misstatements of American history, for George Drouillard could shoot on equal terms with old D. Boone, and Lewis would soon be relying on the half-breed to feed the entire expedition.

With the above note between commanders, Drouillard, as was his wont, slipped out of notice, to be mentioned but seldom until the expedition was ready to leave for the Pacific; then he was suddenly remembered when he delivered $99 but lost a letter addressed to Lewis, which a "Country man" eventually found and handed over.

Finally the expedition was on its way, but the first leg of the journey, as far as the Mandans, was purely routine. A military chain of command was set up; they visited Daniel Boone at his homestead on the Missouri; they looked at Indian petroglyphs and "found a Den of Rattle Snakes"; and they met "old Mr Durioun [whom] . . . we questioned until it was too late to Go further. . . ."[5] In the morning Pierre Dorion, Sr., for it was he, reversed his track and turned upstream with them, thus giving the Americans the second of their famous interpreter-guides.

Presumably, Dorion and Drouillard were acquainted. The fraternity of interpreter-guides was never large, and it is unlikely that men of the rank of the senior Dorion and Drouillard would be total strangers. And since all interpreters were notorious storytellers, their tales enlivened the dull but grueling labor of cordelling. Even the generally taciturn Drouillard said one day with a straight face, and Lewis and Clark recorded it as fact, that "ab$^t.$ 5 Miles below here . . . Passed a Small Lake in which there were many Deer feeding. he heard in this Pond a Snake makeing goubleing noises like a turkey. he fired his gun & the noise was increased, he heard the indians mention this Species of Snake, one Frenchman gives a Similar account."[6]

On another occasion Drouillard hung a deer and a bear on a limb overhanging the river so they could more easily be taken aboard the boats. ". . . during the time I lay on the sand waiting for the boat, a large Snake Swam to the bank immediately under the Deer. . . . I threw chunks and drove this snake off Several times. I found that he was determined on getting to the meet, I was compell^d. to kill him, the part of the Deer which attracted this Snake I think was the Milk from the bag of the Doe."[7]

But there were more serious diversions, too. As noted above, discipline was causing trouble, and on August 7, 1804, the commanders "dispatched George Drewyer, R. Fields, Wm Bratten & Wm Labieche back after the Deserter reed with order if he did not give up Peaceibly to put him to Death &c. . . ."[8]

Orders which should be remembered.

In addition, La Liberty (doubtless a nickname), one of the non-military personnel and probably Drouillard's companion, when he had tried to find the "otteaus and Panies" (Otos and Pawnees) a few days before, was also missing in the vicinity of Council Bluffs.[9] Ten days later, Labiche, to give him his correct name, reported that Reed was being brought in alive and that La Liberty had been captured but had escaped.* Here is a faint hint of collusion. George Drouillard was a hard man, and we shall see that at another time he was far from lenient when sent after a deserter. That on this occasion one runaway should be brought in and another, but recently Drouillard's companion, allowed to escape raises a question.

Anyway, Reed readily admitted his guilt, asked for mercy, and was sentenced to run the gantlet four times in the presence of the Indians, and henceforth to be considered as not belonging to the expedition although allowed to accompany it. This sentence released Lewis and Clark from all legal responsibility for Reed's well-being and at the same time averted the stigma of abandoning a lone man.

Other difficulties arose. The interpreters insisted on the right to trade and trap on their own account and be excused from guard duty and other camp chores. It was not surprising that the demands caused ill-will; or that there was "Gealousy between M^r Gi[b]son one of our int^r and George Drewyer last evening, &c."; or that Drouillard and John Colter got into a row when Lewis bought a colt for supper and turned it over to them to care for until butchering time; or that Drouillard was accused of "several similar fracases."[10]

---

* La Liberty was not again seen by Lewis and Clark, although a man by the same name was with Wilson Price Hunt on the Astorian expedition of 1811.

But it is more difficult to understand why Drouillard was held responsible for situations beyond his control and outside his duties. He had been hired as an interpreter-guide, and yet he did most of the effective hunting, and he and George Shannon sometimes went after lost horses which should never have been allowed to stray in the first place. On one such occasion Shannon got lost, and the commanders had to upset work schedules and hunt him, with subsequent bad humor all round.

All in all, however, George Drouillard was seldom mentioned. He became ill, was given sage tea, and was bled; he killed a bear and saved Charbonneau's life; he supplied skins for the iron frame of Lewis' impractical riverboat; he drank his share of the last whiskey; he hunted Shannon again; he chased an Indian who had stolen his gun, recovered it, and in turn robbed the Indian to teach him a lesson; and he used his superb knowledge of sign language and Indian psychology to pave the way for Sacajawea's famous meeting with her brother.

He gave quiet advice on the location for the winter camp at Clatsop; he awed the Indians with a brilliant display of marksmanship; he killed the bulk of the 131 elk and twenty deer which fed the expedition during the winter on the Pacific.

Then, when it was time to start home, devoid of food and trade goods but with the chiefs happy and the Indian girls well paid for favors granted, it was George Drouillard who collected enough Indian food, where and how only he knew, to serve until he could kill more substantial fare. "I scarcely know how we Should Subsist, I believe but badly if it was not for the exertions of this excellent hunter," said Clark.[11]

It was Drouillard who negotiated with Chief Twisted Hair for the return of the horses left with his Indians on the outward journey. It was Drouillard who taught Lewis how to geld the half-wild stallions so they could be used to carry. It was Drouillard who looked at the sky and the trees and the crusted snow and said it was much too early to get through the mountains on the return journey—albeit the commanders ignored his advice and were then forced to retrace their steps, as he knew they would. And it was he who secured the local guides necessary to make the dangerous crossing when the sun was high and the drifts partially gone.

On July 18, 1806, it was Drouillard who was ordered to chart Maria's River, and .it was the information supplied by this well-educated half-breed on which Clark relied when he drew his celebrated map of the West in August of 1808.[12]

And when the expedition disbanded in St. Louis, it was George Drouillard to whom Manuel Lisa turned for help in organizing the first great American trading venture on the upper Missouri.

United States of North America with the British and Spanish territories, 1809. *Courtesy Library of Congress.*

GEORGE DROUILLARD AND
MANUEL LISA

1807–1810

ST. LOUIS was the crossroads for the greatest frontier in history. Her front lawns entertained the silver buckles of Colonial society; her back porches gave egress into a wilderness. Up and down her dusty streets tramped every sort of man and woman. Perfumed and lace-cuffed noblemen rubbed elbows with flea-infested Osage chiefs; international scientists drank raw alcohol with illiterate interpreter-guides; polished belles competed with black-haired squaws who more than held their own in a contest where fire and lack of inhibition were the twins of preferment. It was a raw, sprawling agglomeration of sin and frontier preachers, squalor and booming fur trade. A quarter of a million dollars changed hands annually. A handful of blue beads bought a $6 beaver pelt. A cup of diluted whiskey purchased a buffalo hide.

Manuel Lisa understood this city of extremes and made it his own. He never achieved popularity with its elite, but he did achieve envy.

Manuel was the son of Christopher Lisa, Spanish government servant, and was born in New Orleans, the City of Sin, on September 8, 1772. He left there perhaps as early as 1790 and drifted to St. Louis, where with the help of his father he soon obtained an exclusive trade with the Osages.

But that range was far too restricted for his genius, and he was casting about for a wider sphere when Lewis and Clark returned from the Pacific.

William Morrison and Pierre Menard, both of Kaskaskia, were doubtless flattered when Lisa invited them to join him in mounting a

St. Louis, 1835. Oil on canvas by Leon Pomarede. *City Art Museum of St. Louis, Arthur Ziern Jr. Collection.*

Manuel Lisa. *The State Historical Society of Missouri, Columbia.*

Two-story stone warehouse of Manuel Lisa, built 1818.
Walker-Missouri Tourism.

venture to the Blackfeet and Crows, 2,000 miles north and west of St. Louis. But Drouillard, who was still loafing about the city, was not overly impressed by the same offer; he expected to be associated with the most important projects.

George Drouillard was no modest underling.

Lisa proposed to head his own expedition in the field. Drouillard was to be his chief support and to represent Morrison and Menard. In addition to a trading post, they intended to set up their own trap-lines. With that in mind, Lisa recruited forty-two employees, including the former Lewis and Clark men John Potts and Peter Wiser, and departed St. Louis on April 19, 1807, with $16,000 in goods aboard.

At the mouth of the Osage River Ed Rose, the mulatto interpreter, joined the party, but one of the *engagés,* Antoine Bissonette, deserted. It was no spur-of-the-moment action. He had signed with Lisa to serve three years; but even before they reached the mouth of the Osage on May 14, and only 120 miles up the Missouri, Bissonette had been systematically stealing supplies to make a getaway. When the expedition tied up at the Osage landing, Bissonette took his clothes and the pilfered articles and secreted them ashore. He then returned to routine duties. While the commanders were occupied with the details of trade, he stole into the brush bordering the river, picked up his cache, and slipped away.

The events immediately following were described by one A. Dubreuil in a sworn statement before Justice of the Peace Thomas Riddick in St. Louis on August 5, 1808. Said Dubreuil:

The day that we were to leave the river of the Osages to continue our trip, Mr. Manuel Lisa ordered the crew to cast off, and soon as the crew had swung away the crew yelled that one man was missing from aboard. Mr. Manuel Lisa asked who that man was, he was told that [it] was Bazine. Mr. Manuel disembarked to go for Bazine and said to Mr. George Drouillard, George, go look for Bazine and bring him back dead or alive. Mr. Drouillard took his carbine and left accompanied by Benito. Shortly after they had left I heard a . . . shot. And about half an hour after Mr. Drouillard returned and said that he came to get someone to bring the wounded man to camp. He then took some men and went to get him and bring him back. Mr. Manuel Lisa had left on his part saying that he was going to . . . where he thought that he would find him, he had taken a canoe and two men and on leaving he said if I find him at sight of [him] I fire upward [as a signal]. He returned two or three hours after to the area and as soon as he embarked, George Drouillard announced to him that he had wounded the man. He said good he is a rascal who got what he deserved. He was near Bazine and spoke to him in an angry voice reproaching for the situation in which he had been put and that it was his own fault. The man remained until the next day when he sent him with someone from St. Charles whose name I do not recall.[1]

Dubreuil's statement, although somewhat confused, makes it clear that Drouillard was issued dead-or-alive orders; that Lisa himself went after the deserter with the same intentions; and that, despite his anger, Lisa attempted to save Bissonette's life by returning him for medical care. Neither Drouillard nor Lisa considered it any of their responsibility when Bissonette died en route to aid—he should not have deserted.

Being a man of temper, Lisa was not always consistent in the treatment of his employees. When Jean Baptiste Bouche returned to camp after four days' hunting without permission, Lisa let him off with a tongue-lashing. Bouche, instead of recognizing his good fortune, determined to get even. During the night (it is not clear whether it was the same night or later), George Drouillard heard a suspicious noise, and creeping stealthily to the keelboat he caught Bouche in the act of setting it adrift. Drouillard seized the craft and presumably reported the incident to Lisa, who again failed to give Bouche a major punishment. A few nights later Bouche tried again, and again Drouillard caught him.

Why Lisa ordered Bissonette shot but used none of the severe punishments against Bouche which the frontier would have considered proper is a riddle, one which must have made Drouillard wonder with what manner of man he was associated.

In the meantime, the expedition proceeded upriver. At the mouth of the Platte, they recruited John Colter, who had been released from the eastbound Lewis and Clark command. He had been trapping on his own and was but now paddling down to St. Louis with reports of fabulous beaver valleys tucked away in the mountains west of the Mandans.

He was easily persuaded to join Lisa and Drouillard.

There was no trouble until they reached the Arikaras,[2] who were just then having a pleasant little war with their neighbors, the Mandans. Two hundred Arikaras fired shots across Lisa's bow to emphasize their objection to any trade with the Mandans. Lisa cautiously nosed the keelboat ashore and was relieved to see Arikara squaws arrive with bags of corn as tokens of trade. These were no sooner dropped on the ground, however, than they were knifed open by several warriors as a sign of war. Lisa immediately trained the boat guns on the Indians but did not fire. At this turn of affairs, the chiefs rushed to Drouillard and said the sack-cutting was the act of "bad men" who had had no sanction from the chiefs. Lisa and Drouillard pretended to believe the excuse, but they realized that profitable trade was unlikely under the circumstances, and they turned the keelboat into the current and departed for the Mandans—considering themselves lucky to escape with no damage beyond a few minor thefts.

But the Mandans, too, were in a nasty anti-white-man mood. Since Lisa never used force if subterfuge or persuasion would serve the same end, he now fell back on Indian psychology. Extreme bravery invariably won their respect. Leaving Drouillard to get the keelboat past the Mandan warriors as best he could, Lisa hitched up his leggings, muttered an imprecation on all savages, and walked boldly and alone the full length of the Mandan towns.

Not a shot was fired.

Despite the fact that Drouillard had been very popular with the Mandans during the Lewis and Clark days, Lisa's bluff took raw courage on the part of both men, for Drouillard must force his reluctant boatmen to pole their clumsy craft close to shore in order to use the current eddies, thus exposing them to a dangerous fire from the warriors on the riverbanks.

This first American trading venture to the upper Missouri had one near miss after another. Lisa and Drouillard had barely outbluffed the Mandans when they saw on the high ground bordering their route an estimated 4,000 to 5,000 Assiniboines whooping it up for trouble.

It was no time to dally, and Lisa and Drouillard started firing— over the heads and beyond the range of the natives. The Indians, not knowing they were being tricked, quickly asked for a parley, and Drouillard conducted the usual double-talk ceremonies which both sides knew were but face-saving formalities.

Thus, without actual violence but with constant warlike demonstrations, Lisa and Drouillard arrived at the mouth of the Big Horn on November 21, 1807, and erected Fort Raymond, a small stockaded post on the right bank. It was the first post and the first white man's building in Montana.[3]

Drouillard and Lisa had intended to establish trade with the Blackfeet, but to do this they should have remained on the Missouri instead of ascending the Yellowstone to the Big Horn. Now they were in the very heart of the territory of the Crows—deadly enemies of the Blackfeet—and by the rules of Indian thinking had just made themselves enemies of the Blackfeet. Only an enemy would trade with a Crow!

If either Lisa or Drouillard was perturbed by their predicament, they did not show it, for Lisa immediately sent John Colter alone and with only a thirty-pound pack on a cruise to solicit the Crows.

It was on this journey that Colter discovered the wonders of Yellowstone Park.

The activities of Lisa and Drouillard while Colter was gone are heavily tinged with conjecture. Some authorities credit Drouillard with retracing Colter's route: up the Big Horn to Pryor's Fork, to the Shoshone, to the Absaroka Range, into Yellowstone, up the Yellowstone to the lake, south to Jackson Lake, to the Green and Big Sandy rivers, across South Pass, and back to the mouth of the Big Horn.[4] In the spring of 1808 he is said to have left Fort Raymond again and ascended the Little Big Horn, visited the upper Tongue River, and turned north to the Rosebud and back west to his post with the report that the tribes were receptive and beaver plentiful.[5] There is no proof.

Other scholars believe that both Lisa and Drouillard remained close to the Fort until the following August, when they embarked for St. Louis with a satisfactory catch.[6]

All are agreed, however, that American trade was established with the Crows, that Colter had seen live steam spouting from frozen riverbanks and bubbling mud surrounded by mountain meadows, that beaver were plentiful; and that the Blackfeet were implacable foes.

Perhaps Lisa did not know why this last was true, but George Drouillard did. He was half Indian. On the night of July 27, 1806, Meriwether Lewis had caught a Blackfoot brave crawling on his belly into camp intent on stealing American guns. Lewis had aroused the camp, and Reuben Fields had stabbed the Indian to death. Since that moment, Drouillard knew, the Blackfeet regarded all white men as enemies and himself and Lewis as devils.

Such considerations, however, did not dampen the happiness with which Lisa and Drouillard poled swiftly down toward civilization, past the Mandans, the Arikaras, the Osages, Daniel Boone's homestead, and St. Charles, to home.

St. Louis—a hot bath (which meant a good deal to even these hardened men), good food, better liquor, and the heady perfume of a clean woman.

With these visions George Drouillard stepped from the keelboat to the dock, was met by Constable Alexander Belliseuine,* and was arrested for the murder of Antoine Bissonette![7]

Even today there is no satisfactory explanation for Drouillard's arrest. In 1808 there was precious little law anywhere on the frontier, and less on the New Orleans–St. Louis–Mandan sector. Shootings were so common in New Orleans they were not even topics of conversation, and shooting a deserter on the Missouri was in the same category as hanging a horse thief. Perhaps someone thought a murder trial would reflect adversely on the unpopular Lisa. Perhaps someone just had a sudden surge of righteousness.

The case brought out the legal elite. Drouillard was tried by Attorney General John Scott before Judge J. B. Lucas; Associate Judge René Auguste Chouteau, a very prominent St. Louis businessman and fur dealer; and a jury of Drouillard's peers—all men who knew the rules of frontier life.

Drouillard was defended by Edward Hempstead, William C. Carr,

---

* His signature is partially illegible.

and Rufus Easton, who argued for three hours that Bissonette's desertion was premeditated, and if allowed to go unpunished would tempt others to do the same and thus endanger all expeditions; that Bissonette agreed he had been well treated by Lisa; that he readily admitted his guilt; that Drouillard was a hero of the Lewis and Clark Expedition, was used to military orders, and would obey a commander without question; and that the Bible said if a thief were killed while being apprehended, his blood should not be avenged.

The jury took fifteen minutes.

Not guilty.

Nevertheless, the trial raises unpleasant conjectures. Testimony showed that Drouillard's bullet entered Bissonette's back near the shoulder, with the obvious inference that he had been given little chance to surrender; and the large number and importance of both prosecution and defense forces hints that more than a routine frontier killing was at stake.

In any event, the trial was a financial blow to Drouillard, who had to pay for his own defense. In fact, the following spring, he was reduced to signing on March 25, 1809, a six-month note made out to Joseph Kimball for the paltry sum of $19.

Two months later he wrote his sister as follows:

St. Louis, May 23, 1809

MY DEAR MARIE LOUISE:

You have without doubt learned of the misfortune which happened to me last spring on my way to the Upper Missouri. I admit that this misfortune was very fatal to us but at the same time, I would have you observe without trying to excuse myself, that this has not been done through malice, hatred or any evil intent. Thoughtlessness on my part and lack of reflection in this unhappy moment is the only cause of it, and moreover encouraged and urged by my partner, Manuel Lisa, who we ought to consider in this affair as guilty as myself for without him the thing would never have taken place. The recollection of this unhappy affair throws me very often in the most profound reflections, and certainly I think it has caused a great deal of grief to my family for which I am very sorry and very much mortified. That I have not lost the affection of my old friends proves that they did not believe me capable of an action so terrible through malice and bad intent.

I would have had the pleasure of seeing you all last winter if it had not been for the lack of money to cover the expenses of such a voyage. The expenses which I had through my lawsuit for the affair above mentioned have absorbed all my savings that I had made in the upper Missouri; this obliges me now to return to this part of the country with the brother of Governor Lewis who continues to employ me as before for the United States—(I mean the last one).*

I do not think I can return from the Upper Missouri before three years and just as soon as I return I shall be delighted to see you all. If some of my family will be kind enough to write to me they will address their letters to Monsieur Pascal Cerré at St. Louis. He and his wife although not known to my family in Detroit join with me and beg you to accept their civilities. They are the best friends I possess in this country. My respects to our Mother who I embrace well, also all my brothers and sisters who I would very much like to see.

> Your very affectionate brother,
> GEORGE DROUILLARD

P.S.   Remember please to Madam Maisonville and her family. Madam Jacque Parrent, Detroit, Sandwich.[8]

Perhaps the letter reflected public opinion in St. Louis, too, for when a new and stronger company, the St. Louis Missouri Fur Company (the "St. Louis" was soon dropped) was organized to continue the Crow-Blackfoot venture, George Drouillard was again chief interpreter.

Manuel Lisa was not liked by his fellow entrepreneurs, but he was much too powerful to be ignored, and the new Missouri Fur Company automatically included Lisa, Morrison, and Menard from the previous organization. All the really important fur men of St. Louis belonged: Benjamin Wilkinson, Jean Pierre Chouteau (half-brother of René Auguste), his son Auguste Pierre Chouteau, Reuben Lewis (brother of Governor Meriwether Lewis), William Clark, Sylvester Labadie, Dennis Fitz Hugh, and Major Andrew Henry.

Clark was to act as agent in St. Louis; Governor Lewis was to negotiate a contract between the federal government and his brother's new fur company calling for the payment of $7,000 to return Chief Big White and his interpreter, René Jusseaume, to their Mandan

---

* That is, Meriwether Lewis, now governor of the Louisiana Territory, still employs him.

homes after a visit to Washington;* and Jean Pierre Chouteau was to command a force of 125 militiamen to protect the total staff of more than 200 voyageurs, clerks, and trappers.

Further to ensure commercial success, Governor Lewis promised to withhold trade licenses from anyone else until the new combination was firmly established.

Excepting Morrison, Clark, and Wilkinson, all the partners were signed with the field expedition when it left St. Louis on June 15, 1809.[9]

Just beyond the mouth of the Knife River, Lisa built Fort Mandan, after which he and certain others returned to St. Louis, where they arrived just before Thanksgiving.

Another segment went to the mouth of the Big Horn, arriving there about the end of October.

In March of the following year, 1810, Pierre Menard and Andrew Henry, with Colter as guide and Drouillard as interpreter, left Fort Mandan with a party and headed for the Three Forks of the Missouri to force the Blackfeet to trade whether they wanted to or not. Despite storms, snow blindness,[10] irregular food supplies, and unfamiliar terrain, the detachment erected a stockade on the Three Forks early in April.

Two days later the Blackfeet struck. Five men were killed, several horses stolen, and many traps and pelts lost. The Indians kept up a steady pressure. Menard forbade lone trappers or even small parties to move outside the immediate area of the post, with the result that no commercial quantities of beaver could be taken.

Nor would the Blackfeet come in to talk.

Finally someone (Menard is often credited with the idea) conceived a crafty ruse: the neighboring Snake tribe would be tricked into warring on the Blackfeet; the Snakes would capture a Blackfoot brave and deliver him to Menard; Menard would load the captive down with presents and turn him loose; the warrior would be grateful and convert his brothers to peace and trade—with Menard.

A scheme so devious was much too complicated to succeed, and it never got beyond talk. Meanwhile, the Blackfeet were striking hard and often. The post was substantially under siege. Despite that, Drouillard, laughing at Menard's caution, made two successful trips

---

* See pages 155–160.

Three Forks of the Missouri. Pencil sketch by A. E. Mathews. *Montana Historical Society, Helena.*

into beaver valleys. "I am too much of an Indian," he said, "to be caught by Indians."[11]

But one bright May day, the corpses of two Shawnee companions and the savagely mutilated and decapitated body of George Drouillard were found behind his dead horse not far from the stockade. A warm spring wind blowing away from the Fort had prevented Menard from hearing the guns, and this fact had turned the fortunes of Drouillard.

Legend says that the Blackfeet mutilated Drouillard's body because they were infuriated with his marksmanship, while at the same time they were so awed by his courage they sought to partake of it by eating choice bits of him, some raw, some boiled.[12]

The Missouri Fur Company never fully recovered. Menard returned to St. Louis in July of 1810, and Andrew Henry evacuated the stockade and moved to a promising site near the modern St. Anthony, Idaho. But this venture also failed, and Henry returned to the Arikaras where, either by design or by happenstance, Manuel Lisa met him.

Other members of the Menard party drifted away—some to find their niche in the fur trade, others to leave no record.

And George Drouillard barely escaped that anonymity, for he was essentially a colorless and tragic figure. More sagacious than a dozen Sacajaweas, more trustworthy than a tribe of Jusseaumes, he lacked the changing lights and shadows which might have made him more than a name.

He was a major factor in the greatest American expedition, but through no fault of his and no design of hers, an illiterate Indian girl stole the spotlight in one dramatic moment; he was associated with every important entrepreneur of his day, but is virtually unmentioned in their memoirs or the thousands of pages written about their affairs; highly literate himself, he left no journal of his own, and no Boswell wrote his story; he tramped and paddled over an empire, but no chart details his wanderings. Even death denied him the balm of heroism, for his killing served no worthy purpose.

Yet despite all this, George Drouillard was one of the mightiest of the breeds and half-breeds who sculptured America.

14

TOUSSAINT CHARBONNEAU

1758?–1804

OF all the New World explorations, the one led by Meriwether Lewis and William Clark has received the most attention. It is unnecessary to dwell upon the major characters and scenes of this, the greatest of American expeditions. Its history has been drummed into every schoolboy with patriotic vigor if not always with complete candor.

Thomas Jefferson, Meriwether Lewis, and William Clark all richly deserve the honor the expedition brought them, but unfortunately there is generally silence and sometimes ridicule for the men who kept the expedition on the proper trails, hunted food, and smoothed the contacts with the Indians.

If millions of words have been written about the leaders of the expedition, only a few less have been printed about Sacajawea,* the Bird Woman. But few of her admirers could name her husband. In fact, there is almost a legend that she was a frontier Madonna without husband or other earthly attributes.

Doubtless there were days when she wished this were true, for she was married to one of the less noble characters on the Missouri, the Frenchman Toussaint Charbonneau.

The record is neither clear nor uncontested. There are those who refer to Charbonneau as one of the half-breeds who roamed over the western fur lands. Others say, with equal surety, that he was a Frenchman from Montreal, and the evidence is strongly in their favor.[1]

---

* Historians and linguists have argued for years over the proper spelling and pronunciation of this name. We have chosen the present spelling without prejudice as to its validity.

Some would have Charbonneau a harmless, simpleminded, and friendly squaw man, capable enough if he were not asked too much, but a nonentity nevertheless.[2]

At the other extreme is Charbonneau the panderer, boaster, liar, brawler, coward, wife beater,[*] and wife trader, a foul-minded and useless bit of frontier scum whom Lewis and Clark tolerated solely for the purpose of acquiring the services of his newest and youngest wife, Sacajawea.[3]

This last is patently a fiction, because Charbonneau "wished to hire as an interpiter" on Sunday, November 4, 1804, and Sacajawea did not become his wife until February 8, 1805; nor is there any evidence that Charbonneau had any plans for marriage in November.

Obviously, it is too late now to ascertain the whole truth about Charbonneau, but we may say that he was almost certainly a Frenchman from Montreal born about 1758, of medium height and heavily built, with brown eyes, a swarthy skin, and a face adorned with a huge mustache.

One of his many wives is reputed to have insisted that Charbonneau possessed a nasty temper, but a careful reading of the journals left by those who knew him fails to disclose evidence that he was cursed with more than the normal French fire and Indian disrespect for womankind.

When Lewis and Clark hired him, he was in his early forties. Though he had lived for many years among the Gros Ventres and other Missouri River tribes, he still affected the plaid shirt with trousers of the French voyageurs rather than the robe and legging costume of the natives.

No one knows when or why Toussaint Charbonneau left Canada and took up Indian life, but ten years before he came to the notice of the lower Missouri River entrepreneurs, his abilities were recognized by Canadian traders like Peter Pond, Peter Pangman, the three Frobisher brothers, Simon McTavish, and others who had formed the loose organization called the North West Company. Long before Lewis and Clark, the North Westers were operating as far south and west as the Dakotas. In 1793–1794 Toussaint Charbonneau was

---

[*] One casual entry by William Clark, "I checked our interpreter for striking his woman at their Dinner," has been blown into gigantic proportions by some writers (see Elliot Coues, *New Light on the Early History of the Greater Northwest,* 3 vols., New York, Francis P. Harper, 1893, II, 497n).

master at their Pine Fort on the north side of the Assiniboine River, not far from the present Carberry, Manitoba. It was the Company's southernmost post at the time, and it served the Gros Ventres and the Mandans, who were twelve days' tramp still farther south.[4]

That Charbonneau held this small command argues that he was not considered an incompetent.

Two or three years later, Charbonneau moved to the Minnetarees on Knife River, north of Bismarck, North Dakota, and settled down at their central village, Metaharta. Whether he was a free trader or was still employed by the North West Company is not clear. In any event, he was a resident white man and correspondingly important because most of the middle Missouri River trade, especially that of the Mandan towns with which the Minnetarees were associated, was with the North West Company via one or another of their Canadian posts.

But Charbonneau did not have a monopoly. Hugh McCrachan had been to the Mandans many times. Spanish traders from Santa Fe and Taos were not unknown, and there was a body of other white traders steadily visiting the fleshpots of the Indian towns. David Thompson remarked that "it is almost their sole motive for their journey hereto: The goods they brought, they sold at 50 to 60 p^r cent above what they cost; and reserving enough to pay their debts, and buy some corn; spent the rest on Women."[5]

As we have seen, René Jusseaume was Thompson's interpreter when the latter visited the Mandans in 1797. Charbonneau may well have been on hand to welcome them, for it is certain that the long association of Jusseaume and Charbonneau began about that time. The friendship is significant to the extent that some of the less commendable doings of both men occurred when they were together or with another interpreter. For example, there is the unproved story that Ed Rose once suggested to Charbonneau that they seize several Indian girls and take them to the cities for prostitution; and the charge is oft repeated that Charbonneau and Jusseaume regularly sold the pleasure of their current wives for a bit of extra cash.[6]

During the trading season of 1803–1804 Charbonneau was again with the North West Company, in command of the small but important factory at Pembina, almost astride the 49th parallel. With him at Pembina was Alexander Henry the younger, a keen judge of men and

Toussaint Charbonneau's old post, Pembina on the Red River, as it looked in 1822. From a watercolor by Peter Rindisbacher. *The Public Archives of Canada.*

business opportunities, who was not given to suffering association with those who could not hold up their end of responsibilities. *

Thus it appears that contrary to the picture which some writers give of Toussaint Charbonneau as certainly incompetent, if not a fool and a rogue,[7] the record does not quite bear out these indictments. And though a story somehow got started that the North West Company had terminated Charbonneau's services because he had betrayed its interests to the Hudson's Bay Company,[8] later events would seem to contradict this also.

Following his tour of duty at Pembina, Charbonneau returned to Metaharta, where he was living a robust middle life when Lewis and Clark came poling into view in the fall of 1804.

All the way up the Missouri, the Americans had added and deleted detachments. Some were Indians whose goodwill was valuable in passing through the next contiguous territory; some were free white traders stopping for a chat; some were Indian "womin verry fond of carressing our men &c"; and some were interpreters. George Drouillard had joined the expedition before it reached the Missouri, and Pierre Antoine Tabeau, Joseph Gravelines, and the Dorions, father and son, had all been with the command for various lengths of time.

---

* Also attached to Henry's command about this time was one Etienne or Louis Charbonneau whose relationship, if any, to Toussaint Charbonneau is unclear (see Coues, *op. cit.,* I, 49–50).

These accretions of interpreters are worth noting, for inasmuch as Lewis and Clark already had their services available, why did they also hire Charbonneau when the time came, if he were as useless as often pictured?

On October 22, 1804, the expedition camped near the old Mandan towns, a site later occupied by Fort Lincoln, although the vagaries of time and Missouri River floods have long since erased all traces of the exact spot where the Americans camped.

A week later Lewis and Clark chose the location for their winter quarters, on the east bank of the Missouri River seven or eight miles below the mouth of the Knife, and hired René Jusseaume. Never one to overlook a few months of easy living, Jusseaume hurried home, rounded up his squaw and their two offspring, and moved in with the Americans, as we have seen.

On Sunday, November 4, "a M^r. Chaubonie, interpeter for the Gross Ventre nation Came to See us, . . . this man wished to hire as an interpiter. . . ."[9] Modern authorities are in substantial agreement that Charbonneau, who never learned to speak much English, was not so accomplished a linguist as he thought; but he had been among the Indians many years, and his experience "fit him to be of great value to the expedition."[10]

The new interpreter and Jusseaume took Lewis on a visit to several Indian towns. On their return, F. A. Larocque and Charles McKenzie,* traders from the North West Company, as well as some Hudson's Bay Company men were with the Mandans, ostensibly for trade but more significantly to scout American intentions. They remained all winter, and Lewis and Clark had to contend with their divisive influence.

Larocque was presently clerk at Fort Assiniboine, and had already been as far west as the Yellowstone.[11] Not long after the Americans hired Charbonneau, Larocque "Spoke to Charbonneau about helping as interpreter in the trade to the Big Bellies, he told me that, being engaged to the Americans he could not come without leave from

---

* For four or five months in the summer of 1805, Larocque toured the Rocky Mountains. He then retired from frontier life and entered business in Montreal. McKenzie, however, never left the American West. He traded with the Gros Ventres on the upper Missouri in 1806, and when the North West Company merged with the Hudson's Bay Company, he remained with the new organization until 1846. He died in 1854.

Captain Lewis, and desired me to speak to him, which I did, with the result that Lewis gave consent."[12] This exchange of civilities is important as it seems to dispose of the slur that the North West Company discharged Charbonneau for disloyalty—at least at that date.

Charbonneau's record becomes hazy at this juncture. He is supposed to have been sent almost immediately after Lewis and Clark hired him to apprehend a Sioux who had killed a Mandan, while early February is also suggested as the date he and Clark set off after the Sioux.[13]

In any event, the culmination of the manhunt, if it ever took place at all, never assumed much status in the journals because the chase was overshadowed by the Frenchman's wedding. On February 8, 1805, the fortyish Toussaint Charbonneau married the teen-age Sacajawea, who had been a slave of the vicious Le Borgne, chief of the Minnetarees, when Charbonneau had purchased her some five years previously.

She was about to bear Charbonneau her first child.

Her groom already had several wives. Joseph Whitehouse, chief teamster for the expedition[14] and one of the few men who bothered to keep a journal, says that Charbonneau had three wives in the Mandan towns;[15] and the commanders' own journal for November 11 says, "two Squars of the Rock mountains, purchased from the Indians by a frenchman [Charbonneau] came down. . . ."[16]

There is a favorite story that Lewis or Clark, or both, required Charbonneau to marry his slave girl to salve the Puritan mores of the command.[17]

Be that as it may, the excitement of the marriage, barely preceding the birth on February 11 of little Pomp, a common Shoshone name for firstborn sons, excluded further interest in Sioux murderers as far as the journalists were concerned.

Christmas had brought a discharge of firearms, hunting, and dancing among the men, with no women allowed except Charbonneau's three wives, who were permitted to watch. Then on New Year's Day the commanders relented and permitted the men to visit the Mandan towns, with the usual results—someone claimed his squaw had been stolen, and an officer had to hurry over and soothe ruffled feelings.

As the winter wore on, Lewis and Clark were increasingly involved in affairs which had little direct connection with their major objective but which needed to be resolved lest the mission fail through the accretion of adverse details.

Charbonneau went to Turtle Hill on the Little Missouri River; he learned that the Hudson's Bay Company was busy undermining the importance of the American expedition in the minds of the Indians, and that the North West Company was planning a post on the Little Missouri. One of Charbonneau's squaws became ill and Clark gave her stewed fruit, a favor which infuriated another wife, and Clark had to compromise that. Charbonneau and Drouillard both became ill, and Lewis forgot to order the boats out of the water so that they were nearly crushed by the ice, which could be neither chopped away nor melted with hot stones. And as if all this were not worry enough, Charbonneau visited the Gros Ventres where the North West Company had a post and returned with tales of lavish entertainment, lengths of gay cloth, fancy garments, 200 rounds of ammunition, and almost ten feet of tobacco! Toussaint Charbonneau was not ill considered by the Canadians.

This esteem so annoyed Clark he accused Charbonneau of accepting a bribe from the North West Company, which only added weight to a pocket of ill will which had been building between the Frenchman and the American commanders. George Drouillard, as an interpreter, had been excused from all guard duty and common labor, and Charbonneau believed he should be treated the same. Furthermore, he insisted on his right to trade privately when he chose.

In view of this dissension, Charbonneau did not take Clark's accusation with equanimity, and there was talk of his leaving American employ. Clark had not expected this reaction to his charge of bribery. Both he and Lewis had but recently broached the subject of taking Sacajawea on the transmountain trek, but obviously they could not have her services if Charbonneau quit them.

With pretended magnanimity, they gave Charbonneau overnight to consider his loyalties.

At this late date, it is impossible to know which side was the more worried that March night. Charbonneau very much wanted to go to the Pacific and be paid for his pleasure, frontier life being no hardship for him. And Lewis and Clark needed the Frenchman's abilities, especially since they believed Sacajawea would be of help if they made contact with her people far to the west.

The contestants retired for the night, each doubtless hoping the other would give in. Next day Charbonneau said he had decided not to accept the American terms of employment, and Ordway wrote in his journal for March 14, 1805, that the commanders hired Gravelines to take Charbonneau's place.

Neither Lewis nor Clark evinced any public concern, and the matter rested—Sacajawea's figure growing more valuable day by day, the glamour of the Pacific shining brighter and brighter night after night.

A week late Charbonneau asked "thro our French inturpeter . . . to excuse his Simplicity and take him into the cirvice. . . ."[18] The matter was not referred to again, but Lewis and Clark were careful to treat Charbonneau with reasonable consideration for his position as interpreter; and we shall see that the relation of Charbonneau and Clark evolved into one of mutual liking, if not deep respect.

By the end of March the expedition was ready to leave winter quarters, but first Charbonneau had to settle a family row. His entourage was to include only one wife—Sacajawea—and those to be left behind set up an unholy racket, hoping thereby to be included in the expedition. Charbonneau stood firm, and all the disgruntled women could do was annoy Sacajawea with their jealousy.

April 7, 1805: Dispatches had been sent to Washington and Mandan farewells said, and Lewis wrote of "this moment of my departure as among the most happy of my life."[19]

New routines had to be established. The military formalities of the past months would give way to more practical arrangements, whereby each man would be assigned the duty he could best perform regardless of former prestige or rank. But there were certain notable exceptions. A close reading of the expedition journals will quickly disclose that Charbonneau was very often given tasks for which he had no ability with nearly disastrous effects, and that Lewis, despite a manful and sincere attempt, never forgot that his regular commission outranked Clark's and automatically assumed the preferred positions and less arduous tasks. He often rode the pirogues while Clark tramped the shores, as we mentioned, and Drouillard, as the greatest hunter and most valued adviser, had already become Lewis' almost constant companion and confidant.

It was left for Charbonneau and Sacajawea to attach themselves to Clark, and as the miles wore past an interesting triangle developed. Lewis, Clark, Drouillard, Charbonneau, Sacajawea, and little Pomp all slept together in "a tent of dressed skins," said Lewis. But Sacajawea had no interest in anyone except her Pomp and the red-haired William Clark, whom she adored.

Nothing was too good for him. She hunted the wild artichokes cached by the gophers; she collected serviceberries; she made special Indian dishes to please him. And Clark would have been less than the man he was had he not responded in kind. Nor did Charbonneau mind: he saw no reason for jealousy; and the Charbonneau-Clark-Sacajawea triangle was never strained. If there were some developments which might have more than one interpretation, historians have charitably avoided dwelling upon them.

As the expedition moved slowly westward, the commanders, for some now unknown reason, put Charbonneau as steersman on one of the pirogues. It would have been difficult to find a position for which he was less fitted. Charbonneau's incompetence and the commanders' poor judgment came near causing fatal accidents. Since the poor Frenchman knew nothing whatever about handling a pirogue, it was not surprising that when one of the Missouri's sudden gusts hit the crude sails, he was helpless. While the boat tipped and plunged, the supposed steersman did everything wrong. Just before the craft turned bottom up, Lewis ordered Drouillard to take command.

But it was a narrow escape. Lewis, Sacajawea, Pomp, all the valuable papers and instruments, and both interpreters were aboard. Had the pirogue gone under, the heart of the expedition would have been lost, and historians would be blaming a clumsy Frenchman.

Perhaps Lewis sensed this injustice to Charbonneau, for as they crossed the mouth of our present-day Indian Creek, between Shell Creek and Little Knife River, he named it Charbonneau Creek in honor, he said, of the Frenchman's having hunted there previously. Sergeant Ordway gave the interpreter more credit: "the above small River . . . is named after our Int^r Charbonae river as he has been to the head of it which is farther up the Missourie Than any white man has been." [20]

On Thursday, April 25, Lewis decided to cut overland to the mouth of the Yellowstone with Drouillard and three or four others; Clark was to bring up the pirogues. Such a move gave Lewis extra time for his observations, he said. Also, it would make him instead of Clark the first American on the Yellowstone.

Making note of the commercial value of the Yellowstone site, the expedition moved on, with Clark, Charbonneau, and Sacajawea

Map of part of North America, "from the authorities of the best informed travellers . . . and from Indian information," by Meriwether Lewis, 1806. *The National Archives, Record Group #77.*

trudging along the shore fighting the spring mosquitoes. But Sacajawea was happy. There were wild fruits for Clark, and a few days
later, on the Milk River, she came radiantly into camp with a meal
of "white apple"* for the entire crew. Lewis called Sacajawea's offering insipid but admitted that "our epicures would admire this root."

If Lewis thought little of Sacajawea's "white apples," he was more
impressed by "what our wright hand cook charbono calls the *boudin
blanc,* or white pudding":

About 6 feet of the lower extremity of the large gut of the Buffaloe is the
first mo[r]sel that the cook makes love to, this he holds fast at one end
with the right hand while the forefinger and thumb of the left he gently
compresses it, and discharges what he says is not good to eat, but of which
in the s(e)quel we get a moderate portion; the mustle lying underneath
the shoulder blade next to the back, and fillets are next saught, these are
needed up very fine with a good portion of kidney suit; to this composition
is then added a just proportion of pepper and salt and a small quantity of
flour; thus far advanced our skilfull operater . . . sceizes the recepticle
. . . and tying it fast at one end turns it inward and begins now with
repeated evolutions of the hand and arm, and a brisk motion of the finger
and thumb to put in what he says is *bon pour manger;* thus by stuffing and
compressing he soon distends the recepticle to the utmost limits of it's
power of expansion . . . and all is completely filled with something good
to eat, it is tyed at the other end, but not any cut off, for that would make
the pattern too scant; it is then baptised in the missouir with two dips and
a flirt, and bobbed into the kettle; from whence, after it be well bolied it
is taken and fryed with bears oil untill it becomes brown, when it is ready
to esswage the pangs of a keen appetite or such as travelers in the wilderness are seldom at a loss for.[21]

Thus again, Charbonneau is found performing a task in no way
associated with his rank as interpreter, but by some quirk of his
simple mind he appeared to enjoy cooking, and there is no record
of a serious protest on his part.

---

* Called *pomme blanche* by the French and *Psoralea esculenta* by the scientists.
These roots were eaten raw or cooked in any manner convenient at the moment.

15

ACROSS THE CONTINENT

1804–1806

DESPITE their earlier experience, Lewis and Clark again assigned Charbonneau to the helm of a pirogue. One day early in May, both commanders went ashore, leaving all valuable equipment in the craft controlled by the Frenchman, "perhaps the most timid waterman in the world," said Lewis.[1]

Sacajawea, with Pomp on her back, sat quietly nursing her own thoughts, which almost certainly had nothing to do with her spouse. Long ago she had transferred any sentiment of which she was capable to William Clark. If she thought of Charbonneau at all, it was with a smoldering hate, the cause of which is only partially clear. True, he had bought her for a slave, fathered Pomp without benefit of clergy, used corporal punishment, and probably offered her to the men with Lewis and Clark. But reprehensible as all these were, they were widely accepted as inevitable by Indian women, and it is difficult to assess Sacajawea's special hate for Charbonneau.

F. G. Burnett, once a teacher at Fort Washakie on the Shoshone reservation in Wyoming, said years later, "Sacajawea rarely spoke of Charbonneau. When she did mention his name, it was with bitterness and in rememberance of his temper and abuse. . . . She spoke of Charbonneau as being a bad man who would strike her on the least provocation. . . . Clark . . . would not allow Charbonneau to abuse her."[2] Also, Burnett continued, if she had been given to Lewis and Clark's men, she would have been disgraced and have had her nose cut off. This is open to debate, because the mutilation could hardly have been effected in the presence of the American commanders as well as in the absence of her own tribe to enforce such a code.

Sacajawea's relationship with Charbonneau is extremely confused for many reasons. Neither Sacajawea nor Charbonneau was literate, and all quotations from either are therefore indirect. Charbonneau entered into domestic relations with numerous Indian girls, and it is seldom possible to know positively which of his consorts was involved in a given situation. And there is no unanimity regarding the date of Sacajawea's death, some having it as early as 1812, others 1837, and still others as late as 1884.

All these factors becloud any evidence attributed to "Charbonneau's wife"; for instance, the above quotations from Burnett were reputedly made many years after some authorities believe Sacajawea to have died. Obviously, if she died in 1812, the remarks about Charbonneau attributed to her in her later life were made not by Sacajawea but by another Indian woman who lived with him at some time. Or if the 1884 date is correct for her death, then the charges of misuse which she leveled against a husband may have referred to another of the several men with whom she is said to have lived after she reputedly ran away from Charbonneau while she was still quite young. If she lived to the age of 100, the memory of early spouses would likely have taken on the inaccuracies of old age.[3]

But all these discrepancies of history were far in the future. For the moment Sacajawea sat motionless, as a good pirogue passenger should, while Charbonneau steered the craft.

And then it happened again. Like a mighty hammer a squall hit broadside, and long before Charbonneau could collect whatever wits he had, the pirogue was on her side, saved from turning bottom up only by the sail.

Blind, trembling panic seized the Frenchman, and there he huddled with fear-frozen hands, too terrified to do anything. He was "still crying to his god for mercy" when one of the crew cut the sail loose and the pirogue righted itself, full of water to within an inch of the gunwales.

Everyone was shouting orders. Even Lewis lost his head and plunged into the river fully clothed in an attempt to help, but he came to his senses and returned to shore before he was caught in the current.

And Charbonneau prayed.

Finally Pierre Crusatte, acting as bowman that day, pulled his pistol and threatened to shoot Charbonneau if he did not do his duty. In the meantime, Sacajawea was leaning over the side of the pirogue busily scooping up every article within reach; she saved some of the most valuable expedition records and supplies.

Crusatte, without much help from Charbonneau, got the pirogue ashore, dumped it free of water, and spread the freight out to dry.

A ration of grog went the rounds that night.

This episode is one of those always cited to prove Charbonneau a coward. It is a picturesque interpretation of an unchallenged occurrence, but it does not present very good historical balance. Certain important items are generally omitted: Sergeant Ordway, not a man to hide his opinions, says little more about the accident than that the pirogue was hit by a squall and turned on her side, with no particular imputation of guilt; Toussaint Charbonneau, like the majority of his fellow Frenchmen, could not swim, and to fall in any water deeper than his head meant almost certain drowning; and perhaps most important, it was as much a psychological truism then as now that every human being has an area of paralyzing fear peculiar to his own ego. It may be great heights, or battle, or fire.

For Charbonneau it was water. It held a mortal terror for him which he was as powerless to resist as many a better man has been unable to combat the panic of fire.

It was on the Pacific journey, too, that another episode occurred that has contributed to Charbonneau's reputation as a coward. One day when he and Drouillard were surprised by a grizzly bear, the animal chose to chase Charbonneau, who fired his gun in the air and hid in the nearest thicket while Drouillard killed the beast.

Here again no one disputes the facts, but their interpretation may be questioned. Charbonneau's customary weapon was a knife; he was a poor shot and seldom carried a gun, one authority saying he never did.[4] Furthermore, climbing a tree or hiding were accepted defenses against grizzlies. Captain Lewis said he would rather fight two Indians than one grizzly, and Sergeant Ordway tells how six of his hunters once wounded a brown bear, far less dangerous than a grizzly, whereupon it chased two of the hunters into a canoe while a third jumped into the river to escape—and no one accused them of cowardice.

Now, all this is not to say that Charbonneau was a noble and fearless frontiersman. But neither was he an abject coward. If he feared more things than some men, by that very token it took a larger measure of bravery just to endure the day-by-day dangers of the American frontier.

When the expedition reached the forks of the Missouri, digressive excursions were made to determine which was the main stream. When this was decided the commanders, not too confident of their opinion, secretly agreed that Lewis and Drouillard would lead a small detachment overland seeking the rumored Great Falls, which, if found, would vindicate their judgment. Clark, Charbonneau, and the remainder of the men would continue moving their bulky craft up the shallow stream.

But it was killing work. The cordelle or towline was the only means of moving the boats. Raw, human muscle must overcome the pull of the river. Barefoot, naked, wading in water often up to their armpits, the men pulled and hauled and stumbled and cursed. But each night they were a little nearer the Pacific. By the first of June, they were eating supper only a few miles below the Great Falls.

In many respects the next two weeks were the most trying for the expedition. Lewis and Drouillard were seeking the Falls, leaving Clark with the poorer interpreter and a short food supply.

Sacajawea was ill and Clark bled her, which did not help; he did it again, and she got worse; he moved her under cover on a pirogue; he switched from bleeding to a "doste of Salts," and "the Indian woman [was] verry sick." Lewis, having reached the Falls on June 13 "about 12 OClock having traveled by estimate about 15. Miles," dropped downstream to find Sacajawea "excessively bad," which concerned him greatly "from the consideration of her being our only dependence for a friendly negociation with the Snake Indians on whom we depend for horses to assist us in our portage from the Missouri to the Columbia river."[5]

Meanwhile, Lewis, apparently without consulting Clark, chose a sixteen-mile portage around the Falls. Whatever Clark's private thoughts were regarding this somewhat high-handed decision, he said nothing, and set about making crude wheels from the cross-sections of giant cottonwood trees. The wheels were to be used on a vehicle it was hoped would lighten the labor of the long portage.

Sacajawea was no better, and Lewis gave her two "doses of bark and opium," which improved her pulse, but a relapse followed. Both commanders then became unreasonable and said that if she died it would be the "fault of her husband."[6] There was little justification for this. Sacajawea's illness almost certainly stemmed from a severe cold contracted at an unfortunate time, and Clark's own journal admits that Sacajawea finally took further medication on orders from Charbonneau. But the contradiction lends weight to the idea that the Frenchman was not well liked, at least by Lewis, and that it was customary to put him in as bad light as possible.

Lewis followed his opium with "15 drops of the oil of vitriol," and Charbonneau made Sacajawea a meal of "white apple," after which her fever rose and Lewis castigated Charbonneau for preparing the delicacy for his wife. Poor Charbonneau could only shrug his puzzlement while Lewis switched from "oil of vitriol" to dilute niter and laudanum!

Frontier medicine was always crude, seldom scientific, and surprisingly effective. Those who were fit survived.

While Lewis was doctoring Sacajawea and damning her husband, Clark was finding the sixteen-mile portage far more difficult than Lewis had thought. The men were exceedingly tired. Prickly pear, insects, and the summer heat were taking a dangerous toll in human strength, and it is doubtful whether Charbonneau's cooking helped matters.

Next to the last day in June, a sudden storm trapped Charbonneau in another of the events which have been turned to his disadvantage. He, Clark's Negro servant York, Clark himself, and Sacajawea were upriver just above the Falls when a black sky warned them of an approaching storm. With the exception of York, they took shelter in a narrow, dry canyon, where they were almost immediately engulfed by the cloudburst runoff racing down the narrow confines.

Water! Charbonneau was as terrified as ever, and with his plaid shirt plastered to his back and his great mustache dripping, he froze midway between life and drowning, clutching Sacajawea by the hand while little Pomp hung wide-eyed from his mother's neck. Charbonneau had instinctively grabbed his wife's hand in a protective gesture and as instinctively failed to do anything but endanger her life. They were perched halfway up the steep walls of the canyon when Clark pushed them both to safety. *

---

* Referring to still another mishap in which Clark saved Charbonneau's life when he was knocked off his feet by a swift current, the vitriolic editor of the Lewis and Clark journals Elliot Coues said, "On most occasions Captain Clark showed . . . rare judgement. . . . Today he was not up to the mark, and the cowardly wife-beating tenderfoot still lived" "Tenderfoot" indeed! Toussaint Charbonneau had already lived many years among the Indians and was the undisputed dean of the interpreter-expatriates on the Upper Missouri. Whatever he was, he was no "tenderfoot." (See Elliot Coues, *History of the Expedition Under the Command of Lewis and Clark,* 4 vols., New York, Francis P. Harper, 1893, II, 442.)

While Clark was saving the Charbonneau family from drowning, the men on the portage were in equal danger from the giant, two-inch hailstones which accompanied the storm.[7] Said Lewis:

Saw a black cloud rise in the west which we looked for emediate rain we made all haste possible but had not got half way before the Shower met us and our hind exeltree broke in two. We were obledged to leave the load Standing and ran in great confusion to Camp the hail being so large and the wind so high and violent in the plains, and we being naked we were much bruuzed by the large hail. Some nearly killed one knocked down three times, and others without hats or anything about their heads bleading and complained verry much.[8]

Nothing was going too well on the portage. Lewis had insisted on bringing the iron frame for a knockdown boat, which, after Drouillard had killed enough animals to supply hides to sheath it, proved impractical and had to be sunk in the river to await the return of the expedition. "I fear I have committed another blunder," said Lewis.[9]

He had.

Swarms of insects allowed little rest, day or night; Lewis suspected what Charbonneau could have told him—that they could not reach the Pacific and return that season, and that as the mountains closed in, game would become scarce and the "white puddings . . . lost and Sharbono out of employment." York was sick; clothes were worn out; and beyond the portage, which was completed July 4, 1805, Clark must build smaller canoes before they could move on.

After this Pryor dislocated a shoulder for the second time; Lepage became ill, and Charbonneau had to relieve him aboard the boat— this time without mishap.

As they neared Snake country, the commanders led small detachments in search of the Indians, from whom they wished to buy horses to use in crossing the Continental Divide. In view of the legend that Sacajawea was indispensable, it is interesting to note that Clark took neither her nor Charbonneau on his excursion. And when, after passing the Three Forks, food was in dangerously short supply and no Snakes or any other tribesmen had yet been found, Lewis took Drouillard and Charbonneau, but not Sacajawea, in a desperate bid to contact the Indians.

Illness, ineffectual sanitary precautions, and accidents had so delayed the expedition that it was August 3 before they arrived in the vicinity of Butte, Montana. Three days later Lewis and the two interpreters again went searching for help.

Lewis would remember the day: a canoe overturned; Clark missed a direction signal; the medicine got wet; Whitehouse fell in the river and narrowly missed death when the plunging canoe passed directly over his head; some powder was missing; and George Shannon got lost again because the commanders had left no direction markers for him, and it had taken him three days to backtrack and pick up their trail.

Near Grayling, Montana, Lewis agreed it was useless to attempt further navigation of the river, and again went in search of the Indians. Shortly thereafter he reached the headwaters of the Missouri, "in surch of which we have spent so many toilsome days and wristless

Meriwether Lewis called this scene "Gates of the rocky mountains." Pencil sketch by A. E. Mathews. *Montana Historical Society, Helena.*

John M. Stanley's lithograph of the site where Lewis and Clark crossed the Continental Divide. *Report of Explorations and Surveys ... 1853, U.S. Senate, 36th Congress, Executive Documents, Phillips Collection, University of Oklahoma Library.*

nights," and the same day crossed the Continental Divide, where "I first tasted the water of the great Columbia river." * [10]

The story of the first contact of the Americans with Sacajawea's people and her joy at finding her brother, Cameahwait, who in turn furnished the horses needed for crossing the mountains, needs no retelling here. It is the *pièce de résistance* of every history of the Lewis and Clark expedition. It is enough here to note that Sacajawea recognized her nation, and that Lewis used "Labuish, Charbono and Sah-cah-gar-wea" [11] in the long-drawn-out negotiations which eventually resulted in the acquisition of the horses; and that when the Americans took temporary leave of the Snakes in order to reunite the several segments of their command, they left both Charbonneau and Sacajawea to continue bargaining for help.

Between the period of negotiations and the expedition's return to the Mandans, Charbonneau and Sacajawea ceased to be of particular significance, and fulfilled only routine duties. From time to time they are mentioned: On August 24, Lewis said, he gave "the interpreter some articles with which to purchase a horse for the woman he had obtained," but the journalist failed to say which interpreter—his favorite George Drouillard or the Frenchman Charbonneau. [12]

Some horseplay between Charbonneau and the two Field boys ended in a dispute serious enough for Clark to record, and he also spoke to Charbonneau "about his duty"; Lewis took "a belt of Blue Beeds which the Squar had," purchased pelts, and reimbursed Sacajawea with a blue cloth coat; at the council held to determine the location of the winter camp on the Pacific, Charbonneau's name is followed with a dash, indicating that he either was not permitted to vote or declined, the latter a most unlikely thought.

Sacajawea made from a minute bit of flour saved for her baby a tiny loaf of bread for Clark, which "I eate with great satisfaction"; on Christmas day the red-haired commander received "2 Doz weasels tales of the Squar of Shabono"; [13] and the Frenchman himself was detailed to help clear the stockade of Indians before the gates were locked for the night.

Charbonneau and Sacajawea begged to be allowed to go see a whale washed up on the beach, the woman saying it would be hard to have come all the long miles and be denied the sight of the ocean or the

* This is not strictly true since Lewis was on the Lemhi, a branch leading to the Snake River.

great fish; Charbonneau brought the commanders an "Oregon robin" (varied thrush) for their specimen collection; and on the return trip, Charbonneau and Drouillard negotiated again for the horses.

Once Charbonneau embroiled Lewis in a row with the Indians over a stolen animal and pilfered goods; Pomp got what appears to have been the mumps; and when Clark digressed to explore "636 Miles of [the Yellowstone]. . . . I descended in 2 Small Canoes lashed together in which I had . . . John Shields, George Gibson, William Bratten, W. Labeech, Tous.ᵗ Shabono his wife & child & my man York."[14]

"The Squaw brought me a large and well flavoured Goose berry" and some other fruit, said Clark;[15] and as they reentered Mandan territory, Charbonneau was sent to bring the Minnetarees to a pow-wow, while Drouillard was to collect the Mandans and invite René Jusseaume to rejoin the expedition as an extra interpreter.

With such isolated entries, the Frenchman and the Bird Woman are dismissed from the journals between the time the expedition made contact with the Snakes and the return to the Mandans, where Charbonneau was paid off with 320 acres of land, "500$ 33⅓ cents," and a gift of blacksmith tools which would add greatly to his prestige among the Indians.

Clark offered to take the Charbonneau family on to St. Louis as unemployed attachments to the expedition, or, if they preferred, to take Pomp and rear and educate him. Toussaint at first declined, saying that interpreting and Indian trade were the only things he knew and civilization would have no need for his services, and that the separation of Pomp from the family must be deferred because the little fellow was still nursing.

The following letter reveals the friendship and respect which the long months and hard miles had built between the illiterate Frenchman and the future governor of the Missouri Territory:

On Board the Perogue Near the Ricara Village
August 20th 1806

CHARBONO

SIR: Your present Situation with the Indians givs me Some concern— I wish now I had advised you to come on with me to the Illinois where it most probably would be in my power to put you in Some way to do Some-

thing for your Self— I was so engaged after the *Big White* had concluded
to go down with Jessomme as his Interpreter, that I had not time to talk
with you as much as I intended to have done. You have been a long time
with me and have conducted your Self in Such a manner as to gain my
friendship, your woman who accompanied you that long dangerous and
fatigueing rout to the Pacific Ocean and back, diserved a greater reward
for her attention and Services on that rout than we had in our power to
give her at the Mandans. As to your little Son (my boy *Pomp*) you well
know my fondness for him and my anxiety to take and raise him as my
own child. I once more tell you if you will bring your son Baptiest to me
I will educate him and treat him as my own child— I do not forget the
promis which I made to you and Shall now repeet them that you may be
certain— Charbono, if you wish to live with the white people, and will
come to me I will give you a piece of land and furnish you with horses
cows & hogs— If you wish to visit your friends in *Montreall* I will let you
have a horse, and your family Shall be taken care of untill your return—if
you wish to return as an Interpreter for the Menetarras when the troops
come up to form the establishment, you will be with me ready and I will
procure you the place— or if you wish to return to, trade with the indians
and will leave your little *Son Pomp* with me, I will assist you with mer-
chandize for that purpose and become myself concerned with you in trade
on a Small scale that is to say not exceeding a perogue load at one time—.
If you are desposed to accept either of my offers to you and will bring
down your *Son* your famn Janey had best come along with you to take care
of the boy untill I get him— let me advise you to keep your Bill of Exchange and what furs and peltries you have in possession, and get as much
more as you can—, and get as many robes, and big horn and Cabbra
Skins as you can collect in the coarse of this winter. and take them down
to S\t Louis as early as possible in the Spring— When you get to S\t Louis
enquire of the Governor of that place for a letter which I shall leave with
him for you— in the letter which I shall leave with the governor I shall
inform you what you had best do with your firs pelterees and robes &c and
derect you where to find me— If you should meet with any misfortune on
the river &c. when you get to S\t Louis write a letter to me by the post and
let me know your Situation— If you do not intend to go down either this
fall or in the Spring, write a letter to me by the first oppertunity and inform
me what you intend to do that I may know if I may expect you or not.
If you ever intend to come down this fall or the next Spring will be the

best time— this fall would be best if you could get down before the winter—. I shall be found either in St Louis or in Clarksville at the Falls of the Ohio.

Wishing you and your family great suckcess & with anxious expectations of seeing my little dancing boy Baptiest I shall remain your friend

WILLIAM CLARK

Keep this letter and let not more than one or 2 persons see it, and when you write to me Seal your letter. I think you best not determine which of my offers to accept untill you see me. Come prepared to accept of either which you may chuse after you get down.

M^r. Teousant Charbono, Menetarras Village.[16]

The letter was a sincere tribute bred of shared dangers and mutual help, and Charbonneau was not unappreciative. He accepted Clark's generous offer, and arrived in St. Louis at the end of the same August of 1806 with two wives and two sons!

And with that turn of affairs, history becomes involved in another dispute. Which wives and which children? The record is incomplete and contradictory. As noted, Charbonneau had other wives and children whom he left with the Mandans when he joined Lewis and Clark, and which of these he brought to St. Louis is in question.* At bottom it doesn't matter, for almost immediately Charbonneau repented of his decision to reenter civilization and joined a trapping and trading party somewhere southwest of St. Louis, probably on the Red or the Arkansas River.[17]

---

* As might be expected, even Charbonneau's contemporaries were confused about his family relations. Willard E. Smith said that Pomp was actually the son of William Clark ("Journal While with the Fur Traders Vasquez and Sublette in the Rocky Mountain Region, 1839–1840," *Oregon Historical Quarterly*, September, 1913), while T. D. Bonner said only that "The Red-headed Chief [Clark] adopted the child . . . , and on his return to St. Louis took the infant with him, and baptized it John Baptiste Clark Chapineau" (*The Life and Adventures of James P. Beckwourth*, New York, Alfred A. Knopf, 1931, p. 364). A scrutiny of dates and events will disclose obvious discrepancies in such tales, of which there were many, but they illustrate the opinions held by some of Clark's fellow frontiersmen.

16

CHARBONNEAU

AND THE WAR OF 1812

As might be expected in the life of one who could neither read nor write and who was unaware of his role in the building of America, there are numerous gaps in Charbonneau's record. A month here, a year there. Wives came and went. He hired to whoever paid the best wages and offered the best fleshpots. For Toussaint Charbonneau was unashamedly a man of the flesh—he never pretended to glib respectability.

After his trip to the Red or Arkansas, he appears next in late October of 1810, when he acquired some land in St. Ferdinand township on the Missouri River, presumably with the intention of settling down to husbandry. But he could no more stick fast to that than he could overcome his fear of water. Five months later he bought fifty pounds of "bequit" (hardtack), sold his parcel of land to William Clark for $100, and was on his way up the Missouri with Manuel Lisa and Henry Marie Brackenridge, on the voyage culminating in the famous race between Lisa and Wilson Price Hunt of the Overland Astorians. *

---

* For details of this race, see Chapter 22. Here again, there is confusion over details. Grace Raymond Hebard says that Charbonneau took Otter Woman, who was another of his wives, and their four-month-old child with him as he returned to the Mandans, leaving Sacajawea and Pomp in the care of Clark (*Sacajawea*, Glendale, Arthur H. Clark Co., 1933, pp. 100–115). In the appendix of John C. Luttig's *Journal* we find that "When Charbonneau and the Bird Woman returned to the Mandan village," they may have left their son in St. Louis (*Journal of a Fur Trading Expedition on the Upper Missouri, 1812–1813*, ed. Stella M. Drumm, St. Louis, Missouri Historical Society, 1920, pp. 133–134). W. J. Ghent states that Charbonneau and Sacajawea accompanied Lisa, but he does not mention another wife or children (*The Early Far West*, New York, Tudor Publishing Co., 1936, p. 138). And Olin D. Wheeler

Sufficient here to note that Lisa sent Charbonneau overland to Hunt to urge his cooperation, and that Charbonneau returned a week later believing Hunt had agreed. How Hunt dishonored this implication and left Lisa to enter dangerous Indian country alone is detailed elsewhere.

Following this, Lisa built Fort Manuel between the Arikaras and the Mandans and made John Luttig post commander. Charbonneau was one of the employees.

One day in mid-September of 1812, Charbonneau came flying into the Fort shouting that François Lecompte, another employee, had just been killed by the Indians. Luttig, who did not like Charbonneau, jumped to conclusions and accused the Frenchman of cowardice, saying he had "run off and left the poor fellow, the Indians spoke to Lecomte and they told him to go about his business."[1]

Charbonneau paid no attention to such rebuffs, and two days later he and his questionable friend René Jusseaume headed for the Gros Ventre country looking for horses supposedly stolen by the Big Bellies. They found the horses without difficulty, but they had not been stolen by the Gros Ventres—rather by the Mandans, the white man's friends!

Luttig wryly remarked, "a lesson to take care of our property, no matter friend or Ennemy."[2]

Shortly thereafter Manuel Lisa arranged for Charbonneau to take over the Gros Ventre trade, but Luttig did not share Lisa's confidence in the Frenchman.

Charbonneau & Jessaume Keep us in Constant uproar with their Histories and wish to make fear among the Engagees, these two rascals ought to be hung for their perfidy, they do more harm than good to the American Government, stir up the Indians and pretend to be friends to the white People at the same time but we find them to be our Ennemies.

. . . some Rees [Arikaras] arrived which were enraged against Charbonneau & Jessaume, . . . they said that C & J were Lyars and not to be considered as good frenchmen, and if Mr Manuel Lisa would send them

---

quotes Brackenridge as saying, "We had . . . a Frenchman named Charbonneau, with his wife, . . . both of whom had accompanied Lewis and Clark to the Pacific" (*The Trail of Lewis and Clark*, 2 vols., New York, G. P. Putnam's Sons, 1926, I, 128).

to the Grosventer with a pipe they would not consent such Credit have these Men amongst the Indians— they find their Character gone and try every Scheme, to Keep themselves alive like a Men a Drowning. . . .[3]

These harsh words bothered Charbonneau none at all, nor did they influence Lisa, for when intertribal war was about to explode as a reflection of the American-British hostilities of 1812, it was the old "rascal" and "Lyar" Toussaint Charbonneau, accompanied by two other emissaries, who was sent to arrange peace among the tribes.

Historians quite properly credit Manuel Lisa with keeping the Missouri River Indians either friendly to the United States or neutral during the War of 1812, but they generally choose to forget that it was the "coward," "Lyar," and "rascal" who risked his life to go among the quarreling Indians and on whom Lisa relied for his contacts with the tribes—contacts which only a trustworthy interpreter could give. As the war spread beyond the Great Lakes and the weight of Indian arms became more and more important, Charbonneau was constantly among both friendly and hostile tribes.

On November 23, 1812, he was talking trade and peace to the Sioux camped near the Arikara towns; a month later the war touched his own family when "the Wife of Charbonneau a Snake Squaw, * die of a putrid fever she was a good and the best Woman in the fort, aged abt 25 years she left a fine infant girl"[4] (perhaps Lizette), who was hastily given into the care of the Indians living at Fort Manuel lest she fall into the hands of unfriendly savages. †

His child thus cared for, Toussaint and a companion set "off for their stations" with the Gros Ventres on February 21, 1813. He returned shortly with the glad news that Le Borgne, perhaps the most bestial chief ever to live on the Missouri and Sacajawea's former master, had at last been dethroned by his own people, and was now begging Charbonneau for twenty-five pounds of powder and twice that amount of shot with which to honor a promise to the North West Company that he would side with the Canadians in the present war.

---

* This wife was probably Otter Woman, although some authorities are positive it was Sacajawea (see Luttig, *op. cit.*, p. 106; Hebard, *op. cit.*, pp. 110–111; and Ghent, *op. cit.*, p. 149).

† Lizette and possibly a brother, Toussaint, Jr., were later taken to St. Louis by Luttig, who believed Charbonneau was dead because he had not returned on time from "one of these expeditions." The child or children were given into the guardianship of William Clark (Luttig, *op. cit.*, pp. 133–134).

Inexplicably, the old chief had also promised only to steal from the Americans, not to kill them. Why he needed ammunition to implement such a promise is a nice bit of Indian rationalization.

As animosities beyond the Mississippi intensified, Lisa believed Charbonneau should have some protection, but the Frenchman was unconcerned. Nevertheless, when the Cheyennes near Fort Yates, North Dakota, warned him there were unfriendly Sioux nearby, Lisa ordered him "escorted by 5 of our Men, untill he would be out of Danger," said Luttig.[5]

Lisa valued his interpreter even if Luttig did not.

Throughout the war Lisa and Charbonneau used their very considerable influence in favor of the American cause, with the result that the Missouri Indians never seriously challenged American arms. To that extent, Lisa the Spaniard and Charbonneau the Frenchman deserve our thanks.

When the war was over, Charbonneau's insatiable craving for new trails and new faces, especially feminine ones, resumed sway, and when Auguste Pierre Chouteau and Jules de Mun turned their fancies from the Missouri to the Rio Grande, Charbonneau was close at hand.

The faint foundation lines across the small creek are believed to be the remains of Manuel Lisa's sanctuary for infirm River Sioux near Cedar Island on the Missouri River, circa War of 1812. *Photo by author. Courtesy of William Arch, owner of the site.*

CHARBONNEAU
GOES TO SANTA FE

1815–1817

IF Mandan towns and Minnetaree fleshpots were steady sources of profit and pleasure, nevertheless, the dream of many a Missouri riverman was to cross the prickly pear fields to the southwest, climb the long, blazing sand reaches of the Spanish mountains, and enter the fabled valley running from Taos to Santa Fe, magnificent every fall with golden foliage symbolizing the material desires of all fur men. There were the streams teeming with luxurious pelts; there were the

Santa Fe, 1846, looking north. Fort Marcy on the far hill was not there when De Mun and Charbonneau visited the town. *Museum of New Mexico, Sante Fe.*

soft summer nights and tingling winter dawns; there were the clean beds and the lithe, perfumed companions to share daytime laughter and nighttime ecstasy.

It is no use pretending that gold and pelts were all that lured these men to Taos. Puritan America and prim chronologists like to sweep unholy facts under the historical carpet, but the interpreter-guides were less sanctimonious. They made no bones about the multiple lure.

Thus far, however, those who had dared the desert, the mountains, and the Spanish laws against foreign traders' entering the Taos–Santa Fe corridor had generally landed in jail and lost their goods, and were indeed lucky to escape with their lives. But the fur trader was essentially a gambler and adventurer, and after the Louisiana Purchase in 1803, it was a rare season when some reckless band did not turn southwest instead of toward the Sioux and Mandans.

On September 10, 1815, Jules de Mun and Auguste Pierre Chouteau led a party to trade at the headwaters of the Arkansas, close by Spanish domains.

On the way they bought out Joseph Philibert, who was returning to his men with supplies and horses for the purpose of bringing out his own catch of the previous year.

At the mouth of Huerfana Creek, De Mun found that Philibert's men, under pressure of starvation, had crossed the mountains into Spanish territory.

De Mun seized the chance to follow them to Taos. He found them safe and well received, went on to Santa Fe to seek permission to trade and trap, was encouraged to believe his request would be granted, and then returned to Huerfana Creek, where he, Chouteau, and Philibert sat down to consider their situation.

They still had more men than their supplies would support, and it was decided that De Mun, Philibert, and one other should return to St. Louis to replenish their needs. They were to meet Chouteau at a rendezvous on the Kansas River.

Forty-six days later De Mun wrote, "I bought the goods and engaged men for a new expedition, and, having taken another license, started on the 15th July [1816] to go by water to the Kansas river, where Mr. Chouteau and I appointed to meet."[1]

John Luttig says that Toussaint Charbonneau was a member of this second De Mun expedition.[2] The fragmentary De Mun journal makes no mention of Charbonneau by name. But Luttig generally knew whereof he spoke, and Charbonneau swore he was on the journey.[3] Hence it is safe to assume that the virile old Frenchman, wrinkled with the trails of fifty-eight summers, hitched up his none-too-tidy britches again, tucked in his plaid shirt, and shouldered his full share of the second De Mun expedition, an expedition which quite possibly represented the first white man's crossing of the Front Range into the "Bull Pen" area of the North Platte.[4]

Without mishap, except for a brush with 200 Pawnees, De Mun met Chouteau, arranged to ship their catch to St. Louis, and headed for the mountains with Charbonneau and some two dozen men.*

By this time both De Mun and Chouteau were planning how best to crack the Taos–Sante Fe barrier, and when some chance-met Spaniards told them there were unfriendly Utes and Apaches nearby, De Mun abandoned local trapping, left Chouteau at Sangre de Cristo pass, and rushed headlong toward Taos again.

But this time he encountered official opposition, even if clothed in Castilian courtesy. He was stopped before reaching his destination, and although he was allowed to send a request for permission to plead his case before the governor, he was told to stay on his own side of the fence in the meantime.

The American West was not conquered by men who paid overmuch attention to such orders, and when De Mun missed Chouteau at the pass and had to trace "him up the Rio del Norte [the upper Rio Grande] near where it enters the mountains,"[5] he was all the while mulling over how best to circumvent the Spaniards.

That his own life and those of his men might be forfeit never entered his head. Death was a daily specter in the mountains, and one got used to the sight of the Scythe.

When a courier from the governor brought a denial of all De Mun's requests, he and Chouteau accepted the rebuff and outlined a trading trip to Crow country instead—a region less strange to Charbonneau than Taos or Santa Fe, and by that token less appealing.

Before the Crow expedition could get under way, however, De Mun

---

* There is the possibility that Charbonneau was sent to St. Louis with the pelts, but since he was paid $200 for the year July, 1816, to July, 1817, this fact would argue that he remained with De Mun.

risked another trip to Taos in March, 1817. There he found wild rumors regarding his intentions in the mountains. To prove his good faith, he led a detachment of Spanish soldiers back over his trail to show that he had built no fortifications and had no soldiers under his command.

By the time the Spaniards were convinced he was a peaceful trader, it was too late to get to the Crows, so the Americans decided to forward what pelts they could to St. Louis and make a new start next season.

Before these good intentions could be put into execution, another detachment of Spanish troops arrived with orders to arrest the Americans and take them to Santa Fe to stand trial. There De Mun and Chouteau were thrown into dungeons, and presumably Charbonneau and his comrades received like treatment.

After they had spent forty-four days in irons, a court-martial was held in which the Spanish commandant acted as prosecutor-judge, presiding over a court "Only one of [whose] . . . six members appeared to have some information [education], the others not knowing even how to sign their names."[6] The court routine consisted largely of threats to blow out De Mun's and Chouteau's brains. Finally a verdict was announced: the Americans were stripped of $30,000 worth of goods which they had cached on American soil but which had been stolen by Spanish troops and brought to Santa Fe; they were made to kneel and kiss the document providing for the theft; and they were to be given an emaciated horse each and allowed to make their way home as best they could.

It would be difficult to overstate Charbonneau's disappointment. Prison, or a few welts across a bare back, or a bit of personal indignity —these were but the hazards of a good adventure. But to be denied access to the dusty streets of the oldest town in North America, to be kept from its grogshops where there were liars as great as he, to bed down at night alone on a cold floor—that was cruelty indeed!

But then, this was not the first adventure which showed no financial profit or personal pleasure, and there is no record that Toussaint Charbonneau brooded over his lot. Once back on the Missouri, no richer, almost two years older, but still the adventurer and interpreter-guide, he cast about for new employment, which for him was never difficult to find.

CHARBONNEAU, MAJOR LONG,

AND PRINCE PAUL

1819–1823

THESE were the years of the United States's adolescence. In two short generations we had effectively, if ruthlessly, shoved our own peculiar civilization to the midcontinent and were now entering our trans-Mississippi expansion.

Toussaint Charbonneau played his little part.

When the Treaty of Ghent closed the War of 1812, several ventures were soon afoot to control trans-Mississippi Indians, protect the traders, and neutralize the influence of the British traffickers on the Upper Missouri. Among these ventures was the expedition of explorer-engineer Stephen Harriman Long.

Congress appropriated funds, and in early May of 1819 Long went to Pittsburgh to study how best to conquer that part of the American West on which only the red man had as yet built a fire.

Despite fewer funds than he had been promised and a bit of Army meddling, Long assembled a staff of prominent specialists: Major John Biddle, journalist; Dr. William Baldwin, physician and botanist; Dr. Thomas Say, zoologist; A. E. Jessup, geologist; T. R. Peale, naturalist; Sam Seymour, painter; and Lieutenant J. D. Graham and Cadet William H. Swift, topographers. With these he went to St. Louis in June, 1819. There he was joined by Benjamin O'Fallon, Indian agent; John Dougherty, O'Fallon's interpreter—and Toussaint Charbonneau.

The old man never traveled in poor company.

Exactly when Charbonneau was attached to the Long expedition is uncertain, but after it was on the move and Dr. Say cut across from the Osage villages to the "Konza" (Kansas) towns, as he called

Stephen H. Long, leader of the western expedition of 1820. *U.S. Signal Corps, Photo 111-BA-1790, The National Archives.*

The interior of the United States as it was known to official Washington following Major Stephen H. Long's expedition of 1820. Long reported that the western plains were worthless for white habitation. Note the "Great Desert" east of the Rocky Mountains. *The National Archives, Record Group #77, U.S. 62.*

them, Charbonneau was already out on the prairies talking to the Kansas tribes and urging them to a council with Say.[1]

Excepting a brush with the Pawnees late in August which Charbonneau had no trouble in controlling,[2] nothing of interest happened, and the Long expedition went into winter quarters near Old Council Bluffs.

When the expedition started toward the Continental Divide the following season, there were twenty men, including "Dougherty and four other men to serve as interpreters, baggage handlers and the like," and on the Loup River two Frenchmen were also engaged as interpreters.[3]

Was one of these six interpreters Charbonneau? Presumably. Yet, except for the fact that he positively was with Long on the Missouri River, no one knows whether he was with him at Old Council Bluffs, whether he went with the expedition up the Platte to the mountains, or whether he climbed Pike's Peak and drifted down the Arkansas to La Junta, Colorado, where Long split his command into two parts on July 24, 1820.

No one knows whether the uninhibited old blade was looking at pretty ankles all the way along the Cimarron and the Canadian rivers to the Texas–New Mexico border with Major Long or was with Captain Bell, who had been detailed to reexamine the Arkansas Valley, already explored by Zebulon Pike.

Perhaps neither. Perhaps Toussaint had found a "Konza" girl and a warm tepee and had settled down to a happy winter.

It is all confused. At the very time Charbonneau was certainly with Long, he is also reputed to have been on the payroll of William Clark, Indian Affairs superintendent, St. Louis, for a fee of $200 covering service from July 17 to December 31, 1819. Furthermore, there is some indication that he was with Stephen Watts Kearny, frontier Indian fighter and United States Army man, during his tour of duty on the Missouri.[4] Of course, these apparent conflicts may not be real, for all these reputed employers were government-sponsored and Charbonneau may have been loaned by one to the other.

Anyway, the blood of Toussaint never lost its fever, and one day sometime before the New Year, 1820, he was back in St. Louis with a new wife, Eagle, from the Minnetarees. In the city he picked up a second spouse, believed by some to have been Sacajawea,[5] and hired out to another fur company. But there are no details.

While in St. Louis Charbonneau must have talked at length with Clark, for about this time the latter, now governor of the Missouri Territory, wrote that he had paid tuition for two Charbonneau sons to two separate St. Louis schoolmasters. Perhaps these boys were Jean Baptiste (Pomp) and Toussaint, Jr., son of Otter Woman, who had died in 1812. But as noted, there is seldom agreement regarding Charbonneau's children or the identity of their mothers. Only their paternity goes unchallenged—an unusual twist to a timeless problem.

None of this historical confusion bothered Toussaint. He went away again and came wandering home with still another woman, a Ute, who, according to one interpretation, was a troublemaker.[6] The Ute girl immediately became embroiled with another wife (Sacajawea?), and Toussaint lost his patience at their wrangling and beat the older woman, whereupon she ran away—to live with three or more men in her turn and give birth to a hazy number of breeds and half-breeds, some of whom became valuable guides and interpreters all the way from Oklahoma to Idaho.

And none of this bothered Charbonneau either. His was a lusty life, and with it he expected certain domestic irregularities and differences. He spanked the offender and forgot it—or went on another excursion and came back with a new love, not infrequently costing as much as $250.[7]

In the present instance he headed for the Great Salt Lake; crossed the Rocky Mountains to Wind River, the Big Horn, and Yellowstone; and thence turned back to the Missouri and down to the Gros Ventres. It was on one such ramble that he may have discovered South Pass.[8]

It would be easy to think of Toussaint Charbonneau as nothing more than a squaw-chasing French renegade because almost every time his name appears, he is living with another woman. But such a judgment would be unjust. The very inclusion of his name in so many journals argues that he was more than he seemed. Perhaps the most remarkable thing about this extraordinary man was his talent for being sought out, employed, and appreciated by so many notable figures over so long a time.

When Paul Wilhelm, Prince of Württemberg, made the first of his five visits to the American West in 1822–1823, he met Charbonneau, a wife (just possibly Sacajawea), and Pomp at the mouth of the Kaw on June 1, 1823, and was much impressed by the old Frenchman. The Prince was journeying up the Missouri aboard a "French Fur

South Pass City, ghost town just northeast of the most famous of passes across the Rockies. *Wyoming State Archives and Historical Department.*

Company keelboat,"[9] the only reasonably sure and minimally comfortable transportation available despite the advent of steamboats on the river three years before.

When Paul arrived at Fort Recovery on August 23, 1823, the factor at Fort Kiowa, a few miles upstream, sent Charbonneau to invite the royal visitor to Kiowa.[10] The Prince accepted, and took an increased fancy to the Charbonneau family. This encounter developed into an expensive attachment for Paul. Before he left the Missouri, he had arranged to take Pomp to Europe to receive a classical education—to become fluent in English, German, French, and Spanish in addition to the almost limitless Indian languages and dialects he already knew.

When the Prince and his twenty-four-year-old protégé returned to the Missouri six years later, he generously purchased tobacco and ammunition for the "interpreter, Charbonneau," and saw Pomp launched on his own career as interpreter-guide.

Young Charbonneau was superbly equipped to follow in his father's path. He did so, but with two notable differences: he was not to experience the luxury of association with the great and celebrated figures and events his father had so casually enjoyed, nor was he to build the legend of rakish adventure which adds so much color to old Charbonneau. Instead, the younger man tramped prosaically over most of the American West, leading detachments of traders or sight-seers over trails already worn deep by others.

Legend says that he died on the Wind River, Shoshone Reservation, 1885; that his body was carried to a nearby mountain, lowered forty feet down between two great crags, and covered with boulders; and that a subsequent mountain slide erased the burial site.[11]

CHARBONNEAU AND MAXIMILIAN, PRINCE OF WIED

1832–1834

WHEN Colonel Henry Leavenworth went to the relief of the fur trader William Henry Ashley, who had been attacked by the Arikaras, he found Toussaint Charbonneau, then in the service of the "French Fur Company" (Berthold-Pratte-Chouteau) at Fort Kiowa,[1] a willing go-between, and sent him with the following communication to the Indians on August 14, 1823:

RICARAS:

You see the pipe of peace . . . in the hands of Mr. Charlonnau, and the flag of the United States.

These will convince you that my heart is not bad. Your villages are in my possession; come back and take them in peace. . . . You shall not be hurt if you do not . . . molest the traders. . . .

> H. LEAVENWORTH
> Colonel   U. S. Army[2]

This chore done, Charbonneau returned to Kiowa, and was there when the mountain man Hugh Glass crawled into the Fort following an attack by a grizzly and desertion by his companions, John S. Fitzgerald and Jim Bridger.

Meanwhile, Joseph Brazeau was organizing at Kiowa the first attempt to ascend the Missouri since Ashley's recent defeat. It was to be a small party, composed of Antoine Citoleux, or Langevin as he is often recorded, in command, and Jean Eymas, Joseph A. Sire,

Toussaint Charbonneau, and two others. At the last moment Hugh Glass joined them, despite his still bothersome wounds.

The seven men left Fort Kiowa October 10, 1823. Neither Citoleux nor Charbonneau believed they could get through the Arikaras, and five days later, while the party was still some thirty miles below the mouth of the Teton River, Citoleux made his will, anticipating the worst.

However, the men did reach the Arikara villages, but found them deserted and burned. Years of wary association had taught Charbonneau an almost infallible sense of Indian psychology, and he told Citoleux that the Arikaras had doubtless gone to the Mandans and would attack the whites at the first opportunity.

No one paid any attention.

One day before reaching the Mandans, Charbonneau announced he was leaving the river to continue by land, where the chances of survival were better. His companions snorted their disgust at such cowardice, as they saw it, but made no attempt to dissuade him.

Then Glass went ashore to hunt, and Citoleux apparently started off alone through hostile country.[3]

Within minutes Glass was ambushed by the Arikaras but was saved by a friendly Mandan who galloped by, swooped Glass to the back of his pony, and raced for a nearby trading post.

Before this excitement had subsided, Charbonneau walked into the same stockade, unharmed.

Citoleux never arrived.[*]

Except for casual notice by Stephen Watts Kearny and Henry Atkinson, United States Army commanders on the Missouri, no further mention is made of Charbonneau until the spring of 1825 or 1826, when one of the Missouri's great floods came roaring down from the north and west. Charbonneau went fleeing from the thing which robbed him of all coherent thought—water.

He tore off blindly across country as if the demons of hell were snatching at his faded plaid shirt. Two miles away he clawed to the top of a pile of Indian corn, where he sat shivering from ice, spring

---

[*] Dale E. Morgan says that none of Citoleux's party were ever seen again (*Jedediah Smith and the Opening of the West*, Indianapolis, Bobbs-Merrill Co., 1953, p. 100); but John C. Luttig refers to affidavits made later by Eymas and Sire (*Journal of a Fur Trading Expedition on the Upper Missouri, 1812–1813*, ed. Stella M. Drumm, St. Louis, Missouri Historical Society, 1920, pp. 156–157).

snow, and terror for three days.[4] He claimed the water was twenty-five feet deep, and it doubtless was—at river flood, but not out on the prairie where he was hunched on a pile of old corn stalks.

These lapses of manhood, if such they were, did not keep Charbonneau from full employment. Between November 30, 1828, and September 30, 1834, John F. A. Sanford, United States Indian agent on the Upper Missouri, said the Frenchman was paid $2,437.32 in wages as an interpreter—an amount roughly equal to that paid United States Government Indian subagents, and a princely sum since Charbonneau would be trading on his own account, either with or without his employer's permission.

By 1833, the bulk of the Indian trade was controlled by three groups: Lisa's old forces (he had died in 1820) held the Upper Missouri; the Columbia Fur Company, with James Kipp as commander in the field, ruled the middle river; and John Jacob Astor's American Fur Company dominated the St. Louis area.[5]

The Columbia Fur Company was absorbed by the American Fur Company in 1827. Kipp remained as administrator for the new combination, and when he visited the Mandans in 1833, he hired Charbonneau as his personal interpreter. His wisdom in doing so was challenged by Mr. Laidlaw, also of the company, who said, in a letter dated January 14, 1834, at Fort Pierre, "I am much surprised at your taking old Charbonneau into favor after [his] showing so much ingratitude upon all occasions. The old knave, what does he say for himself?"[6]

These various employments in no way interfered with Charbonneau's association with important people. During the first quarter of the nineteenth century, the American West attracted the wealthy who were bored with the stale limits of the European grand tour; big game hunters and scientific junkets moved up the Missouri to the heart of the continent; and royalty, coming to see the "Wild West," engaged in sport or serious study.

Maximilian, Prince of Wied, arrived in America in 1832 just as the American Fur Company's *Assiniboine* was ready to make her maiden voyage up the Missouri.* Since Astor and Maximilian repre-

---

* The *Assiniboine* was built in Cincinnati and destroyed by fire only two or three years after launching (*Travels in the Interior of North America*, Vols. XXII–XXIV of Reuben Gold Thwaites, ed., *Early Western Travels*, Cleveland, Arthur H. Clark Co., 1906, XXII, 240; XXIII, 178n).

sented similar social circles, if not bloodlines, it was to be expected that the Prince would "explore" the West aboard Astor's newest boat, which in theory would make the royal journey comfortable and safe.

Exploding boilers, river pirates, and endless delays while the countryside was combed for provisions and wood to feed the ever-hungry fires did not always validate this confidence in speed, safety, and comfort, but nevertheless the steamboat gradually increased the pleasure of river travel.

Maximilian planned to go to the mouth of the Yellowstone, making such side excursions as his fancy might choose. Somewhere along the Mandan sector of the route he met Charbonneau, "the old interpreter . . . who had lived thirty seven years in the villages . . . near this place,"[7] and an easy rapport was soon established between the Frenchman and the Prince. Charbonneau knew everything Maximilian wanted to learn. He was perhaps the first white man ever to live with the Minnetarees,[8] and had come among them long before the men from St. Louis plied the Upper Missouri. He had found the Indians using the shoulder blades of the buffalo for hoes; and now, thirty-odd years later, he could encourage them to accept the as yet unpredictable steamboat as something beneficial to their life.

And so the Prince and the interpreter-guide toured Indian towns where the braves greeted Charbonneau cordially and shook hands solemnly with the Prince. Such familiarity was hardly in keeping with royal etiquette, but Maximilian accepted it in the spirit in which it was offered. Only when a young blood became overzealous was there any friction. It came about when Maximilian refused to exchange a compass, which he carried on a cord around his neck, for a horse and the warrior's best clothes, and the Indian attempted to effect the sale by force. It "was only by the assistance of old Charbonneau that I escaped a disagreeable and, perhaps, violent scene," said Maximilian.[9]

Charbonneau did not accompany Maximilian up the Missouri. Instead he went on another of his wanderings. Captain R. Holmes, United States Army, found him among the western mountains during the season of 1833, and he is sometimes reported with Sublette at the Green River rendezvous of 1834, although this Charbonneau was almost certainly his half-breed son Baptiste.[10]

When Charbonneau returned from the mountains, he found his domestic affairs in an uproar, and during October of 1834 he rushed to the Gros Ventres "in quest of one of his runaway wives . . . for I

Minnetaree Indians at the arrival of Maximilian at Fort Clark, 1833, probably by Karl Bodmer. *U.S. Signal Corps, Photo 111-sc-92838, The National Archives.*

must inform you he had two lively ones. Poor old man," said Francis Chardon, clerk at Fort Clark.[11]

"Poor old man" indeed! There was still more life and zest for adventure in the heart of the old Frenchman than in a dozen Chardons.

By the time the difficulty of the runaway wives was resolved, Maximilian was returning downstream. Near the mouth of Knife

River, he was hailed from shore by Charbonneau, who was temporarily serving as interpreter for Joseph L. Dougherty, clerk at the newly established post of William L. Sublette–Campbell Company not far from Fort Clark.[12] The captain of the boat immediately pulled ashore to accommodate his royal guest, and Maximilian and Charbonneau began a conversation which lasted so long no attempt was made to proceed that day.

Even the next morning the old interpreter and the Prince went blithely off across four miles of Missouri countryside to look at a petrified tree, leaving the ship's commander to fidget. At their convenience they rejoined the boat.

As the vessel pulled into the Mandan towns about three o'clock in the afternoon, Charbonneau "hid himself, that they might not recognize him and invite him ashore. He had five names among these Indians—the chief of the little village; the man who possesses many gourds; the great horse from abroad; the forest bear; and fifth, which, as often happens among these Indians, is not very refined," said Maximilian.[13]

Why Charbonneau should suddenly become self-conscious before the Mandans is unknown. Certainly it could not have been because he was unaware of their numerous names for him. Long ago he had been accepted as the chief of a Minnetaree village; very early his refusal to mix all his food in a single gourd had earned him the name "man of many dishes"; the tall tales he told as he returned from his incessant wanderings fell on unbelieving Indian ears, and "the great horse from abroad" was but their derisive summation of these travels; he never pretended to exceptional bravery and would rather run from danger, as did the "forest bear"; and the fifth name was simply some earthy reference to his dealings with women, a facet of his life he never so much as bothered to defend.

All these were known for thirty years. All these he had accepted as a sort of reverse compliment from a people who understood him and whom he understood, a situation not unlike the profane names given and accepted as tokens of affection by sincere but unpolished men everywhere.

Despite these peculiar actions, Charbonneau continued to serve Maximilian. He helped the Prince make a glossary of Mandan words and, said Maximilian, "Mr. Kipp and Charbonneau, with some of the others . . ., daily assist me, . . . with much patience and kindness, in this work."[14]

The Prince was also given reviews of Mandan and Minnetaree life and legend ranging from their versions of sin, virgin births, and the creation, to the intimacies of their sex mores.

The Mandans believed they were often inhabited by animals, and Charbonneau told Maximilian the story of the Indian girl who refused to get married. One night a brave lay down beside her, but she repulsed him and he left wrapped in a white buffalo robe. On each of two succeeding nights, she rejected him. On the fourth day she stained her hand red, and as he again approached her that night, she struck him with her stained hand. Next day she vainly searched for a brave with her mark on him. Instead, she found her print on the glossy coat of a great white dog. In time she gave birth to seven pups.[15]

Once Maximilian saw a young man boastfully display a bundle of small sticks, with one end of each painted red. Another had a larger branch with red and white circles painted thereon. Charbonneau explained that each small stick or circle represented the conquest of a

Loaded dogsled of the Mandan Indians on the frozen Missouri, not far from Fort Clark. A woman with a burden is walking ahead, a child is sitting on the sled. Water color by Karl Bodmer, 1834. *Northern Natural Gas Company Collection, Joslyn Art Museum, Omaha, Nebraska.*

chosen girl, and that the stick in the center of the bundle with the jaunty feather signified the favorite conquest.[16]

If Toussaint Charbonneau was a man of the flesh, his chosen people were no less so.

But obversely there was the beautiful Minnetaree version of the creation. All was water until a huge, red-eyed aquatic bird which had been sent by the first man, Eh sicks-Wahaddish, dived into the depths and brought up the earth, after which an old grandmother helped populate the new world with sand rats, toads—and two cooking pots.

As a climax to Maximilian's frontier tour, Charbonneau arranged an invitation to a great Indian medicine feast thirty miles away "among the Manitaries, an invitation which I gladly accepted," said the Prince.[17]

Toussaint Charbonneau was now seventy-four years old. His eyes lacked the luster of the days of Lewis and Clark, but his spirit and body seemed untouched by fatigue. Without thought he led Maximilian and one or two others over river ice only twenty-four hours thick and on across thirty miles of prickly pears to the Indian rites. The Prince slithered across the flimsy ice as courageously as Charbonneau, and when his royal footwear gave out, he donned a pair of moccasins and tramped on.

North American Indians were often jealous of their religiomedical rites, but Charbonneau had joined with them many times, and people he sponsored were accepted. Once arrived at the rites, Charbonneau quickly introduced the visitors, and all joined the circle about the ceremonial fires inside the great earthen lodge.

The feasting began; the braves made speeches; they sang their monotonous chants; and they danced their rude shuffling steps to the rhythm of their mounting passions.

Two hours later each brave's wife solemnly approached her spouse, untied her leathern girdle, removed her undergarments, and handed them all to her husband. Then, with the lodge held in ritualistic hush, she approached another male of her choice, slid her hand softly down his arm, and turned and walked slowly from the lodge. The chosen man followed to consummate what was, for the Indians, a part of their ageless rites to woo from their gods fertility, good crops, and good hunting, but for Puritan America only a degrading orgy.

Who knows which was right?

TOUSSAINT CHARBONNEAU
GROWS OLD

1836–1839?

IF the first quarter of the nineteenth century was marked by nobility's interest in the American West, it was also replete with those who saw therein a possible solution for all the ills of mankind. And dreamers, honest and dishonest, set afoot all manner of schemes. That they generally failed in no way dimmed the color or excitement of their dreams.

While Charbonneau was off to the Gros Ventres trailing a runaway wife—and shortly thereafter getting mixed up in a tribal war in which he narrowly missed death when two shots intended for a nearby companion passed instead through the crown of his battered old hat—a visionary scheme was being hatched in Buffalo, New York, for freeing the American Indians from white domination and Texas from the thralldom of Mexico.

James Dickson (no one knows who or what he really was[1]) believed that by marching boldly into the wilderness, he could recruit zealots along the way, rally the braves to his banner, throw out the white rascals, establish man's humanity to man—and leave a name for himself—Montezuma II.

Leaving Buffalo on August 1, 1836, he headed west leading sixty Canadians, some of whom had joined his pennant merely for safety. "As yet I know little of this man, but if I may judge from so short an acquaintance, he is somewhat visionary. . . . *N'importe* I wish to go North and Westward and will embrace the opportunity," said Martin McLeod, one of Dickson's majors.[2]

The famous Albert Gallatin map, 1836, of North American Indian tribes is also notable for depicting the incomplete knowledge of Arctic geography. *American Antiquarian Society.*

It was already far too late to start toward the mountains, but Dickson gave it no thought. In mid-October he was at the west end of Lake Superior, ready to strike overland across Minnesota. Before he realized his danger, he was surrounded by deadly winter.

The Hudson's Bay Company on the Red River refused help because it nurtured the absurd fear that this starving, freezing band might in some mysterious fashion undermine its hold on the Red Valley. And so the dreamers died one by one and were left where they fell. The living stumbled on, suckling the hope that Pembina, Charbonneau's old command, might have food. Instead it had no garrison. Only Dickson and two followers remained. Some had deserted. The rest had died.

Whatever his faults, James Dickson was neither coward nor weakling. With a heart worthy of a greater vision, he fought across Minnesota snow, and turned north toward Fort Garry (Winnepeg), and, with nine deserters who had rejoined him, staggered into the Canadian post, heading an even dozen strong.

After an unusually long and severe winter, "the Liberator" headed for the Missouri and the Minnetarees. He hoped to go up the Missouri, up the Yellowstone, through South Pass, and on to Santa Fe. In so doing the Cherokees would be rescued from a worthless reservation, New Mexico would fall to righteousness, and California would be taken from the dons and given to Yankee traders.

But somehow it didn't work out.

Close by the "Little Village" on the Missouri, old Charbonneau found "the Liberator" prostrate on Minnetaree soil. Montezuma II was tired! Tired of dreaming! Tired of walking!

He had lain down to die.

Or so legend says. No one really knows. All that is certain is that Charbonneau was again involved in some small way in another episode which would always be retold in any serious history of the great Missouri.

One more adventure and one last valiant fling at romance were to be granted the old dean of Missouri interpreter-guides. As a final great hazard, he must survive the smallpox epidemic of 1837—a visitation which killed and killed and killed until entire Indian towns vanished; until fathers tomahawked their families rather than see them suffer; until a suicidal death lust led men and women to cut their throats, hang themselves, or put a gun in their mouths and pull the trigger; until the stench and terror drove brave men mad. ". . . only grog keep me alive," said Francis Chardon.

The pox had been brought by a company steamboat just before July 4, 1837, and because the Indians had refused to stay away from the annual celebration, the disease was soon out of hand.

Chardon did the best he could, but the Indians declined to be quarantined, and modern vaccination, while known, was not in common use. An isolated case or two of crude vaccination or plunging the open sores into hot ashes were not enough to halt the plague. By Christmas it had invaded every Indian tribe from the mid-Missouri west to the Blackfeet and beyond.

While there was still hope that a few might escape the disease, Chardon sent Charbonneau on his last mission—to search for a band of Minnetarees who had not yet returned from their summer hunt, and beg them to stay away from the river towns and thus perhaps avoid the pox.

That they refused was no fault of Charbonneau's.

At the same time, the old interpreter must drink his own bitter cup. He must go once more to the Gros Ventres and find there, too, the stench; must pick his way among the unburied dead; must beat off the scavenging dogs; must hear the screams and see the agonies; must bear the laments of those who would live to hate their pox-marked skins.

He must walk into his own tent to find a wife bloated and still; must turn and drop the tent flap with whatever grief he could know on that bit of his own domesticity, and journey slowly back to the Minnetarees.

Long since, the natives had blamed the white man for the Terror, and Chardon's Fort Clark was under virtual siege. Vengeance-minded Indians stood stolidly waiting with guns at the ready for Chardon to leave his quarters so they could kill him and by this revenge perhaps appease their angry gods.

Mandan Chief Four Bears used his last hours inciting his braves to retaliation:

My Friends one and all, Listen to what I have to say—Ever since I can remember I have loved the Whites . . . and to the best of my Knowledge, I have never Wronged a White Man . . . Which they cannot deny. I have done everything that a Red skin could for them, and how have they repaid it! With ingratitude! . . . I do not fear Death my friends. You Know it, but to die with my face rotten, that even the Wolves will shrink with horror at seeing Me, and say to themselves, that is the 4 Bears the Friend of the Whites. . . .

Listen well what I have to say, as it will be the last time you will hear Me. Think of your Wives, Children, Brothers, Sisters, Friends, and in fact all that you hold dear, are all Dead, or Dying, with their faces all rotten, caused by those dogs the Whites, think of all that My friends, and rise altogether and Not leave one of them alive. The 4 Bears will act his part.[3]

But death was too near. No war party arose, and the old warrior tried to kill Chardon alone. Failing, he staggered to his village and died, as he had said he would.

Meanwhile, the Sioux raided cornfields and butchered the living. And in March of 1838 the Arikaras took advantage of the worse plight of the Mandans and seized and occupied their village, leaving forty of their own old women to starve in their abandoned Arikara town.

Francis Chardon sent them one meal.

Nine of every ten Mandans died, and the tribe never recovered. Today there are no full-blooded Mandans, and few persons of Mandan extraction.

The epidemic caused amazing havoc. Alexander Culbertson, agent on Maria's River, wondering why not a single Indian had come to trade all summer, investigated and found, deep in Blackfoot land at Three Forks, a village in which every living thing, man and beast, had died, save two insane old women crawling among the rotting corpses.

Thousands lay unburied across the Missouri prairies. No one knows the total dead: Mandans, Arikaras, Minnetarees, Sioux, Assiniboines, Blackfeet—certainly 15,000, perhaps five or six times that many.

But Toussaint Charbonneau survived. Survived without ill effect except such scars as may have been burned into his soul by the horrors he had seen.

As the plague drifted into the autumn of 1838, the pitiful fragments of once-proud tribes resumed whatever they could of normal life. But they were in a nasty mood.

When Charles Larpenteur, clerk for the American Fur Company at Fort Union at the mouth of the Yellowstone, started downriver with one companion and two canoemen to visit his family in Baltimore, they were repeatedly harassed by the Indians—the Assiniboines, the Arikaras. Along the banks of the river the red men were "running back and forth" in a most hostile manner, said Larpenteur. Doubting his own leadership, he landed on the opposite shore and magnanimously released his three companions of any responsibility for his safety, telling them to pursue whatever course they thought best to ensure their own escape.

They agreed to stay together, keep to the river—and hope.

Fort Union, 1833, by Karl Bodmer. *U.S. Signal Corps, Photo 111-sc-90803, The National Archives.*

Piling tobacco on the bow of their canoe as a token of peaceful intentions, the four men shoved off again and began paddling, one eye on the river, one on the growing number of Indians running along the shore. Larpenteur's fright was increasing with every stroke of the paddles, and he had no very real expectation of ever enjoying his furlough.

Exactly when his dejection was at full tide,

when our fears were at the highest pitch we perceived an individual with pants and a red flannel shirt on, looking very much like a white man. To our surprise and joy we found it was old Mr. Charbonneau who had been 40 years among the Missouri Indians. He used to say that when he first came on the river it was so small he could straddle it. Imagine our joy to find ourselves befriended instead of butchered. . . .[4]

Charbonneau told Larpenteur which Indians to present with tobacco, and that done, the four men passed in safety downstream.

We have said repeatedly that Toussaint was a man of the flesh who pretended to nothing else, and it came as no surprise to his contemporaries (or to those who have chronicled his years) that the fetor of the pox did not deter him from embarking on his last romance.

On October 27, 1838, Francis Chardon sold Charbonneau a fourteen-year-old Assiniboine girl who had "roused a spring fret in the blood of this man of many wives," and the "young men of the Fort and two rees [Arikaras] gave the Old Man a splendid Chariveree, the Drums, pans, Kittles &c Beating; guns fireing &c. The old gentleman gave a feast to the Men, and a glass of grog—and went to bed with his young wife with the intention of doing his best," wrote Chardon in his Fort Clark journal.*[5]

A few months later Joshua Pilcher, who had come to St. Louis during the War of 1812, had held many positions since, and was now superintendent of Indian Affairs for the Missouri, paid Charbonneau, "tottering under the infirmities" of eighty winters, a last claim for six months' wages as a government interpreter although the post had been

---

* Following a not uncommon custom, Charbonneau is purported to have shared his new bride with the men of the Fort the following night (Grace Raymond Hebard, *Sacajawea,* Glendale, Arthur H. Clark Co., 1933, pp. 105-107).

abolished, unknown to Charbonneau. "This man faithful servant of the Government—though in a humble capacity," said Pilcher.[6] He paid the claim August 26, 1839, because the old Frenchman was in want (Missouri rivermen never saved), and Pilcher believed Charbonneau deserved consideration for his life of service to the United States, for after all, he had been born a French Canadian.

No one knows positively where or when Toussaint Charbonneau died, but the 1839 transaction is the last recorded.

Toussaint Charbonneau: perhaps the first white man to live in the Mandan-Minnetaree towns, associated with the earliest traders at Pembina—Lewis and Clark, Sacajawea, Auguste Chouteau, Brackenridge, Luttig, Manuel Lisa, Jules de Mun, Long, Kearny, Prince Paul, Colonel Leavenworth, General Atkinson, Maximilian, John Jacob Astor, "the Liberator," Larpenteur, Pilcher—every name important to the Missouri prairies.

The old Frenchman knew and served them all.

All the West and all its Indians, three generations of chiefs and traders, had engrossed on his mind an incomparable pageant. He had come to these parts early in the last decade of the eighteenth century and, if with no spectacular success and not too much praise from a catalogue of employers, he had been working for fur companies, the United States Army, and the government ever since. Long ago he had developed a distaste for his own race. He was an Indian now, a good one, and lived with his own people, not at the fort. He was as bent as a scrub cedar on a bluff, his face was as seamed as a clay bank, but he was more sagacious than his overlords . . . and could travel river or prairie forever, winter or summer.[7]

And just perhaps out there somewhere on those prairies where the buffalo bulls no longer stomp and roar but where the long, lean coyote still cries across the snow—just perhaps, we say—the soul of old Charbonneau still wanders Missouri trails.

PART III

RIVER TRADERS AND
MOUNTAIN MEN

THE story of mankind is a saga of nobilities and de-
pravities, ennuis and adventures—lives motivated more
often by greed than by the arts, sometimes .lonely, frequently unique. One Moses led his people, one Caligula
disgraced an empire, one Isadora Duncan thrilled a
world with her nimble feet and died with a knotted scarf
around her neck. And in this company of saints and
sinners the New World mountain man, the great Missouri
River traders, and the interpreter-guides who served them
stand straight and high, living the last chapter in the Age
of Discovery—as contradictory as the tribes they feared
and loved, as mean as the debaucheries they encouraged,
as magnificent as the rivers and mountains they called
their own. We shall not see their kind again.

PIERRE DORION, SR.

1780–1807

THREE generations of Dorions served the American West. They guided civilization from the Missouri to the Pacific, and their lives spanned history from an unexplored wilderness to the State House on the Willamette.

Pierre Dorion, Sr., was a member of a prominent Quebec family, at least one branch of which was interested in public affairs. Reputedly he was born sometime before 1750, and left the comforts of Quebec and came to Cahokia, Illinois, before 1780. He was therefore well toward middle life (old age came early in the 1780's) before he ventured to the frontier.

Why he left Quebec is unknown. It may have been nothing more than the urge to go west and make a fortune. It may have been something more personal. The survivors of unpopular duels often changed addresses; judges looked the other way when a troublesome character left town; gambling debts stood little chance of being collected west of the Mississippi; and nagging wives seldom followed decamping husbands to the wilderness. It is all conjecture, but Pierre the elder certainly cut his ties with civilization relatively late in life and in a dramatic fashion. He remained at Cahokia but a short time, moved to St. Louis briefly, and then gave up all pretense of civilized connections and went to the Yankton Sioux and took a squaw. He never left the Indian life except for occasional trips to St. Louis.

The Missouri marked the line between civilized society and total wilderness, albeit a wilderness not entirely unknown. Spaniards and Frenchmen had long tramped the plains of the Dakotas and, farther to the west, had trembled, as did the natives, at the mighty noise which came from the far reaches of the "Stony Mountains"—a great crashing reverberation which was heard by many a mountain man, and which remains unexplained in any very convincing fashion even to this day.

It was this wilderness which the elder Pierre Dorion adopted when he dropped his white man's civilization, chose his Yankton woman, and founded the family which became a legend.

Very little is known of his first twenty years on the Missouri beyond the fact that he was engaged in trade and became sufficiently important to cause concern among rival traders.

Beginning in early August of 1799 and continuing for several months, an exchange of letters passed among Dorion, Spanish Governor Charles Dehault Delassus, and L. Honoré Tesson (or Taisont as he sometimes wrote it), a trader with a post at the present Montrose, Iowa.

The burden of these exchanges was Dorion's request of Delassus for a grant of land on the Des Moines River with privileges of trading with the local Indians, and Tesson's warning to Delassus that Dorion was a foreigner, from Mackinac, and probably represented British interests, and even more probably would cause trouble.

Therefore, what should he, Tesson, do?

The initial letters were followed in rapid succession by urgent notes: Dorion had arrived via the Illinois River; Dorion was trading; now he was with the Iowas; *now* two sons of Dorion's had arrived armed with a license to trade issued by their own interloping father, but probably they were working for a man named Crofeurte or Croford or—anyway, an Englishman who had already caused trouble on the river and was most assuredly behind this Dorion fellow; and you just ask Mr. Loisel (a Spanish trader on Cedar Island in the Missouri), and he will tell you all about it.[1]

Tesson told Delassus that he personally had met Pierre the elder at the mouth of the Des Moines River and caught him trading with the Iowas. Some action certainly should be taken against such a formidable rival.[2]

As if Delassus could do anything to stop the Dorion breed! Nor did he. They continued to trade.

Pierre Dorion, Sr., learned Indian languages easily. He loved Indian life, and he married a number of times and begot sons—how many no one knows. The river and mountain men chose their Indian women according to the code of each tribe, and married and deserted them according to that same code.

Indeed, where could Dorion or any other frontier "sinner" have found a clergyman to murmur a ritual?

And so the elder Dorion begot sons, and one of them, Pierre Dorion, Jr., carried on the family tradition as interpreter-guide. And his son, Baptiste Dorion, did likewise. We need feel no shame for them even if they did not always obey the moralists.

But is was a ribald and riotous family. Old Dorion and his half-breed sons often got drunk together. Once when he, young Pierre, one or two other sons, and an assortment of squaws were all home at one time, the boys and their father got drunk and engaged in a "friendly fight"—a common diversion among the voyageurs, mountain men, and Indians, especially after the last learned the use of whiskey.

There was no particular ill feeling in these brawls, at least in their early stages. Old men, young boys, and, if the truth were known, the squaws too, often put on magnificent bouts fatal only if they got out of hand. On the present occasion, young Pierre bested his father, grabbed his scalping knife, and was about to use it when the pater-familias sobered enough to cry, "Hold, my son, you are too brave, too honorable to scalp your father."[3] If the story is perchance apocryphal, it is nevertheless in the image of the Dorions.

By the time Lewis and Clark left St. Louis on their westbound journey, Pierre the elder had been with the Indians at least twenty years and Pierre the younger was a strapping half-breed assigned to managing a trading post among the Yankton Sioux for the Chouteau family, St. Louis traders. The elder Dorion was also trading along the Missouri, and was just coming downstream with two rafts loaded with buffalo hides and tallow as Lewis and Clark were starting up the river. Under date of June 12, 1804, Sergeant Ordway wrote, "We Got an old Frenchman to go with us which could Speak Several languages, among the indians for a long distance."[4]

The Americans recognized the advantage of having Dorion smooth their route through Sioux country, and as previously noted, they placed great importance on having Indian chiefs visit Washington. They hoped Dorion could arrange for several such guests. He was therefore hired to leave his rafts, reverse his route, and return to the Sioux, meanwhile acting as another interpreter-guide between the modern Glasgow, Missouri, and Yankton, South Dakota. A guide was not in any sense necessary, and Dorion was almost exclusively an interpreter of Indian life, but in this role he was exceptionally skilled. He knew river customs, and was well informed on various natural phenomena—the stone breastworks six or seven feet high and a hundred yards long which, though often attributed to glacial deposits, were believed by the Dorions and many other trained Indian observers to be of Indian origin; or the Pipestone quarries in Minnesota from which the Indians made their ceremonial pipes, and which were a sanctuary for friend, foe, or tribal criminal.

On the last day of August, Sergeant Pryor and Dorion arranged a council with the first band of Sioux, and found with them Pierre Dorion, Jr. Young Dorion, five chiefs, and about seventy warriors came to talk and to give the Americans parcels of general information about the Yanktons and their home territory—information which either of the Dorions could have supplied without the formalities of a council, but these meetings were accepted protocol.

However, the explorers did not understand certain other facets of frontier protocol, and they committed a serious faux pas. At the council they gave young Pierre a flag, clothes, and other provisions as prepayment for services he was engaged to perform, but they neglected to invite his father to the feast following the council. The senior Dorion was "much displeased that we did not invite him to dine with us" said Clark.[5] This oversight wounded the older man's pride, and he immediately withdrew from expedition service, except that he agreed to fulfill his previous promise to enlist Sioux chiefs to take the long and, for them, dangerous journey to Washington.

These excursions could become complicated. The Indians were not used to traveling under the white man's conditions, and they often became unbelievably homesick and physically ill. They could not understand such disabilities, and the resultant fears bred distrust of any suggestion made by their escort which deviated ever so little from the original promises.

After several months the Dorions got a delegation ready and took them to St. Louis. In the meantime Lewis and Clark were urging still others to visit the "White Father," and a number of Arikara chiefs actually got to Washington, independently of the Dorions. There one of the chiefs died in 1805.

This death had to be explained to the folks back home if a war of revenge were to be averted. Joseph Gravelines, another longtime interpreter on the river but one about whom little is known, was given

An Arikara Indian. Painting by Karl Bodmer. *U.S. Signal Corps, Photo 111-sc-92840, The National Archives.*

a free hand for this not too promising task. As a beginning he collected a sizable package of presents as an indemnity for the chief's death. To get these past the Sioux and to the Arikaras was the first hurdle. Gravelines asked that the elder Dorion help in the talks with the Sioux.

Both interpreters were to travel upriver with a trading company under the command of one of the several Robert McClellans who were engaged in Indian trade.

On the way they were to inquire for news of Lewis and Clark. The lapse of so many months was considered evidence of total disaster by most national figures—Jefferson being an exception—and the attitude itself was mute testimony to the general ignorance of the vastness of North America 300 years after Columbus.

The negotiations among Dorion, Gravelines, and McClellan had taken so much time that on September 12, 1806, their party going up the river met Lewis and Clark as they were coming home.

Events now become confused, for at this point we must resume the story of René Jusseaume.

When Lewis and Clark returned from the Pacific, they naturally stopped at the Mandans again. Aided by Jusseaume and perhaps one of the Dorion family, they induced Chief Sheheke, or Big White, and his family to visit Washington. We have seen that Jusseaume was chosen to accompany Big White as interpreter. The entire party left the Mandans on August 17, 1806.

To Jusseaume's credit, he took his charges to Washington, called upon Jefferson, saw the sights, and returned to St. Louis without too much difficulty. Here the troubles began. As noted, one Arikara chief had died in Washington, and Big White could not have been kept in ignorance of it; he had been away from his people for a long time, and now he was told he must wait until a military escort could be provided for his further return.

Lieutenant Joseph Kimball was to go with the Indians as far as the Sioux, and Ensign Nathaniel Pryor and George Shannon, former Lewis and Clark men, were to continue the escort to the Mandans. Each officer was to have a small force of men. Kimball and Pryor were to be supported further by Auguste Pierre Chouteau, West Point graduate and son of the St. Louis merchant Jean Pierre Chouteau, and Pierre Dorion, Jr., each of whom would command a trading party. Altogether there were ninety-four persons, including the women and children.[6]

The extreme irregularity in the use of Christian names makes any identification of Chouteau portraits suspect. The above is probably René Auguste, 1749–1829, one of the founders of St. Louis. *The State Historical Society of Missouri, Columbia.*

Sheheke, or Big White. Crayon portrait by C. B. J. F. de Saint-Memin. *Courtesy of The New-York Historical Society, New York City.*

It all appeared simple enough until the elder Dorion returned to St. Louis following his aid to Gravelines.

In the National Archives at Washington is a letter headlined St. Louis, May 18, 1807, from William Clark, Indian agent, to General Dearborn, Secretary of War, in which Clark refers to the senior Dorion as an Indian subagent for Missouri appointed by General Wilkinson. But the important item, said Clark, was that Dorion had arrived in St. Louis "a fiew days ago" with fifteen Sioux *on their way to Washington.*

Clark was having Indian trouble. Big White was on his hands, and now Dorion had showed up with fifteen Sioux. Since Clark had no instructions to finance their further journey, he told Dorion to take them home and stay with them until he received further orders.

Dorion then demanded his wages—contracted to be $1.50 per day, almost twice the usual rate, which readily indicates his reputation. He also asked reimbursement for goods he had used as presents while coaxing the Sioux to leave their homes. Clark paid the wages, and wrote that "Mr. Deirion has great influence with the Sicous haveing resided near thirty years with those people and can be of great service to the government in keeping those vicious tribes at peace."[7]

Despite this praise, Clark haggled over the goods Dorion had bought, and finally refused to pay "Two of his accounts . . . which he was not positively ordered to expend in his instructions, . . . altho I think that it might have been necessary to give such things &c. . ."[8]— a tortured bit of rationalization apparently designed to make Clark's cash account look good at Dorion's expense.

When all details were arranged, the Kimball-Pryor-Chouteau expedition to return Big White finally began. Trouble on the lower Missouri was now rare, and the combined commands reached the Arikara villages without incident on September 9, 1807.

There the Rees and a considerable force of Sioux allies opened hostilities, apparently catching Kimball and Pryor by surprise.[9] Why the military should have been unaware of the Indian temper is a minor mystery. That all three interpreters failed to sense trouble and so gave no warning is a hypothesis too absurd to be taken seriously. More likely, Chouteau and the military refused to listen to underlings better qualified than they to judge Indian behavior.

Ensign Pryor thought the Indians had been incited by the British, but this idea was considerably undermined when a captive Mandan

Pierre Chouteau, Jr. *The State Historical Society of Missouri, Columbia.*

squaw stole to Pryor and told him that the Rees, the Sioux, and her people were just then engaged in one of their eternal wars, and that this accounted for the general ill will.

Chouteau now suggested that perhaps the Indians could be soothed by seeing his gaudiest trade goods, whereupon the "Two interpreters, Dorion and Jusseaume, went by land through the villages,"[10] and nearly lost their lives—for the Indians rejected the baubles and opened fire. It was here that Jusseaume probably received the wound for which he later petitioned "Monsieur le Président" for a pension.

The military returned the fire, hoping to cover the reembarkation of the several men who had gone ashore. But the whites were out-gunned and outnumbered, and a retreat was ordered. Chouteau's boat got stuck on a sandbar and was dragged to safety just in time; Shannon eventually lost a leg from his wounds; and at least four whites were killed and twice that many were wounded.[11]

It was here, too, that Big White refused to detour overland to avoid the Arikaras, and Jusseaume and Pryor had no choice but to return their charges to St. Louis.

Big White was no closer home than he had been a year before. And there we must leave him and René Jusseaume until their story can be resumed a year later.

Both Dorions apparently remained upriver when Big White returned to St. Louis, and Dorion the elder became a somewhat hazy figure in the journals of the river.

Pierre Dorion, Sr., was a trustworthy interpreter and Indian sub-agent; he must have participated in many of the stirring events which made Charbonneau's life one long adventure. But Dorion lacked Toussaint's flare for publicity. Royalty, river captains, and military commanders all surely used his ability, but they often neglected to mention it. He never moved beyond the footnotes of notice in the annals of the West.

Toward the end of his life, he lived in a tepee outside the walls of Fort Pierre, South Dakota. Tradition says that his tent was a flamboyant red and had scalps fluttering from the center poles, and that "Old Pierre" loafed about in the garish clothes of the voyageurs, telling tall tales of the past and wishing he were young again. But variations of the same stories are told about one or more of his half-breed sons, so we had best leave it as tradition.[12]

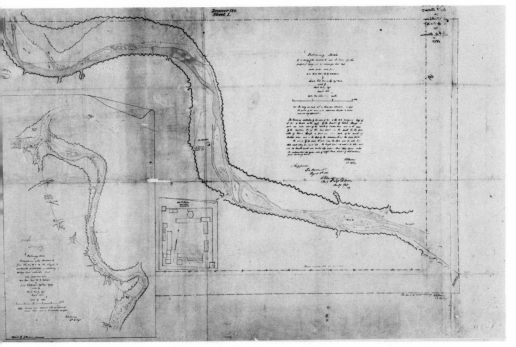

U.S. Army survey of the Missouri River near Fort Pierre, 1855. The modern Pierre, South Dakota, is across on the east bank. Inset shows the plan of the old post. *The National Archives, Record Group #77, Dr. 126-1.*

Fort Pierre, 1832, site of the present Pierre, South Dakota. *U.S. Signal Corps, Photo 111-sc-92851, The National Archives.*

PIERRE DORION, JR., AND
WILSON PRICE HUNT

1804–1811

WASHINGTON IRVING says Pierre Dorion, Jr., the best known of the Dorion family, was a "loose adventurer," a somewhat unsavory character; Coues says he "appears to have been a sulky brute"; Brackenridge called him a "worthless fellow"; and other contemporaries said he was dark-browed, sullen, and quarrelsome, drank excessively, and beat his wives. Doubtless. Of course Pierre the younger was not exactly responsible for his complexion, and Indian stoicism could have been taken for sullenness. But it cannot be denied that he drank, quarreled, fought, and beat his wives. Every half-breed and many a white man did the same. On the other hand, Dorion is credited with a devotion to his families not always found among Indian men.

Regardless of his personal traits, the younger Pierre was acknowledged as the best Sioux interpreter on the Missouri and was in constant demand.

No one knows where or when he was born, but he was a Sioux trader when Lewis and Clark went up the river. Unlike his father, his life-span was short, violent, and tragic. Excepting his role in the Lewis and Clark and Big White excursions, he was attached to only one historical venture in any notable sense, that of the disastrous Overland Astorians. The record of that expedition and the story of young Pierre Dorion's adult life are inseparable.

When John Jacob Astor entered the trans-Mississippi fur trade with his dream of an empire at the mouth of the Columbia, he thought to guarantee its success by sending one expedition by sea and one by land to build his first post, Astoria. The maritime detachment under Captain Thorn on the *Tonquin* does not concern us here.

For the overland venture, Astor chose Wilson Price Hunt of Trenton, New Jersey, a cultured and successful gentleman of the Atlantic seaboard but one completely ignorant of the Indian trade. There were other partners whom we shall encounter from time to time, men who owned small amounts of shares and held equally small authority. Some were experienced Indian traders; others were primarily gentlemen for whom Astor had a predilection, perhaps in contrast with his own very humble beginnings.

From first to last, Hunt committed one blunder after another. He

Wilson Price Hunt, leader of the tragic Overland Astorians. *Missouri Historical Society, St. Louis.*

and Donald McKenzie, a former North West Company servant and one of several traders with the same name, went to Montreal in July of 1810 to recruit men and buy equipment. The North West Company was already fighting a bitter battle with the Hudson's Bay Company and did not welcome another competitor. It did everything it could to hinder Hunt and McKenzie, and it effectively prevented all first-class voyageurs from joining the Astor flag. The crew Hunt finally collected was distinctly second-best.

However, he got his thirty- to forty-foot canoes loaded; assigned a foreman to the bow, the oarsmen to the center, and the steersman to the rear; and paddled to the Chapel of St. Anne, named for the patron saint of the voyageurs. Here simple rituals prepared them for the wilderness. The conclusion of the rites signaled a gigantic thirst, and Hunt barely managed to get beyond Montreal.

At Mackinac he hoped to expand his crew to sixty men. It was the last stop before entering the wilds, and the voyageurs made the most of it. They always received a large portion of their wages in advance, and these were immediately spent on gaudy clothes, women, and rum. After the advance wages were gone, the boatmen ran charge accounts at the local shops, knowing that custom compelled their current employers to pay these bills before they would be allowed to leave town. Thus, the voyageurs and the shops colluded to perpetrate a profitable swindle, and Hunt "bought" his employees a second time at Mackinac.

Donald McKenzie and Ramsy Crooks, who joined Hunt at Mackinac, were familiar with the routine. Why they did not prepare Hunt for the experience is unknown. Perhaps they tried. Hunt had a habit of not listening.

In mid-August the Astorians left Mackinac and paddled for St. Louis via Green Bay, the Fox and Wisconsin rivers, Prairie du Chien, and the Mississippi.

At St. Louis Wilson Price Hunt ran head on into Manuel Lisa. *
Henry Marie Brackenridge, in his rare *Views of Louisiana* published in 1817, three years before Lisa's death, says the Spaniard had gone as far as the Big Horns, and Washington Irving credits him with traveling to the very source of the Missouri. The point is unimportant

---

* About this time Joseph Miller, a well-educated Baltimore citizen, joined the Astorians.

here except to stress that Hunt was entering into competition with a master completely familiar with the battleground.[1]

It was much too late to start for the Pacific during the present season. Hunt, hoping to curb expenses, decided to winter his men at Nodaway, a few miles above the modern St. Joseph, Missouri, where prices were lower and temptations fewer. Two days after they arrived there, the river froze over, and the men squatted down to while away the winter. Hunt went back to St. Louis and enlisted Robert McClellan, a former partner of Ramsy Crooks, and John Day from the backwoods of Virginia.

Sometime during the winter it dawned on Hunt that he might need guides and interpreters. The delay was a serious blunder, because Manuel Lisa knew the value of the interpreter-guides, and when Hunt at last made overtures to Pierre Dorion, Jr., Lisa began a series of maneuvers designed to prevent any such association.

Young Dorion loved three things in life: a good fight, women, and liquor. He had recently gone to Lisa's upriver store and purchased several items on credit, including whiskey at $10 a quart—a fantastic markup even on the river. When Pierre sobered up, he refused to pay the bill on the ground of an overcharge. Lisa did not press the matter at the time, but when Hunt tried to hire the interpreter, Lisa let it be known that he intended to have Dorion jailed for nonpayment of debts. An interpreter in jail was of no value to Hunt.

But Pierre Dorion, Jr., was also versed in the tricks of the river. For two weeks he played Lisa against Hunt, until the latter agreed to give him wages of $300 per year, $200 to be paid in advance, and allow him to be accompanied by his pregnant wife, Marie, and two small sons*—all expenses to be paid by Hunt, of course.

To add to Hunt's troubles, five men from his Nodaway camp drifted into St. Louis and spread a tale of mistreatment intended to induce others to desert. The men were in fact on a diet of "lied corn hominy for breakfast, a slice of fat pork and biscuit for dinner, and a pot of mush with a pound of tallow in it, for supper."[2] This diet and the boredom were the real causes of discontent.

---

* Pierre had earlier married a Yankton girl, Holy Rainbow, but had left her and was now attached to Marie, an Iowa girl. Marie had a long, wild life of her own, encompassing three "husbands" and half a continent. The facts of her life rival the fictions of Sacajawea's, but Marie never acquired a good press agent.

About the only bright spot for Hunt was the attachment to his command, as paying guests, of John Bradbury of the Linnaean Society of Liverpool, and Thomas Nuttall, the English-American botanist. These gentlemen, out to see the West, were in no way under Hunt's orders except that they would not be permitted to break the rules of safe travel.

When Hunt left St. Louis on March 12, 1811, Bradbury and Nuttall stayed in town an extra night to await the mails and have a last bit of fun. During the evening they heard that Lisa had a warrant for young Dorion's arrest which he planned to serve upriver at St. Charles after it was too late for Hunt to obtain another Sioux interpreter. Bradbury and Nuttall naturally threw their sympathies to Hunt, and at two o'clock in the morning rushed overland to warn him of Lisa's plans.

When Pierre learned of the trick, he quickly outlined a ruse to circumvent the arrest. He and his family would leave the boats at once, circle inland, bypass St. Charles, and rejoin Hunt farther upriver. Hunt did not trust Dorion, and said he never expected to see him again if once he left the boats. But since there was little real choice, he agreed, and shortly got an agreeable surprise when Pierre did exactly as he had promised.

Except that when he rejoined the Astorians he was alone. Marie had absconded in a huff with the children because Pierre had lost his temper and given her a sound spanking.

Normally this discipline was accepted by Indian women with total equanimity; in fact, its omission was sometimes considered proof that their husbands placed no value upon them. But Marie was different. Any one of the three men with whom she is known to have lived could attest to that—but this is the story of Pierre Dorion, Jr., not Marie.

Pierre was disturbed at Marie's defection—not because she was gone, for wives were easy to come by, but because she had his personal goods with her and he was bankrupt. Hunt understood and sent one of his men after Marie, but it did no good. Pierre slept alone that night. Just before daybreak a repentant Marie and two big-eyed little boys showed up of their own accord, and Hunt took them aboard. Pierre forgave, if he did not forget, and the Overland Astorians went on to Charette, sixty-eight miles above St. Louis.

From there they moved to Fort Osage for three days, April 8–11,

1811. Here Hunt learned that the Sioux were again in an angry mood.

The Osages entertained Hunt, Bradbury, and Nuttall with a scalp dance. This ceremony, and presumably a new male face, so impressed Marie she decided to leave Pierre and move in with the Osages. Dorion knocked that nonsense out of her in short order, and from then on she was a dutiful if not a particularly loving wife. She sulked a few days, but Pierre knew his rights!

In mid-April Hunt picked up his Nodaway section. The united party of sixty voyageurs, hunters, interpreters, paying guests, five partners, and the clerk, John Reed, headed upriver, keeping a sharp lookout for rattlesnakes, which were just emerging from their winter quarters and were in no humor to be trifled with.

One night eleven naked Sioux whooped into camp and set up a great hullabaloo. After their capture Dorion explained that the "warriors" had recently been defeated, and as redemption they must discard all their clothes to the "medicine"* and perform some reckless deed to regain their self-respect. The present night foray had not been notably successful. Hunt's men wished to shoot the braves and get back to sleep, but he vetoed that form of frontier justice.

This little episode pointed up the angry temper of the Sioux and Crooks, and McClellan blamed the trouble on Lisa, contending that he had set the Sioux against all other traders in order to ease his own passage through their lands. McClellan was so sure of this that he had repeatedly said he would shoot Lisa on sight. The rumors of Sioux hostility and McClellan's attitude made the voyageurs nervous and unhappy. As these simple men saw it, the Indians might attack at any moment; McClellan might start a trade war; and Nuttall and Bradbury were silly young men who asked Dorion foolish questions, and spent long hours pulling up weeds along the river and oh-ing and ah-ing over them. In fact, the men suspected they were attached to an unlucky expedition.

These feelings were not lessened when Bradbury cut across land one day and was captured by a small band of Sioux, who seemed uncertain what to do with him after they had him. He seized upon their hesitancy and saved his life by entertaining them with the "medicine" of his pocket compass and microscope until the boats

---

* "Medicine" has no exact synonym in our present-day vocabulary. It was an Indian-frontier term covering ritualistic mores, superstitions, native medicine, and anything the Indians could not understand.

came up. But it had been a tight situation. The Sioux had soon lost interest, and he had had nothing else to divert their attention.

While most of these events were occurring, Manuel Lisa was still in St. Louis. Several details had delayed him. For almost two years Sacajawea and another Indian wife and two children belonging to Toussaint Charbonneau had been living in St. Louis more or less as guests of William Clark. But Sacajawea was unwell and wished to return to the upper river, and Charbonneau had long ago tired of the inhibitions of civilization and wished to go north with Lisa. *³

Also, Henry Marie Brackenridge, whose writings were one day to be valuable sources of early Missouri River lore, wanted to see the West as a paying guest aboard Lisa's boat. Such details took time to arrange, and it was the first week in April before Lisa could leave St. Charles.

In view of this delay and Indian unrest, Lisa sent Charbonneau to Hunt asking him to wait so that the two parties could travel the dangerous territory together. But Hunt, influenced by Crooks and McClellan, thought Lisa could not be trusted, and the New Jerseyite played a very questionable hand. He replied to Lisa in terms so ambiguous that both Charbonneau and Lisa believed the Astorians had agreed to wait.

When Lisa found the contrary to be true, he initiated the longest race ever run in North America. And it was no gentlemen's sporting event. It was in deadly earnest, and the loser might well forfeit his fortune and his life, to either the Indians or his opponent. Lisa was furious at his rival's perfidy, and Hunt was so frightened that he was not entirely responsible for his actions.

The race lasted two months over a course of 1,200 miles. Day after day Hunt pushed his voyageurs in a frenzy to escape the indignant Spaniard. Lisa, in a single keelboat manned by twenty-five superb oarsmen, begged, threatened, and taunted his crew to catch the double-talking Astorians.

During the course of the race, the regular routines were maintained of necessity. Hunters brought in the daily meat; clothes wore out and were mended or replaced; and around evening fires made of green

---

* We have already called attention to the uncertainty regarding which of Charbonneau's wives was involved in this journey. See Chapter 16.

wood whose excess of smoke helped control the mosquitoes, the men laughed at ribald tales or complained of the food or the work.

At one point three white men came paddling downstream—Ed Robinson, John Hoback, and Jacob Reznor, former employees of the Missouri Fur Company who were returning almost reluctantly to civilization. It took little persuasion for Hunt to induce them to join him.

They advised him to leave the Lewis and Clark trail, probably the least practical of all the transmountain routes,* at the Arikara villages, strike overland, and cross the Continental Divide farther south. Hunt accepted their advice.

While these arguments were being considered, minor duties were keeping Dorion busy. Two Sioux spies called from shore and warned Hunt not to attempt to cross their land, and a war party rode brazenly along the high river bank. Hunt's rifles were about to open fire when Dorion's sharper eye saw the buffalo robe signals which indicated a desire to talk rather than fight. At the parley which followed, Pierre is said to have interpreted the speeches simultaneously with their utterance. If this is true, he was a notch above most interpreters, who gave the substance of a speech either at the end or in long segments.

A few days after this council, Lisa hove in sight.

There were to be stirring hours ahead. The quarrel between Crooks, McClellan, and Hunt on the one hand and Lisa on the other, with Pierre Dorion, Jr., the pawn between, had smoldered for several months. Lisa intended to collect for the whiskey Pierre had bought from him—but Dorion had won the first round by evading arrest at St. Charles.

Hunt now believed himself in double jeopardy. He honestly thought Lisa was dangerous in his own right; and if McClellan really shot Lisa as he had threatened, the act would constitute murder, even on the Missouri. Hunt wanted none of it. He was having trouble enough.

---

* This was contemporary opinion, but it is not commonly expressed today. "The route taken by Lewis and Clark across the mountains was perhaps, the worst that could have been selected," said Brackenridge; and Major Andrew Henry of the Missouri Fur Company, referring to the better passes over the mountains, said he thought "loaded horses, or even waggons, might in the present state, go in the course of five or six days, from a navigable point on the Columbia, more easy than between those on the heads of the Ohio." (See Henry Marie Brackenridge, *Views of Louisiana,* Baltimore, Schaeffer & Maund, 1817, pp. 163-164.)

He was to have much more.

At the moment, however, everyone pretended amity. Lisa covertly looked for Dorion, and Hunt covertly watched McClellan. Lisa did not intend for his difference with Dorion (largely wounded pride, since the accusation of overcharge was true and Lisa knew it) to eclipse the insult of Hunt's leaving without him at the beginning of their respective journeys. But for now, he would keep up pretenses and wait.

Meanwhile, Lisa and Hunt were moving upriver with a buffer zone of safe distance between them. But a torrential rain following the Fourth of July upset the arrangement and compelled the two parties to camp not over a hundred yards apart.

Lisa was much too wily to start open war. Instead he invited Dorion for a drink. Whiskey was one of the pleasures the half-breed could not refuse, and Lisa kept the tin cup full. *

Bradbury said:

Mr. Lisa invited Dorion . . . to his boat, where he had given him some whiskey, and took the opportunity of avowing his intention to take him away from Mr. Hunt.

Dorion had often spoken . . . of his debt [for whiskey in] great indignation at the manner it had been incurred, alleging that he had been charged the most exorbitant prices for articles at Fort Mandan, and in particular ten dollars per quart for whiskey. [4]

To take Dorion from Hunt would even two scores: it would put Dorion in Lisa's power again and deprive Hunt of the best Sioux interpreter on the river. But for once, Lisa underestimated his man's capacity. Pierre drank a goodly round of river fire but refused to betray Hunt. Lisa threatened to prosecute, and the half-breed countered by reporting the whole thing to Hunt. Naturally, this convinced Hunt of Lisa's treacherous nature.

Just as Pierre finished his story, Lisa walked into Hunt's camp and asked to borrow a towline. A grand free-for-all flared up. Dorion, fired with whiskey and an innate love for a fight, charged from his

---

* Liquor was measured on the river and throughout the mountains by the tin cup. Unscrupulous traders often handled it in such fashion that a finger or thumb took up a profitable portion of the cup.

tent and struck Lisa "several times, and seized a pair of pistols belonging to Hunt," said Brackenridge.[5]

Lisa shouted, *"O mon Dieu! où est mon couteau?"*[6] (he preferred a sharp knife to a pistol) and rushed to his boat to get his weapons.

Brackenridge stepped in and tried to calm Lisa, but seeing it was futile, accompanied him back to Hunt's camp. Dorion "took his ground the party ranging themselves in order to witness the event," said Bradbury.[7]

This was the chance McClellan and Crooks had waited for. It gave them a chance to kill Lisa in an open fight and avoid the charge of murder. Hunt perhaps sensed this, for "he did not seem to interest himself much in the affair," said Brackenridge.[8]

At this stage of affairs, the three paying guests decided to intervene. Brackenridge wrote later, "I had several times to stand between him [Lisa] and the interpreter, who had a pistol in each hand. I am sorry to say, that there was but little disposition on the part of Mr. Hunt to prevent the mischief. . . ."[9]

However, while Brackenridge was thus occupied, Hunt did dissuade McClellan from shooting Lisa, only to have his good work backfire: at that very moment Lisa made a derogatory reference to Hunt, who immediately reversed his ground and challenged Lisa to a duel.

"He told Lisa the matter should be settled by themselves and desired him [Lisa] to fetch his pistols."

Lisa started for them, and "I followed to his boat, accompanied by Mr. Brackenridge, and we with difficulty prevented a meeting, which in the present temper of the parties, would certainly have been a bloody one," said Bradbury.[10]

Time played to the advantage of the peacemakers. Brackenridge talked Lisa into a calmer attitude, Hunt did not press the matter, Dorion partially sobered up, and McClellan stalked off to sulk and wait for another day. Bloodshed had been avoided but Lisa and Hunt refused to speak to each other.

The intermediaries believed they now held certain advantages which they hoped to maintain: interwhite war had been prevented and the Indians were less likely to attack; Dorion would probably not start a fight unless he got drunk again; and Hunt, they were confident, would not force the issue.

At the same time, they had to consider negative items. The Mc-

Clellan-Crooks combination was potentially most dangerous. Mc-
Clellan was activated by a blind, sustained hate, and Crooks was all
too likely to back any move McClellan made. Brackenridge considered
Dorion a "worthless fellow," and was inclined to sympathize with Lisa
on the whiskey bill. And not only were Bradbury and Nuttall unfamiliar with the ways of the river, but Nuttall remained aloof from
the whole thing as much as possible, thus placing most of the burden
for peace on Brackenridge and Bradbury.

LISA AND HUNT REACH

AN AGREEMENT

1811

UNDER an uneasy truce, the two commands worked slowly up the current along opposite sides of the Missouri, always in sight lest one should reach the Arikaras first and open trade to the disadvantage of the other. Hunt was slightly ahead and Lisa granted this salve to his rival's pride, for the Spaniard's superior crew could have passed Hunt any time they were ordered to do so.

During the second week in July, both parties camped six miles below the Arikara towns. The question of who first should enter the villages could no longer be postponed.

Who was to have the advantage? Who was to decide?

Each possessed certain strengths. Lisa had the experience and the better crew. Hunt had Pierre Dorion, Jr. And we may be sure Lisa appreciated that fact even if Hunt did not. Perhaps that is why the Spaniard accepted with such alacrity when Brackenridge offered to approach Hunt seeking some compromise.

Before any conclusion was reached, however, two Arikara chiefs arrived with their own interpreter* and told Dorion bluntly that the Rees would permit no further progress unless Hunt established a

---

* The identity of this interpreter is clouded. He is referred to as a Frenchman who had lived among the Indians twenty years. Several had done that—René Jusseaume, Toussaint Charbonneau, the Dorions, Joseph Garreau, and Antoine Tabeau, to name a few. Since Charbonneau and one or more of his wives were with Lisa, and Dorion, Jr., was with Hunt, it is doubtful if the interpreter mentioned could have been either of them.

permanent post among them. Dorion countered that such a ruling should not apply to Hunt because he was going to the big water to the west and would leave the river at this point anyway. The Indians were satisfied, and Brackenridge then persuaded Lisa and Hunt to enter the towns separately but simultaneously—a solution which prevented the Indians from suspecting ill will among the whites.

A council followed in which Lisa dropped a most magnanimous remark, often studiously forgotten by Hunt's partisans. Lisa agreed to trade if Ree prices were not too high, and then pointedly referred to Hunt as his friend, saying that in case of any trouble he would be arrayed with Hunt.[1]

While Pierre Dorion, Jr., was interpreting, his eyes wandered searchingly around the council fire. He was uneasy, and whispered to Bradbury, who sat next to him, that many of the head men of the Rees were not present, so that their followers would therefore not be bound by the agreements of the council. Hunt, of course, knew nothing of this, but Lisa did, and it may have been these potentials for trouble that induced him to ally himself with Hunt. However, before the absences came up for discussion, the missing chiefs drifted in one by one and the tensions relaxed.

The Arikaras consented to sell horses at $10 a head in goods at "first cost," a price somewhere between our cost of manufacture and wholesale. This settled, Lisa then offered to trade his horses for Hunt's riverboats, and Crooks, Dorion, and Bradbury went after the horses.

Bradbury was riding a very poor horse which constantly fell behind, and "Dorion . . . and others . . . occasionaly rode after me, to beat him forward"[2]—a sentence that adds another brushstroke to the portrait of Pierre Dorion, Jr. To let Bradbury, whom he liked, ride a worn-out horse which must be beaten to keep it moving amused him. His fun was as simple—and as cruel—as his loves and hates.

René Jusseaume (who was again upriver) met the horse-collecting party, and at first took pains to be courteous to Bradbury, inviting him to a squaw dance. But on the way he reverted to his often unpleasant self, deliberately riding through an Indian corn patch over the protests of both Bradbury and the squaws working there. "I suspected that he committed this aggression to show his authority or importance," said Bradbury.[3]

Following the council, Hunt and Lisa had resumed speaking to each other, and Lisa went to help Crooks and Dorion; Hunt began buying additional horses from the Rees.

But he was unhappy. As each horse was acquired and its tail cropped to mark the sale, Hunt would cast an anxious eye on the heights along the riverbank, where a band of Sioux was riding back and forth, back and forth.

Was it to be war after all?

The several interpreters explained that if the Sioux rode side by side as they were doing, it only meant that buffalo were near. If they began riding crisscross to each other, then it was time to post guards and get the powder out.

But a Sioux was a Sioux to Wilson Price Hunt, and he began buying dogs for food rather than risk hunting buffalo—a move which must have amused Charbonneau and his squaws, to say nothing of Dorion when he returned and heard about it.

The adjustments in package size and distribution of personnel, necessitated by Hunt's decision to go overland, would have taken much longer than they did had not Hunt and Lisa been served by the greatest collection of interpreters available on the Missouri. Charbonneau and Pierre Dorion, Jr., had come all the way from St. Louis; Hunt had recently hired the mulatto Ed Rose (of whom much more later) and René Jusseaume; and one or two others were within call.

It is to be regretted that these men were either illiterate or too busy to set down their versions of the Hunt-Lisa quarrel. But their days were filled with labor and their nights with sin, and history is the loser.

Prostitution was a thriving business. Bradbury said that about eighty squaws were on hand and that it was very common for wives and husbands to put their heads together and discuss the price to be charged. "The Canadians were very good customers, and Mr. Hunt was kept in full employ during the evening, in delivering out to them blue beads and vermillion, the articles in use for this kind of traffic."[4]

The river Indians honored chastity and modesty mostly in the breach.

The Arikaras gave a special prize to any young lady who could prove virginity at a specified age; but she must claim the prize in public, and if she lied the man—or men—responsible for her loss must step forward. Brackenridge witnessed one of these rituals, in which "the daughter of the interpreter (a Frenchman who had resided with the Arikaras upwards of twenty years), a beautiful girl of sixteen came forward, but . . ." a young man stepped out and the "young lady . . . shrunk back confused and abashed, while the . . . crowd was convulsed with laughter."[5]

On another occasion Bradbury' and Brackenridge hired an old squaw to ferry them across the river to visit a Mandan village. They had just shoved away from shore when three young ladies, about fifteen years of age, arrived and demanded to go along. They had not been included in the agreed-upon price for ferry service but they were determined to have their own way. They stripped nude, tossed their clothes in the boat, and dived into the river and swam and splashed around the amused Brackenridge and the blushing Bradbury. They teased and coaxed until the two men got into the game and decided to teach the girls a lesson. When they reached the opposite shore, the men refused to give the girls their clothes.

The outcome of the game is not recorded.

But it was not all fun and frolic. One day all business was halted; a sense of suspense hung over the lodges, and the whites ran half-fearfully to Dorion to ask what it meant. He said a war party, led by Grey Eyes, was returning, and the solemn music and the slow tread of the advancing noncombatants were part of the ceremonies to welcome the heroes and honor the dead. Villagers and their horses marched ten or twelve abreast, each clan to itself. Warriors in full dress pranced into view with captured scalps fluttering from their war poles; an old mother greeted her dying son sitting stiffly astride his horse and staring ahead into eternity; the aged and infirm rubbed their shriveled hands across a hero's legs to share the glory; and those whose sons had not come home slunk off to a nearby hill to grieve and moan, away from the feasting and dancing which would be held in the great lodge for the next two days.

These were stirring scenes for Hunt, his guests, and even the interpreters and voyageurs, who, though they had witnessed them many times, never really tired of the spectacle.

But the summer was well advanced, and if Astoria were ever to be founded, Hunt must be about it.

24

DISASTER

1811–1814

JULY 18, 1811: Hunt was ready. Nuttall was staying upriver; Brackenridge and Bradbury were to return to St. Louis aboard Lisa's keelboat.

The Astorian forces of sixty-four men and eighty-two horses were divided into messes, each with its own equipment. Only the partners, and later the hunters, rode. And Pierre Dorion, Jr. He laid down the flat condition that he have a horse to use as he saw fit. This did not imply that the pregnant Marie was to ride. She trudged along on foot as good squaws were supposed to do.

Washington Irving has left a classic description of the wilderness over which the Astorians were about to pass. And if some of his predictions eventually proved wrong, the travelers were nevertheless to find conditions very close to Irving's dismal picture.

Some portions of it along the rivers may partially be subdued by agriculture, others may form vast pastoral tracts, like those of the East; but it is to be feared that a great part of it will form a lawless interval between the abodes of civilized man, like the wastes of the oceans or the deserts of Arabia; and, like them, be subject to the depredations of the marauder. Here may spring up new and mongrel races, like new formations of geology, the amalgamation of the "debris" and "abrasions" of former races, civilized and savage; the remains of broken and almost extinguished tribes; the descendants of wandering hunters and trappers; of fugitives from the Spanish and American frontiers; of adventurers and desperadoes of every class and country, yearly ejected from the bosom of society into the wilderness. . . .

Irving was willing to admit that "Some may gradually become pastoral hordes, . . . half shepherd, half warrior, . . . but others, it is to be apprehended, will become predatory bands, mounted on the fleet steeds of the prairies, with the open plains for their marauding grounds, and the mountains for their retreats. . . ."[1]

In the beginning of the transmountain journey, Ed Rose was the more important of the two interpreter-guides. His duty was to get the Astorians safely through Crow country. But he had a bad reputation, and it was rumored that he intended to betray Hunt to the Crows.

Hunt was in a dither. He was afraid of the Indians; he distrusted both his interpreters; he did not know how to go ahead, and he dared not turn back. Stubbornly trusting his own infallibility, he blundered along until on the outskirts of the Black Hills Dorion and two companions went hunting and failed to return for three days. Hunt set signal fires. Nothing happened. Justifiable fear for Dorion was intensified by the belief that it was here that Rose intended to ambush the Astorians. It was arrant nonsense, of course, but fear knows no logic.

Thus pressed, Hunt clutched at the absent Dorion as a savior, and shifted his course westward in the hope of making contact with the hunters. Shortly thereafter they came into camp. They had got lost, seen none of the signal fires, and recognized no landmarks.

Even Marie seemed pleased to see Pierre.

This experience pointed up the value of Ed Rose, who was at home here. But after he led Hunt around the Black Hills, traced out the Big Horn Mountains, and located his own Crow camp late in August, Hunt overpaid him and summarily canceled his contract. This was a costly mistake, for it put all the responsibility for interpretation and guide service on Dorion, who never pretended to know anything about the lands beyond the Crows.

The Overland Astorians were not a confident or happy expedition. Their leader was conscientious and brave but unfitted for his task; the partners squabbled; the crew was generally second best; and the greatest Crow interpreter (with one possible exception) had just been dismissed.

But sometimes an amusing incident lightened the general gloom. Once when John Day and a younger boy were hunting, they were surprised by a grizzly bear. Day cautioned the boy to stand still and not shoot. The bear might go away. Instead it reared, roared, and threatened. Day whispered, "Be quiet, boy! be quiet!" Again the grizzly threatened and again Day said no. A third time the bear offered battle, and Day himself shot and killed it. The boy, somewhat confused by the conflict between orders and actions, asked for an explanation, and Day laconically replied, "I will not be bullied."[2]

After Ed Rose was discharged, Hunt and Dorion wandered on into the mountains. It was the last of August, and snow soon blocked the route. Hunt then ordered one of the backtrackings which eventually brought disaster to all and death to some.

Rose heard of their present plight, and despite his recent shabby treatment came to their rescue and set them on a proper trail. It apparently did not occur to Hunt to rehire the mulatto.

Perhaps only the tragic Vitus Bering or Henry Hudson among New World expedition leaders deserves more blame and more sympathy than Wilson Price Hunt. He made one mistake after another. But he was a brave man, and his suffering in the weeks after Rose had left a second time beggar description. He found a roving band of Flatheads, but left them to challenge the Wind River; a local guide thought a single range of hills separated Hunt from the headwaters of the Columbia when in fact a Continental Divide with a thousand spurs stood in his path; he floundered into sight of the Tetons and on to the Green and Hoback rivers; he got to Jackson Hole but left its relative safety for Teton Pass and the Snake. He sent Dorion and Day to explore the Snake because the voyageurs were weary of horses, dry land, and sagebrush and longed for their boats and the toils and perils they were used to, and Dorion and Day came back saying the Snake was unnavigable. The partners voted to go to Andrew Henry's old post near the modern St. Anthony, Idaho, and arriving there found it deserted—and it was October.

But the quiet little river flowing past the empty site, with the Tetons shining across the valley on frosty mornings, was too much for the good sense of the voyageurs and Hunt. They gave their precious horses to a band of Indians, made canoes, and, leaving Hoback, Reznor, and Robinson to trap the Henry preserve, embarked in high spirits on October 18.

Within a matter of hours, catastrophe struck: submerged rocks punched holes in the canoes, and unexpected currents capsized them and scattered everything helter-skelter. Valuable sunshine hours were lost collecting the goods, drying and repacking them, and repairing the canoes. The wilds, supposedly alive with game and Indians, were devoid of both. For 300 miles the expedition encountered not another white man. Now and again they spotted a few Indians far to the right or left, but they were only outlines against the sky. Seldom could Dorion get close enough to be heard. When he could, he did not know their tongue, and sign language was inadequate for the information he needed.

Crooks and Antoine Clappine, probably Hunt's most valuable voyageur, split a canoe end to end, and Clappine drowned. Food was nearly gone, and Hunt divided his command, sending them in all directions with the admonition to find help or get to the Pacific as best they could. This command, in effect, relinquished Hunt's leadership.

Dorion and his family remained with Hunt.

Extra goods were cached and Hunt fought bravely on, hungry, wet, essentially lost, and near total despair. In these days of trial, Wilson Price Hunt rose above his own attributes and displayed a personal fortitude worthy of a greater leader.

Some of those he had but recently sent away returned and said the farther reaches of the Snake were still more wild and unnavigable. Turbulent water was forcing one portage after another, and Hunt abandoned his canoes and decided to walk to the mouth of the Columbia—a thousand miles away! Hunt and the Dorions and the dispirited boatmen. Snow on the hills, frost and cold and hunger. Only forty pounds of corn, twenty of lard, a handful of dry soup, and five pounds of dried meat per man—a pitiful supply for thirty-six humans for a thousand miles. But long ago they had reached the point of no return. Go on or die.

With the Dorions and eighteen men, Hunt started down the north side of the Snake while Crooks and the others took the opposite bank. They hoped that by keeping to the river they would at least always have water. It was a delusion. It was impossible to follow the river that closely. Long before the end, the voyageurs resorted to their own urine in their agonies of thirst.

In mid-November Dorion heard from a band of half-starved Snakes that John Reed, leading one of the splinter parties, had passed by. Hunt bought one emaciated horse and a few days later Dorion bought another for his family. Snow-covered mountains faced them. Famine was very real, and Hunt killed his horse, and the men declared it wonderful food. "So should I," said Hunt, "were it not for the attachment I have to the animal."[3]

December, and three feet of snow. Crooks on the opposite bank was suffering from the last stages of starvation, and Hunt was powerless to help. Marie trudged along, uncomplaining, and the two little boys stoically accepted it all. With old moccasins and an occasional dog, the party cheated death. Crooks retraced his steps but found no relief. Hunt panicked and ordered a retreat into the heart of the Continental Divide in midwinter. Crooks became too weak to travel, and Hunt and five others heroically slowed their pace to wait on him while the Dorions, their skeleton horse, and the remainder went on. For he who could not keep up was left behind: this was the universal code, from the Gulf to the Arctic—cruel, pathetic, and deadly practical. The majority must not die for the sake of the minority.

Hunt begged Dorion to kill his horse, but Pierre refused and was unanimously supported by his companions, who argued that death was not yet upon them and the animal could always be killed later.

Then, from a helpless Indian camp, Hunt seized five horses and immediately sent meat to Crooks and his men on the opposite bank. Starvation had made them frighteningly wild and ravenous; and Jean Baptiste Prévost, insane with hunger, lost all control, upset a makeshift boat, and drowned at the very moment of rescue.

Ice flowed in the Snake. Hunt seesawed first ahead and then behind his separate fragments of command. Christmas came and went, and the Hunt party left the river and headed straight into the mountains. Marie's time matured, and Pierre did the unusual, waiting with her while the others tramped on, and a new Indian baby joined a tragic journey.

Then: a snow-free valley with friendly Indians and food. New Year's Eve, 1811, and Pierre and Marie walked quietly into camp, their two-year-old son proudly riding the family steed. New Year's Day, and in their buoyancy the voyageurs broke into song and dance, garnished with spitted dog and horse. Another day, and the third little Dorion left his new world with as little fanfare as he had entered it. Warmer winds and milder skies told of Pacific slopes as one fragment of the command after the other found the Columbia and straggled to its mouth, defeated and bankrupt but alive.

And the Dorions walked, too, for Pierre became careless and lost his horse to thieves.

The failure of the seaborne Astor enterprise under Captain Thorn, the murder of his crew and the loss of the *Tonquin*, the rivalries among the partners, the advent of the North West Company, the War of 1812, and the sale of Astoria for a fraction of its worth to the North Westers are matters which affected Pierre Dorion, Jr., only in that he heard them talked about.

From mid-February of 1812 until July of 1813, the Dorions received little recorded attention at Astoria. Presumably Hunt took Pierre on his many excursions along the river and into the immediate hinterland, but there is no satisfactory evidence that the guide went with Hunt to Alaska.

Small parties were dispatched from Astoria on various missions; reports were dispatched to St. Louis only to be lost to Indian knavery; trapping and trading units were sent as far east as the Rockies and as far north as the Okanogans; the *Beaver,* the second annual ship from home, arrived; Robert Stuart, Ramsay Crooks, John Day, and a small crew started east with dispatches, and Day went insane and was left with friendly natives to be returned to the Fort, where he died a year later.

Robert Stuart picked up Hunt's westward trail, got lost, and traveled a hundred miles down the Snake in the wrong direction before he came to his senses and realized he was heading toward Astoria and not St. Louis.[4] He found Hunt's caches rifled. Then Crooks became too ill to travel, and Stuart too had to decide for or against leaving a helpless companion. He wrote: "The sensations excited on this occasion . . . are not such as arise in the artificial solitude of parks and gardens . . . [for] the phantoms which haunt a desert, are want, misery, and danger . . . [and] man is made unwillingly acquainted with his own weakness, and meditation shews him how little he can sustain, and how little he can perform."[5] As Hunt had done on the outward route, Stuart refused to leave Crooks. But starvation then became so real that his crew proposed they cast lots that one should die to save the rest.

My thoughts began to ruminate on our hopeless and forlorn situation with the prospects before us untill I at length became so agitated and weak it was with difficulty I crawled to bed. . . .

This . . . led my revery to a retrospective view of former . . . days, when difficulties and distresses were only things imaginary, which convinces me how little a man who knows . . . neither cares nor sorrows, can feel for those of others. . . . Let him visit these regions of want and misery . . . and he will be taught the . . . advantage of prayer.[6]

Stuart floundered on; discovered South Pass and did not know it; reached the North Platte and failed to recognize it; went into winter quarters and lost them to the Arapaho; found another shelter and spent a lonely winter in it; and finally delivered the dispatches to St. Louis on April 30, 1813.

In the meantime, the sale of Astoria to the North West Company had been decided, and on July 5, 1813, John Reed, Giles LeClerc, Pierre Delaunay, the Dorions, and others were sent to the Snake country. Their orders were to find Hoback, Reznor, and Robinson, collect as many pelts as possible, and join the remaining Astor forces as they were returning to St. Louis after the transfer of Astoria to the North West Company.

Reed intended to center his work on the left bank of the Snake but changed his mind and built a small cabin near the mouth of the Boise River. Dorion and one or two others built another shelter four or five days' travel farther on.

By late September Hoback and his partners were with Reed, but even this last effort to save some little of the Astor investment failed. Delaunay, a moody man, left camp one morning and was never seen

Astoria, 1811. *U.S. Signal Corps, photo 111-sc-90797, The National Archives.*

Astoria, renamed Fort George by Captain W. Black of the British sloop of war, *Raccoon,* in 1813. Rendering by Henry James Warre. *The Beinke Rare Book and Manuscript Library, Yale University.*

again; François Landry fell from his horse and was killed; Jean Baptiste Turcot died of syphilis, politely called (as were several other diseases) "king's evil" in those still-Puritan days; then, during the second week in January, LeClerc crawled into Dorion's hut and gasped out that Pierre and Reznor had been ambushed and killed.

Marie caught two horses, helped LeClerc onto one, put herself and her sons on the other, and dashed for Reed's cabin, five days away. Sometime during the third day of fear, LeClerc died of his wounds,* but there was no time to mourn him or perform even the simple Indian rites. The enemy was in sight. Marie and the boys hid and spent the January mountain night without food or fire, an ordeal which would have proved fatal to a lesser breed. At daybreak she hurried to Reed's cabin.

The gruesome remains of a sadistic massacre were strewn about. Only she and her sons were alive.

The whole Astor enterprise had been a failure. Disaster had piled

---

* Hubert Howe Bancroft says LeClere died at the Dorion cabin (*History of the Northwest Coast;* Vols. XXVII–XXVIII of *Works,* San Francisco, A. L. Bancroft Co., 1884, XXVIII, 246–247, 247n).

on disaster, death on death. Twenty-two men had died on the *Tonquin,* Clappine had drowned, the new Dorion baby had quitted life before it had a meaning, John Day had died insane, starvation had driven Prévost mad and he had drowned himself in a frenzy for food—and now only Marie Dorion and her boys were left of the Reed party.

Even her Pierre was gone. He would spank her no more, nor wait while she presented him with a son. Not again would his wild laughter carry across the nights, or his prowess as an interpreter buy her blue beads.

Helpless to aid the dead and fearing for herself and her sons, Marie turned mutely away from the blood and mutilation and started for the Columbia. In midwinter she forded the Snake, but she found the Blue Mountains impassable. With a fortitude rarely matched by any New World heroine, she killed her horses, made a tent of their hides, gathered fuel, dried their meat, and proceeded to survive the winter. When spring came she worked laboriously through the mountains, and arrived at Walla Walla just as the homeward-bound Astorians were moving up the Columbia. She hailed them from shore on April 17, and told them the story we have repeated. *

Marie Dorion was as much an adventurer as any man who ever took a scalp from a writhing enemy. After telling the Astorians of the fate of Pierre and his companions, she said good-bye and started for the Okanogans, 2,000 miles away from her ancestral home. Six years later she married a trapper, one Venier, of whom nothing is known. Whether Venier died or deserted her or she left him is unrecorded, but in 1823 she was living with Jean Baptiste Toupin, an interpreter at Walla Walla. Almost twenty years later Toupin and Marie moved to the Willamette Valley near Salem, Oregon. Advancing age and the proximity of an organized society induced them to have their twenty-year union, and their two children, legalized. Baptiste Dorion, grandson of old Pierre Dorion and one of the two little boys who suffered all the way from the Missouri to the Pacific, and Marguerite Venier were also "acknowledged" by Toupin in the ceremonies of the Catholic faith, July 19, 1841.[7]

With all their flouting of the mores of their society, there was a genuine understanding of human frailties and a willingness to for-

---

* The only record we have of most of these events is Marie's memory. Therefore, the time and place of LeClerc's death and the details of her flight are subject to human error.

give them among the frontiersmen. They understood the basic drives of men and women, their own mates included—and did not quibble.

Pierre Dorion, Jr., was not so stable as George Drouillard; he was not so picturesque as Toussaint Charbonneau; he was neither so reckless nor so invaluable as Ed Rose. But he was a worthy member of the select fraternity of interpreter-guides. He easily ranks among the dozen most important on the Missouri. He was born a riverman and died a mountain man, and by that transition symbolized the shift of emphasis from the Missouri to the Continental Divide.

BAPTISTE DORION

1834-1849

BAPTISTE DORION and an uncertain number of half-brothers and half-sisters rounded out a third generation of the Dorion family. But compared with his father and grandfather, Bapiste was a colorless and indistinct figure flitting across the log pages of the Columbia. He was never associated with a really great cause or even a pathetic failure. He lived during the exciting years when Hudson's Bay Company men, missionaries, settlers, and government agents built the "Oregon question" into an international crisis, but Baptiste played no decisive role; and except for the Whitman massacre, the years themselves were generally safe and prosaic, reflecting political footwork more than frontier heroics.

For years Baptiste Dorion and Thomas McKay, half-breed son of Mrs. McLoughlin, wife of Dr. John McLoughlin, were the two most important half-breeds attached to the Hudson's Bay Company on the Columbia.[1] But the doctor, the Company's chief factor at Vancouver, wrote of events, not interpreters, and his many associates were equally remiss.

From early life until his death, Baptiste was surrounded with rival traders in the Okanogan, on the Columbia, Cowlitz, Spokane, and Willamette rivers; with missionaries of conflicting and intolerant faiths at Waiilatpu, Lapwai, Salem, and The Dalles and in the Cowlitz Valley; and with an ever-increasing flow of settlers—God-fearing, ruthless, sinful, peaceful, and quarrelsome. All his life he was subject to the cross-pulls of divergent faiths, commercial interests, and political entities. Life for him was much more complicated than for his grandfather, old Pierre, squatting among his squaws on the Missouri, or even for his half-breed father, Pierre, Jr., who mastered his craft

Dr. John McLoughlin, Hudson's Bay Company chief factor at Fort Vancouver when Baptiste Dorion served as one of his interpreter-guides. *Oregon Historical Society.*

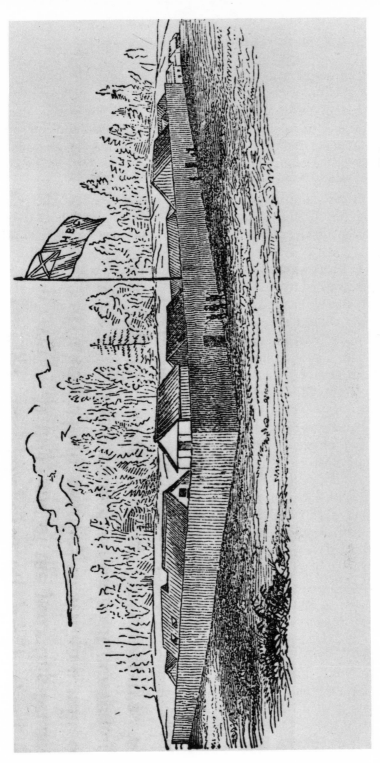

Fort Vancouver when it was a trading post of the Hudson's Bay Company 1841. *U.S. Signal Corps, Photo 111-sc-89870, The National Archives.*

and tramped across a continent and died without ever knowing the stresses of civilization.

No wonder Baptiste was neither quite civilized nor savage, neither wholly upright nor totally treacherous. He had forever to remember that he was more Indian than white, more civilized than savage—a conflict which he controlled largely with honor and a minimum of lapses.

Early in his maturity, Baptiste was employed as an interpreter-guide along the Columbia, particularly at Vancouver, where he was "an important leader among the half-breeds—next to Thomas McKay."[2]

When J. K. Townsend, the noted naturalist, visited the Columbia in 1834 and wished to make a side excursion into the Blue Mountains south of Walla Walla, he chose Baptiste as his guide and mentor; but he said little about Dorion's work.[3]

Seven years later Baptiste was interpreter for the notorious Dr. Elijah White, the "garrulous busybody"[4] who imagined himself with a mission to put the Indians in their place, remove the Hudson's Bay Company from Old Oregon, abolish demon rum, and show the missionaries how to save Indian souls.

White had first arrived on the Columbia by the sea route in June of 1837 as a physician attached to Jason Lee's Willamette mission. Three years later Lee's patience was exhausted, and he dismissed White.

But it was too late. The doctor had evolved a scheme for reorganizing life on the Columbia. He hurried to Washington to arrange official status, and before his neighbors were aware of their danger, he had been appointed Indian subagent and was hurrying west, making speeches, sneering at missionaries, damning the Hudson's Bay Company, and publicizing himself.

He arrived at Elm Grove, southwest of Independence, Missouri, just in time to be elected captain of the wagon train which left there May 16, 1842. Under his command were eighteen wagons and somewhat more than a hundred men, women, and children—and a goodly number of family dogs.

Now, Elijah White was not only a busybody; he was a prude. Within days he had issued a fiat: no swearing, no lovemaking—and no dogs. It is unlikely the good people under his orders would have taken much umbrage at the first two rules. One could always curse silently and make love in secret. But when White tried to legalize his hate of dogs by jamming a motion through camp meeting providing that all family pets be shot, it was too much.

As the beasts yelped and mothers and children cried at the cruelty, irate fathers informed White that any man shooting another dog would himself be shot.*

At the end of the month Elijah was not reelected, and Lansford Hastings became captain. Thereupon the train split into two parts, and the doctor stalked ahead with a small following of his own.[5] However, Indian alarms and the accidents of trail travel kept the two divisions more or less in touch, and at Fort Laramie, Thomas Fitzpatrick agreed to deliver both detachments to the Columbia for $500.

---

* Some say every dog was killed; others insist that the parental revolt saved some of the pets.

Fort Laramie, 1842. Artist unknown. *U.S. Signal Corps, Photo 111-sc-89547, The National Archives.*

When the wagons were abandoned at Fort Hall, White again rushed ahead, and on September 11, 1842, gleefully brought Marcus Whitman, medical missionary at Waiilatpu, the staggering news that his mission was to be sold, his colleagues were to be recalled to the states, and Whitman himself was to desert his Cayuse Indians and start over again among the Spokanes.

White was exultant. He went on to the Willamette, set up his authority, and before long announced he was leading an army to punish the Indians who had invaded Whitman's privacy and burned the gristmill.[6]

Not only did the Cayuse and Nez Percé need correction, said the doctor; they needed laws. And he obliged, with eleven sections of perhaps the most absurd rules ever written to affect the Indians. There was some native support for his edict that the Indians could own no dogs except those used as draft animals (the doctor hated dogs as some spinsters do men—without qualification). He further decreed that braves were to be whipped, jailed, or hanged for offenses ranging from entering a house uninvited to horse-stealing and murder.

McLoughlin, who knew the Indians, and even the missionaries, who did not, were appalled. They begged White to let the Indians quiet down of their own accord. But Elijah White, armored with Righteousness, his laws, and an "army" of six men—Thomas McKay, Cornelius Rogers (a recent recruit of Whitman's), Baptiste Dorion, and three others—moved against the Cayuses and Nez Percé on November 16, 1842, fighting −15 degrees of frost, the coldest in Indian memory.

White passed The Dalles on the twenty-fourth and was at the modern Walla Walla December 1, where he met Mr. McKinlay, the Hudson's Bay Company representative in the area. McKinlay, however, had been ordered by McLoughlin not to accept White as United States Government Indian agent since the Oregon boundary had not been settled and there were honest reasons to doubt White's authority. Furthermore, McKinlay was not to attend any meeting with White or to permit Company buildings to be used for the same.[7]

None of this deterred White. He called the Indians to council; he scolded, he promised, he exhorted, he read his laws. To his delight and surely to Baptiste Dorion's secret amusement, the natives appeared to accept the eleven rules with equanimity—for whatever his failings, the doctor had a suavity which appealed to the primitive mind.[8] What he did not know, but Dorion did, was that the Indian would bitterly

Marcus Whitman mission at Waiilatpu as it looked when Elijah White, Indian subagent, tried to reorganize religious work on the Columbia. *Washington State Historical Society.*

The Dalles, favored salmon fishing and drying site of Columbia River Indians. Mt. Hood in the upper center. John M. Stanley. *Report of Explorations and Surveys . . . 1853, U.S. Senate, 36th Congress, Executive Documents, Phillips Collection, University of Oklahoma Library.*

resent a flogging, first as an insult to his manhood and second because he could not understand why he should be punished for acts he had done all his life without censure. Such punishments put him in the category of squaws, than which there was no lower status except a dog's.

And the brave would expect payments for these indignities, just as Whitman and Reverend H. H. Spaulding of Lapwai, the Idaho mission, and the Catholic fathers "paid" him with food, presents, and special privileges for singing hymns and mumbling prayers.[9]

The Cayuse and Nez Percé also found it inconceivable that White would set out to punish a whole tribe with an "army" of six or seven men. The Cayuse in particular were restless. Both the Whitmans were gone—the doctor back east to plead his cause and recruit immigrants, and Mrs. Whitman to The Dalles for safety. The Cayuse felt deserted.

Open hostility was imminent.

But radiant with pride at his success, White returned down the Columbia, reporting to Mrs. Whitman and Dr. McLoughlin that he had fixed everything.

He had.

He had fixed it firmly in the minds of the Indians that the white man could not be trusted and was probably a fool besides.

Early in March of 1843, the doctor returned to the Cayuses accompanied by some 500 Nez Percé he had collected from Lapwai. Whitman was still absent, and the Cayuse were apprehensive and the Nez Percé angry.

White held another council and mouthed more absurdities, including the hint that he was a direct representative of God.[10]

When news of this latest folly reached the lower Columbia, his outraged neighbors hurried a request to Washington that White, who was also going to the Capitol, be stripped of his power to cause trouble and be kept away from Old Oregon entirely. His commission as subagent was eventually canceled, but he returned to the Willamette in 1850 as a private citizen.

Following Whitman's return with the immigrant train of 1843, the pot boiled steadily among the mission Indians and the settlers on the Willamette and the Columbia. All manner of proposals were offered for the solution of Indian unrest and the problems evolving from the influx of immigrants into Hudson's Bay Company preserves.

The international, national, and even local political infighting which took place over the Oregon question has no place in this volume. Suffice it to say that in 1847 the Indian facet of the problem exploded in the Whitman massacre and the Cayuse War.

The causes were manifold, and no two historians agree either on their number or on their importance. Without prejudice as to their validity or rank, the following may be suggested.

The white man never understood the Indian's values of right or wrong.

The Indians resented the increasing immigration.

They were confused by the conflicting teachings of the missionaries, Protestant and Catholic.

Whitman, knowing that his system of Indian salvation had failed, was plagued by an increasing lack of confidence. This was sensed by the Indians, who demanded more and more concessions.

The Hudson's Bay Company ruled their Indians by the code of an eye for an eye, which the natives understood, while the Americans wrote noble treaties and broke them with a callous disregard for honor worthy of Nietzsche.

The delay in settling the Oregon boundary also delayed the right to maintain troops in the area, and the Indians committed acts they would not have done had force been present.

And perhaps not least among the causes of the war and massacre were the disgruntled half-breeds, who were barred by their birth from living entirely in the world of either of their parents. They were often unemployed and yet lacked the Indian's skill to survive. Robert Newell said there was no "doubt in my mind but one of these kind of men was the cause of the massacre at Waiilatpu."[11] He was referring to Joe Lewis, an educated half-breed who had drifted all the way from Maine to the Columbia[12] and had been a great troublemaker at the mission.[13]

And there were more reasons for the conflict. Marianne Toupin, half-sister of Baptiste Dorion, lived among the Cayuse, and had been a constant harassment to the Whitmans. And Baptiste himself seems to have been a sort of agent provocateur, perhaps in revolt against White's actions, perhaps through some warped sense of eye-for-an-eye justice, perhaps for pure mischief. Anyway, when White returned to the Willamette after his first visit to the Cayuse, Dorion remained upriver.

There is little agreement on how long he stayed or exactly what he did except that, along with Joe Lewis and others, he was accused of inciting the Indians to trouble. He reportedly told them that when spring came, White would return with a fighting army; that Whitman had gone east for the express purpose of bringing yet another army to punish them;[14] and that when this was done, the white men would drive them from their homes and seize their lands.[15]

If Dorion did allege this last, he can be indicted only for telling the truth, for that was exactly what the white man, under one pretext or another, intended to do.

These reports had one seriocomic repercussion. The Indians asked McLoughlin whether the rumors of white intentions were correct. He denied them,[16] and gave the Indians presents to assuage their fears. Thereupon they promptly repeated the cycle, rumor followed by denials and gifts, with every band they met, and these in turn hastened to the nearest Company post to claim *their* gifts.

Open hostilities between the Cayuse and their allies and the whites began in 1847, and a hastily recruited militia, under several commands, rushed up the Columbia to quell the unrest.[17]

Baptiste Dorion, second lieutenant,* First Oregon Rifles,[18] receives a note of dubious honor in the journals. The First Oregon Rifles, commanded by Lieutenant Colonel James Waters and Major J. Magone, went to the Palouse River not far from where it empties into the Snake. Dorion was a member of their force. Waters and Magone hoped to capture one or more of the Indians involved in the Whitman massacre.

In mid-May Waters marched toward the Reverend Spaulding's mission at Lapwai, not far from the present Lewiston, Idaho, where guilty Indians were supposed to be camped. He sent one segment of his men across the Snake and led another to the Palouse River in an attempt to prevent any escape to the Columbia.

Waters, Magone, and Dorion with their men reached a rendezvous on the Palouse where they had been promised ferry service by friendly Indians. However, no Indians were present, and Magone and four others made a raft, crossed to the far side, and scouted to the mouth of the river, where they found their transport.

The Indians ferried the troops across the Palouse to a suitable campsite. While they were there, a local Indian offered to lead Waters to the

---

* However, the official roster of Dorion's company as published in the *Oregon Spectator* (April 6, 1848, p. 4) has him listed only as "duty sergeant."

enemy, and about May 22 the militia started up a dry stream bed toward Spaulding's mission. Around noon they received word that a band of Spokanes were holding a small herd of cattle belonging to the Indians whom Waters was seeking. The Spokanes offered to deliver the cattle to Waters and join him against his enemies.

The militia seemed about to consummate a successful campaign when the following morning Waters learned that his quarry had escaped to the mountains, leaving their stock behind. He immediately sent Magone, Dorion, and about 100 men to seize the animals.

In his official report, Magone said that as they approached the Snake, "an Indian was discovered on the hills, and warmly pursued by Battise Dorio and others who were in front and this was deemed a sufficient signal for a charge. . . . Before I got down the hill that leads to the river I heard the shrill report of the rifles. . . ."[19]

Historians have sometimes absolved Magone of responsibility by saying that "Baptiste Dorion . . . set off at full speed without orders, followed by several others, and the fleeing Indian was killed before the major, owing to his having a poor horse, could call a halt."[20]

Magone, however, said that when he came up, he was told that Dorion and his fellows were shooting at Indians hiding in a canoe and that an Indian camp was nearby.

The spokesman for this camp denied there were any guilty Indians there. Magone accepted this statement but posted a guard and then left on a short errand. By the time he returned, four of his men had killed two of the Indians, and had he acquiesced they would have shot the entire camp—not because they were guilty of any wrong but because they were Indians.

Later, Waters' official report also admitted that "an [armed] Indian" had been killed in cold blood for no offense other than insisting that certain animals which the army had seized were his and in no way connected with the Whitman massacre.[21]

And so the Cayuse War, which "was hardly a war at all,"[22] dragged along in similar episodes, offering little glory to anyone unless it were the negative commendation that with such exceptions as the above killings, the white men behaved with more humanity than was their wont in Indian wars.

The Cayuse affair may be said to have been important more for its causes than for any profound results, leaving aside the question of the subjugation of a minor people.

And Baptiste Dorion, too, remains an unsatisfactory historical figure. He served Townsend in the Blue Mountains; he and his half-breed friend McKay acted as guides and interpreters for McLoughlin and his guests; in 1844 "Baptiste Doria" paid a tax of 85¢ on horses valued at $280; and once he emerges as interpreter-guide in the "Reminiscences of Hugh Cosgrove,"[23] a well-to-do businessman trying to locate somewhere in Oregon about 1847, two years before Dorion died at the age of thirty-one.

Baptiste had his grandfather's sense of rude fun, and one day after Cosgrove had enjoyed a hearty meal, Baptiste inquired whether he preferred cow beef or horse beef. Cosgrove replied that he did not know since he had never eaten horse beef. "Yes you have, that was horse beef you have just eaten," replied Baptiste.[24]

Dorion apparently continued with Cosgrove until the traveler bought a section of land next to the Catholic mission for $800, many times the price several ex-fur-traders, tired of farming and the "civilization" of the Willamette, had been willing to sell their holdings for.

But such fragments do little to build a personal narrative of Baptiste Dorion, grandson of old Pierre, French expatriate, and son of Pierre the younger and Marie of the Iowas. Nevertheless, together they made the clan Dorion, which, if we count only the years spanned and the domains served, was perhaps without peer among the fraternity of interpreter-guides.

Dr. John McLoughlin's house, built at Oregon City in 1846 after McLoughlin resigned as factor at Fort Vancouver and became champion of American rights in Old Oregon. *Oregon State Highway Department.*

ED ROSE

?–1807

IT seems entirely fitting that the city about which more reprobate tales are told than any other in North America and the man about whom so many unproved stories have been circulated should have a modicum of common history: New Orleans and Ed Rose.

When the Sieur de Bienville laid out the colony of New Orleans in 1718, he certainly did not intend to found the most openly sinful city in the New World; nor did the senior Rose and his Indian-Negro mistress intend their child to grow into the notorious mulatto mountain man that he did. But the city and the man both became legends early in their respective lives, and to understand Ed Rose one must have a picture of New Orleans, for the city indubitably formed his character.

There was nothing inherent in the original settlers to cause one to suppose they would establish a unique city or organize sin on such a grand scale. By the time Ed Rose reached manhood and was a resident there, New Orleans was a town of about 10,000 souls. It was a city wracked with yellow fever and cursed with the absence of a police force; a city where the cathedral was used as often for a market as for a place of worship; where wealthy young folks, without too much attention to costume, if any, went swimming at night in the canals; where religious and civil authorities fought incessantly over supreme power; where enjoyment of the opera was offset by fear of an uprising of the Negroes; where the Ursuline nuns ran a school for girls but kept them completely ignorant of the processes of life. It was a city of brute Negroes fresh from the slave ships, and of polished quadroons whose superb females enticed the wealthy whites away from the famous Orleans ballroom while their white wives and sweethearts fumed and vented their fury because their men had deserted them for ladies of color and a livelier show.

New Orleans, of which an Ursuline said, "The women here are extremely ignorant of the means of securing their salvation but they are very expert in the art of displaying their beauty. . . . They paint and rouge to hide the ravages of time . . ."[1]—and, she might have added, to help hide their chagrin at being outcharmed by their quadroon neighbors who exacted "fewer of the troublesome considerations," as Perrin du Lac remarked in his *Voyage in the Two Louisianas*.—Charmers who believed their sole role in life was to please their white "protectors," and who gladly exchanged chastity for a comfortable apartment.

New Orleans, where Canal Street was trimmed on both sides with cypress-lined sewage ditches, cleaned each day by slaves whose jangling chains struck a harsh note in the gaiety of what was to become one of the most beautiful shopping streets in the world; New Orleans, where sailors, soldiers, and Negroes must be off the streets by eight P.M.; where the law forbade greasing cart wheels lest the quieted vehicle be used by smugglers to evade the law; where prisoners were once set free if they would marry prostitutes and thus help stabilize the population; where the dead of the poor were dumped into shallow graves already many times used, and then floated up in water seeping in from the river only a few hundred feet away until they were in turn weighted down with new bones and old earth.

New Orleans, a city of voodoo dances and Congo Square; a city where more than a half-century after Ed Rose left it, Marie Laveau, Queen of the Voodoos, terrorized superstitious Negroes and impressed sophisticated whites with her "black magic"; a city where, only a few years after Rose, thrice-married Delphine Lalaurie, social butterfly, went galloping out of town with a howling mob at her carriage wheels because they had caught her torturing her slaves in the attic of her town house; a city of which Rachel Jackson, wife of the President, said, "Great Babylon is come up before me. Oh, the wickedness, the idolatry of this place! unspeakable riches and splendor,"[2] and which Charlevoix, French Jesuit historian, called a "wild, lovely place."

But most of all New Orleans was the city where the pirate Laffite (or Lafitte) laughed and fought and loved and smuggled and killed and turned patriot and helped Jackson save the city from the British that Christmastime, 1814–1815. The legend that was Laffite would have no place in this chapter were it not that Ed Rose almost certainly came under his shadow.

The Laffite brothers were French-born, adequately financed, and well informed. Their manners were impeccable, their dress fashionable, and their friends the wealthy and influential. They came to New Orleans in 1806, the year before Ed Rose left, and their paths unquestionably crossed.

Long before the Laffites came, Barataria Bay, on the Lower Mississippi, was the headquarters of a horde of piratical ruffians who pillaged river and gulf shipping, although their mass effectiveness was minimized by their intergang wars.

Jean Laffite changed all that. He and his brother, Pierre, established a blacksmith shop on St. Philip Street to feign respectability, and then took over Barataria Bay and Mississippi River piracy with approved "gangster" methods, and openly imported, advertised, and auctioned the spoils of piracy. They taught fencing to rich men's sons and attended the most exclusive balls; won a tactical battle with the law in the United States courts following American acquisition of the Louisiana Territory; received Presidential pardons of all their sins for their bravery and invaluable support to Jackson in the Battle of New Orleans; and when at last they could have lived out their lives as legal and honored citizens of the City of Sin, succumbed again to the lure of free gold and "black ivory," collected their crews, relinquished their control of river and delta piracy, and passed out of the Mississippi story.

Laffite river brigands used a unique method to guarantee success. They first established a hideout where the current of the river compelled all boats to warp close to shore. One of the gang would go upriver, steal aboard a chosen craft, and later punch holes in the bottom of the boat at such a time as to ensure that it would sink approximately in front of his colleagues, who would then swarm aboard, kill the crew, and seize the cargo.

Ed Rose reputedly belonged to one of these gangs.

Rose's father was a white trader among the Cherokees and his mother was a Cherokee-Negro woman. One Captain Reuben Holmes, quoted in an early St. Louis newspaper, says that Rose was born near Louisville, Kentucky, and first went to New Orleans as a boatman when he was about eighteen years old, which would place him there just before the Laffites rose to power. Washington Irving says that

Rose was already a river pirate in 1800, six years before the Laffites arrived.

There is no present confirmation of either statement. However, certain facts, surmises, and opinions bear repetition.

Samuel Mason, a former Continental Army officer, had teamed up with Micajah Harpe, called Big Harpe by those who feared him, and his brother Wiley, or Little Harpe, to create the infamous Mason gang with headquarters at Cave-in-Rock, fifty miles above Paducah, Kentucky.

Mason was at Cave-in-Rock in 1791, and if Ed Rose was born in Kentucky, he could not have avoided knowing about Mason. In fact, Lyman C. Draper, historian of the Mississippi Valley, wrote on the flyleaf of his copy of *Astoria* that "Rose was probably one of Mason's gang."[3]

About the turn of the century Mason left Cave-in-Rock and went to the Natchez Trace, where his reputation for savagery grew to dimensions bordering on the impossible. If Rose was with him, it would put the mulatto in the piracy business on the Lower Mississippi before 1800, the date Washington Irving posited.

Between the activities of Mason and later the Laffites, Governor William C. C. Claiborne of the Mississippi Territory and Manuel de Salcedo, Spanish governor general at New Orleans, were nearly frantic trying to maintain some semblance of order and safety.

On February 10, 1802, Claiborne wrote De Salcedo complaining of new outrages against American citizens. De Salcedo replied that he was fighting the same battle, but that since no arrangements existed whereby either country could pursue the outlaws into the territory of the other, it was a most difficult situation.

Two thousand dollars had been posted on Mason's head, but there had been no claimants.[4] Then, just before the American occupation of New Orleans, the Spaniards rounded up a parcel of river pirates. In March of 1803 Governor de Salcedo reported that Captain of Militia Robert McKay had started for Natchez with a shipload of pirates who were mostly American nationals, but that they had escaped. Samuel Mason, bandit-murderer of the Natchez Trace, was one of them. Although Rose's name was not mentioned, the date and the nature of the crimes are compatible with Draper's assertion that Rose was probably one of Mason's gang and with Irving's further statement that Rose had been outlawed as a river pirate but had escaped.

Cave-in-Rock, one time headquarters for Mississippi River Pirates to which Ed Rose is reputed to have belonged. *Illinois State Historical Library.*

And so the charge that Ed Rose was a river pirate has been generally accepted despite the lack of good evidence to support it.

Pirate or no, Ed Rose grew to full manhood amid the bawdy squalor of the Lower Mississippi and the beauty and glitter of the City of Sin. It all left its mark on him.

Unless new evidence is discovered, we can know nothing more about Rose until we find him lounging at the bars of St. Louis in 1807, with a brand on his forehead and the nickname Cut Nose because someone had bitten out a piece one day because the Marquis of Queensberry was not present to enforce the rules.*

Rose was a big, quarrelsome man. He favored his Negro-Indian mother more than his white father, and when aroused he was a dangerous foe. His black eyes animated a face on which he was said to have deliberately cultivated a fiendish expression to awe his enemies and delight his friends.

Rose's immediate movements after his arrival in St. Louis are also very much in question. He may actually have reached the city several months earlier than usually supposed and then spent the winter of 1806–1807 on the Osage River.[5] If he had but recently escaped from the law, then the Osage area would be as convenient a sanctuary as any outlaw could want. It was well beyond the effective authority of New Orleans, and reasonably adjacent to the pleasures of Ste. Geneviève and St. Louis—and no one there asked questions.

---

* As far as is now known, Rose was illiterate and left no personal narrative. An early biography of Rose written by Captain Reuben Holmes was published in the *St. Louis Beacon* in 1828 and republished in the St. Louis *Weekly Reveille* in 1848. Some of Holmes's statements are unsupported by other authorities.

ED ROSE BECOMES A
MOUNTAIN MAN

1807–1823

ED ROSE was a member of the Manuel Lisa–George Drouillard venture to the Upper Missouri in April of 1807. Before that date, however, he could have been involved in the Big White episode, but the record is not clear.

Certain facts are of record. We know that Auguste Pierre Chouteau planned a trading trip to the Mandans to coincide with the Lisa-Drouillard expedition; that Pierre Dorion, Jr., intended to return to his Yankton Sioux; that acting Governor Bates at St. Louis, upon hearing that Lisa was about to go upriver, requested him to delay his departure so the several parties could travel together in greater safety, and that Lisa refused; and that Lieutenant Kimball and Ensign Pryor, as we have seen, failed to deliver Big White to his home and returned him to St. Louis in the autumn of 1807.

We know, too, that an Indian trader named Ezekial Williams was associated with Lisa on one or more occasions. The sources of our present tale have it that it was Williams, not Kimball and Pryor, who first undertook to conduct Big White to his people, and that Ed Rose was with Williams.[1] The story continues that Williams and his party started for the Mandans but that somewhere along the way Ed Rose saw a pretty Crow girl, gave up his obligations to Williams, and went off to live with the Crows. It may be nothing more than a tale—but there it is, and it does cast doubt on Rose's whereabouts at the time of the Lisa-Drouillard trip to the Yellowstone country.

If the Ezekial Williams story is true, Rose was enjoying life with the thieving Crows, and it was some other mulatto who joined Lisa at the mouth of the Osage when Antoine Bissonette deserted and was shot while being recaptured by George Drouillard.

But since it is unlikely that Lisa could be mistaken over such an identity, Rose was probably working for the Spaniard. The evidence further indicates that though Rose had "one of the blackest reputations in the fur trade,"[2] Lisa put him in charge of a small stock of goods when they reached the Big Horn and sent him to the Crows, with whom he ingratiated himself by means of lavish gifts.

The Crows played upon his ego until he had given away Lisa's entire stock. Rose has ever since been accused of misappropriating Lisa's property.

Now, there does not seem to be a reliable estimate of the value of the goods in question, and the point is of some importance. The giving of valuable gifts was an accepted routine of Indian trade, and it may well be that the merchandise sent with Rose was no more than enough to impress the Crows. But Rose had a bad reputation, and the worst possible interpretation has been put on his act. Years later, Washington Irving accused him of seeking his popularity with the Crows by the misuse of property belonging to Smith and Fitzpatrick, mountain traders.[3] Perhaps both accusations are factual.

In any event, the Crows made Rose a chief, but this honor caused internal bickering with the tribe he "deceived, swindled and deserted"[4] when he returned to Lisa empty-handed in the summer of 1808.

In passing it may be asked how Ed Rose could "desert" the Crows. It was their home ground, and they certainly held the upper hand.

When Rose reported to Lisa, a violent quarrel ensued. Several versions exist, but the one with the most authentic Rose savor is as follows.

Rose returned to the Big Horn at the very time Lisa and Drouillard were ready to take their season's catch to St. Louis. The canoes were loaded and the men assigned, and Lisa was about ready to embark. Since Rose arrived without a single pelt, Lisa demanded an explanation, and Rose replied that the goods had all been used to cement friendly relations. Lisa refused to believe the story, and hot words followed. Rose was not a man to talk when action could be taken, and he attacked Lisa. John Potts intervened to save Lisa but was no match for the big mulatto, and he took a fearful beating before several more men piled onto Rose and bore him down by sheer weight.

When Rose transferred his attention from Lisa to Potts, the former turned on his heel, walked to his boat, issued final orders, and shoved off. This walking out on a fight so infuriated Rose that he broke free, rushed to Fort Raymond's swivel gun, and fired it at the departing canoes.

The story goes that at the very second Rose touched fire to the gun, an extremely long-legged man walked in front of the muzzle, and that the shot passed harmlessly between his legs and landed on one of the canoes without damage. The long-legged one, however, was so frightened he fell to the ground shouting, "I am dead, I am dead!" Rose paid no attention but was frantically trying to reload and get another shot at Lisa while the canoes were still within range. Before he could do so, other members of the post caught up with the fast-moving mulatto and subdued him a second time, none too gently.

Lisa and Drouillard went on to St. Louis in August, 1808, and Rose calmed down. His actions had alienated the men at the post, however, and they ostracized him. This punishment Ed Rose would accept from no man, and he returned to the Crows.[5]

In view of the Blackfoot hostility, Lisa believed only a stronger company could achieve a satisfactory cost-profit ratio. The Missouri Fur Company was the answer.*

Big White was still in St. Louis following his return there by Kimball and Pryor. Lisa knew the federal government was willing to pay handsomely to close the chief's case, and suggested the new company would return the Indian to his Mandan home for $7,000. Washington accepted.

The expedition was ready at St. Charles about the middle of June, 1809. There were 210 men, nine barges, one canoe, Big White and his family, and René Jusseaume and his squaw. By the time the company reached Fort Osage, the last outpost of federal military authority, desertions and releases had cut the force to 172 men. These were sworn in as militiamen to give them more prestige with the Indians and to expand the authority of the commanders.

From the first, Lisa was confronted with a wide difference in diet between the French and American servants, and early on the voyage he was forced to quell a near-mutiny by the Americans, who refused to work on the monotonous fat rations issued the voyageurs. Sugar,

---

* For a review of the organization of this company, see Chapter 13.

coffee, and rum were also items of contention. But gradually the difficulties were smoothed over, and by the time the Sioux were reached the men had formed a united front, which easily overawed the Sioux. A little later the Arikaras also quietly accepted superior power.

In the meantime, Ed Rose had again left the Crows and had drifted over to the Arikara villages. Both Lisa and Rose were too smart to spite their own interests, and when they met at the Ree towns, they conveniently overlooked their recent difficulties at Fort Raymond. Rose rejoined the Lisa fortunes, although more as an aide to Major Henry than as an interpreter for Lisa.

At the mouth of the Knife River, Lisa built Fort Mandan and deployed his trapping parties. In company with some of his men, he then returned to St. Louis on November 20, 1809.

Big White was home and the Missouri Fur Company was richer by $7,000.

The following March, Menard and Henry with Colter and Rose as guides started for the Blackfeet, the same tribe that had killed John Potts from an ambush only a few months earlier. They arrived at the Three Forks in April but never did get into a settled routine. The Blackfeet attacked early and viciously. So savage was their assault that the trappers dared not attend their traplines even at night. George Drouillard was killed, as we have related; Colter and one companion made another spectacular escape all the way back to St. Louis. Late in the spring Menard conceded defeat, and returned to St. Louis in July with approximately half the remaining men.

But Andrew Henry and Ed Rose were cut of different cloth. Henry was a stubborn leader who did not intend to be routed by those he considered his inferiors. Ed Rose was a daredevil adventurer who was willing to go on any excursion as long as it interested him. The question of personal danger seems never to have entered his head in his entire life. And so Henry, Rose, and a few companions held on at the Three Forks until about July 1, 1810, and then started south up the Madison River. Over the Divide they went, into Idaho, past Henry's Lake and to Henry's Fork of the Snake near our St. Anthony, Idaho. Here they built a small post set safely on a gravel bench a few feet above a quiet stretch of the river, rimmed with small deciduous trees and beaver ponds. In the distance across the great valley the Tetons seemed to promise a lavish reward. But by the following spring it was obvious that the post could not be maintained, and Henry abandoned it and returned to the Big Horn. A year later he saw Lisa withdraw all his men from the West and set up a new trading fort near the Arikaras.

The "stronger company" had been almost a total failure. Enormous expenses had precluded profits, and even the attempt to invade the transmountain country had come to naught. Today a crude concrete shaft, unattended and almost unknown, marks the site of Henry's Fort on Henry's Fork of the Snake.

In the meantime, Ed Rose had tired of Henry's authority and dropped out to marry a new Crow girl. He was building his reputation with his adopted people. Already he was Cut Nose, and now some foolhardy act of savage bravery won him the name Five Scalps. Far from the fleshpots of New Orleans, Ed Rose was as happy as it is given his kind of man ever to be. He hunted and fished and fathered, and might well have dropped out of the annals of the fur business entirely had not John Jacob Astor had his dream of a western empire called Astoria.

In this interval Lisa had lost track of Major Henry, and one of the purposes of his 1811 trip to the Mandans was to seek information on the whereabouts of his partner. The Lisa-Hunt race and its subsequent near-fatal violence followed.

Ed Rose was not present at the most exciting moments of either the race or the quarrel, but he heard about them and was disappointed. He liked a fight.

Yet Ed Rose's relations with the Overland Astorians were unbelligerent and on at least two occasions almost magnanimous.

It will be recalled how Hoback, Reznor, and Robinson had joined Hunt after he had left St. Louis but before he had reached the Indian towns on the Missouri. They had recommended leaving the Lewis and Clark trail for a more southerly overland route, and John Colter, of Yellowstone Park fame, had agreed with them but warned Hunt of the dangers of crossing Blackfoot land. Hunt had decided to leave the Missouri, although distrusting Pierre Dorion, Jr., and believing that Ed Rose, whom he had but recently hired, was a "very bad fellow full of daring"[6] who intended to betray the Astorians to the Crows.

As noted, Dorion and Rose managed to keep the Americans out of serious trouble until they reached the Crows, where Hunt's fear of Rose became ridiculous. He schemed to get rid of him by "offering him half of his year's wages, a horse, three beaver traps and some other things . . . [which] he accepted."[7]

Despite this deplorable treatment, Rose arranged a three-day rest for Hunt among the Crows, set the travelers on their way to the Continental Divide, rescued them when they got lost, and again started them on the proper trail. Finally, Rose returned first to the Crows and later to the Arikaras, where Lisa found him again on his upriver trip of 1812.

There are two stories concerning Rose circa 1812. Captain Holmes says that Ed was attached to an Ezekial Williams party which Lisa first sent out to trade in 1810. They had been successful until the spring of 1812, when the Indians turned troublesome and Williams divided his forces to seek out more peaceful fields. Eight or ten of his men crossed the Rockies, and Williams with a small crew skirted southward along the eastern shoulder of the mountains toward Spanish territory. There were exciting brushes with the Spaniards, and the Williams force split into still smaller groups, after which some of them disappeared forever while others were arrested and thrown into Spanish dungeons.

Williams, accused of murdering one of his own men, started east, was captured by the Kansas Indians, escaped, and eventually arrived home on November 30, 1813.

Ed Rose is supposed to have been with the transmountain detachment and to have shared their adventures. Unfortunately there is no proof that he did.

There is a second unproved story that during this same season Rose and old Charbonneau got together over in Crow country. They purportedly hatched an iniquitous scheme to go to the Snake tribe and purchase several Arapaho girl prisoners to be taken to the Missouri and sold or rented to the voyageurs as their hungers and purses would dictate. Whether this villainy was ever carried out is not certain, for Rose is said to have taken advantage of Charbonneau's reputation for cowardice and played several practical jokes upon him which delighted Rose but did not amuse Charbonneau.

At the very same time, Rose is chronicled as being a member of the Reuben Lewis expedition, which on "friday the 11th early rise, the parties prepared to start . . . Mr. Lewis, two engagees and the trappers for the little horn."[8] There follow references to Lewis' men being robbed by the Crows in December, but another message to Lisa four days later said they were "hunting and trading 12 Packs of Beaver in Store."[9]

On this trip with Lewis to the Little Big Horn River, the mulatto is supposed to have stolen so many company goods that he and Lewis quarreled and Rose stalked off on a trading venture of his own. He wandered east and south to the Tongue and Powder rivers, where he met John Dougherty, another Lisa man. They teamed up and drifted slowly back to Fort Manuel at the Arikara towns, where they arrived just in time to find Lisa surrounded by a frenzied mob of Cheyennes bent on killing him. He appealed to Rose for help, and once more the big half-breed used his fearful mien and prestige with the natives to save a life.[10] Lisa and Rose then headed for St. Louis, but an Omaha girl caught Ed's eye and he stopped off for two or three years with her.

Some or all of these stories may be true, due allowance being made for faulty dates and details. Certainly the account book of Manuel Lisa for 1812 has Rose listed as an employee, and there is a ledger page in the accounts of the Missouri Fur Company for parts of 1812 and 1813 on which Rose seems to be posted as a free trader. In any event, he bought more than $200 worth of guns, powder, balls, beads, vermilion, and other items of Indian trade and charged them to himself, not to the company. However, Mr. Lewis, Mr. Dougherty, and others closely associated with Lisa are posted in a manner to indicate beyond reasonable doubt that Rose was still connected with Lewis and Lisa in some manner.

Perhaps the only positive things we can say are that, beginning about 1812, Rose was in and around Crow country and remained there for the duration of the War of 1812, and that Lisa worked hard and successfully to prevent the Missouri tribes from defecting to the British. It is most unlikely that he accomplished this very important service to his adopted country without the aid of his interpreters, and, admittedly, Ed Rose and Charbonneau were among the half-dozen most influential of these.

Either Ed Rose had an amazing capacity for getting into trouble, or he has been lied about more than any man deserves regardless of his character. Ed had hardly settled down with his little Omaha girl before rumors were afloat that he was causing trouble: Captain

Holmes claims he was arrested and taken to St. Louis in irons, leaving his wife and at least two children; Joshua Pilcher, one of the more trusted traders on the river, referred to Rose in an 1823 letter as the "celebrated outlaw" who left "this country in chains some ten years ago," that is, in 1813; and yet another story says that Rose returned to the City of Sin and joined the Gulf pirates.

And all these could be true, too, for we hear no more of Ed Rose until about 1820, when he again shows up with the Arikaras.

Such adventurous perambulations stagger credulity, perhaps, but there are authenticated cases of men who did as much and went as far. These river and mountain men may have been outlaws and drunkards and adulterers and all the rest of the lexicon of sin—but they were men, and America need have no shame for their deeds.

THE ARIKARA-ASHLEY FIGHT

1823

PRESIDENT WASHINGTON had established federal trading posts for the explicit purpose of supplying honest goods at fair prices to the Indians, but to those who wished to cheat the natives as much and as often as possible, these posts were anathema. And John Jacob Astor, assisted by Senator Benton of Missouri, used their financial and political powers to influence Congress to close the posts in 1822. Astor was then ready to make his influence dominant in the already crowded trans-Mississippi area. The Hudson's Bay Company was there; Manuel Lisa had died in 1820, but Joshua Pilcher and the Missouri Fur Company were there; several dozen independent operators with more or less adequate capital were there; and William Henry Ashley was planning to enter the field.

With all this competition, it was apparent that a different method of trading was needed if satisfactory returns were to be realized. The French along the St. Lawrence basin and the Spaniards in the southwest quarter of the continent had learned very early that it was almost impossible to have a good wage relationship with the Indian. But he was peculiarly susceptible to the feast-speech-gift routine. For a few words and fewer beads, he would part with the finest pelts in the world and immediately compel his slave-wife to process more. The Americans would have to follow the French-Spanish technique or develop a new and better one.

General William Henry Ashley believed he had the answer. His plan was to build a small post at each of several strategic locations and send a staff of trader-trappers into the mountains to live and work for several years at a time. They would meet the Indians in great mountain fairs, or rendezvous, buy their pelts at the lowest possible price, and come to the company post only to deliver the furs and get new supplies of beads and crimson yardage.

Ashley had come from Virginia to the Ste. Geneviève region on the Missouri about the time of the Louisiana Purchase. He had tried surveying, had speculated in land, manufactured gunpowder, and played general merchant to the frontier. Twenty years later he was wealthy. He entered politics, and was elected first lieutenant governor of Missouri and appointed adjutant general of the militia—a post which enhanced his position and did not impair his wealth.

The *Missouri Republican* for March 20, 1822, carried Ashley's advertisement directed "To Enterprising Young Men." He wanted "100 young men to ascend the Missouri River to its source, there to be employed for one, two, or three years." Ashley supplied two keelboats, each 100 feet long, with a cargo box of eighty feet plus a galley forward for the cook. The long sweep was operated from the top of the cargo box, and there were oars, a square sail, and the all-important towline. Each boat carried a burden of goods worth approximately $10,000, no mean fortune in 1822.

To manage this new enterprise in the field, Ashley hired Major Andrew Henry, a former Lisa man and an old and trusted friend. Ashley, Henry, and the two keelboats left St. Louis about the middle of April and reached Fort Osage safely. Shortly thereafter one of the boats hit a snag, and Ashley lost the boat and $10,000. He had intended to enter the mountains from a base at the Three Forks of the Missouri, but the present accident plus the loss of fifty horses to the Indians caused him to abandon his original goal and build his post at the mouth of the Yellowstone.

Major Henry went into Blackfoot country, but their hostility forced him back to the Yellowstone in June, 1823. Ashley returned to St. Louis, where he advertised for another 100 employees. This time he acquired the most valuable force of mountain men ever to invade the West at any one time. How it happened that they were in St. Louis, free from other commitments and sober enough to be interested in a new venture, is one of the little coincidences of the mountain fur trade. But there they were, and Ashley hired them: Louis Vasquez, David E. Jackson, Hugh Glass, Thomas Eddie, James Clyman, William L. Sublette; Thomas Fitzpatrick, the Broken Hand of later days; Jedediah Strong Smith, gun in one hand and Bible in the other, so they said;*

---

* Smith may have joined the party upriver somewhere because he was a member of the 1822 venture.

and not the least, Ed Rose.* James Bridger and Etienne Provost were already with Henry on the Yellowstone. The remainder of Ashley's crew may well not have been of this caliber, for there were not a hundred such men in all America, but these few set the tone of the expedition.

It is significant that Ed Rose was included in this elite assemblage. Ashley's losses of the previous year had been serious but by no means crippling, and he could still afford the best—including interpreters.

Ashley's *Yellowstone Packet* and *Rocky Mountains* were loaded and ready to leave St. Louis on March 10, 1823. The days ahead were to hold the same drudgery of poling and towing as every other upriver trip, but they would be lightened now and again by the funloving voyageurs and mountain men.

One evening several of the young men went to a nearby settlement and stole a quantity of poultry and pigs. Next morning the irate farmers descended on Ashley and demanded their property. The General gave them permission to search the boats. They found nothing. After the morning chores were done, the crews got out the towlines and inched the heavy craft slowly upstream. Then, "pulling around a bend the wind became farir breeze and [the sails] wa[r]e ordred unfurled when out droped pigs and poultry in abundance. A man was ordred to Jump in the skiff and pick up the pigs and poultry."[1]

Ashley intended to trade with the two fortified towns built on the high west bank near the mouth of Grand River in modern South Dakota. The lower of the two villages had some seventy earth lodges protected with palisades twelve or fifteen feet high and six inches in diameter. There were dry moats at the base.

The Rees were a big, powerful people, unafraid of their neighbors or the whites. They had been friendly to Lewis and Clark, but later developments had convinced them the traders were an inferior lot. The result of this conclusion was that the tribe was entirely unpredictable. Friendly and eager to trade one day, the Rees might be deadly enemies the next. Any contact with them was fraught with danger. They might do no more than pillage your wares as a sort of tribal

---

* Bernard De Voto states that James P. Beckwourth, the mulatto whose career it is impossible to untangle from that of Ed Rose, was also on this Ashley venture, serving as a blacksmith and wrangler in 1823–1824. (Introduction, in T. D. Bonner, *The Life and Adventures of James P. Beckwourth,* New York, Alfred A. Knopf, 1931, p. xxxii).

prank—or they might murder you. Those were the chances Ashley took when he anchored offshore in front of the lower village on May 31, 1823.

Almost immediately advice and warnings were given Ashley. A few miles downstream Joshua Pilcher had but recently had trouble with the Rees, and he had warned Ashley of their present mood; James Clyman said that "on ariveing in sight of the villages the barr in front was lined with squaws packing up water thinking to have to stand a siege,"[2] a sign of trouble to any experienced Indian man; and Ed Rose knew that something was afoot, and suggested that Ashley move upriver past both villages while it was still possible, before the Rees could begin any offensive move.

These warnings were all disregarded. Why Ashley, who normally evinced a proper appreciation of the advice of qualified personnel, stubbornly refused to listen on May 31, 1823, no one will ever know. Despite Rose's recommendation, both boats were anchored less than 100 feet offshore, between a gravel beach directly below the town and a sandbar beyond. On the sandbar the Indians had erected a log breastwork which would permit them to crossfire on the whites.

Leaving his boats in this precarious position, Ashley took two men, one of them presumably Rose, and went to talk with the Rees on the beach. Here they were met by the Indian leaders, Little Soldier and Grey Eyes. Ashley invited them aboard his keelboat. Grey Eyes accepted, but Little Soldier refused.[3]

Ashley reminded the Indian of the recent trouble with Pilcher, and stressed the fact that he, Ashley, could not be held responsible for that unpleasantness. Both sides agreed that all trouble was in the past and need not affect the present friendly intercourse. At the same time Ashley hinted that any attempt at violence would be dealt with severely. Unfortunately, he was in no position to make good on his threat, and the Indians knew it.

Rose warned Ashley that the Rees were too friendly; the women and children were too quiet; there was not enough exuberance over the arrival of a trader who would exchange priceless powder and shot for a few horses or skins from dead animals; there was too much tension. Things just did not look right to Ed Rose.

But Ashley did not trust Rose. Now, no one denies that Ed sometimes used his employer's goods to buy Indian favors or perchance an occasional bed partner, that he got roaring drunk and picked a quarrel with anyone he could, and that he was not a very pleasant fellow socially. But those traits were not peculiar to Ed Rose. How many other trusted employees used company goods for the same purposes and blamed the shortages on Indian attacks and robbery? If every man who got drunk and started a fight was to be distrusted, no keelboat would ever have left St. Louis.

And so, illogically, Ashley hired Rose, admittedly one of the best interpreters on the river, and then refused either to trust him or to take his advice.

Meanwhile, the Arikaras and Ashley agreed on a price for the horses needed to replace those recently lost by Henry to the Assiniboines. The Rees wished the business concluded inside their palisade, but even in his reckless mood Ashley refused to do that, insisting that the sale take place on the beach.

Early the following morning, Ashley quickly purchased forty horses, after which there was a change in the tone of the relationship. Up to this point all trade had been done without the exchange of guns or ammunition, and it was the Ree insistence on these items that turned the tenor of the feelings.[4]

Again Ed Rose urged Ashley to leave. He had his horses, the Rees were still quiet, and there was ample daylight left to get beyond the worst dangers before night would make river travel extremely hazardous. Instead Ashley left his horses and about forty of his men, including Sublette, Smith, and Jackson (who in time were to become as famous as Ashley), encamped on the open beach.

Late in the afternoon of June 1, the Bear, a principal Arikara chief, asked Ashley to a feast. The General hesitated to go and hesitated to refuse. One course invited personal attack, but the alternative might make the Rees think he was afraid. He took Rose and went. During the long-drawn-out ceremonies, he became convinced the Indians were genuinely friendly. Rose differed and suggested the boats be moved at least to the sandbar, out of range of Indian guns.

Ashley refused. He would leave next morning.

And sometime during these hours, the Ree chief Little Soldier, wishing to curry favor with the whites, told Ashley his tribe intended to attack. *

As the day wore on, bitter thoughts must have come to the big

---

* Harrison Clifford Dale gives Little Soldier the credit for warning Ashley, and by omission implies that Rose did nothing to save the Americans (*The Ashley-Smith Explorations and the Discovery of a Central Route to the Pacific*, Cleveland, Arthur H. Clark Co., 1918).

mulatto, Ed Rose. Twelve years before, Hunt too had refused to listen and had gone on to disaster; and now Ashley was virtually inviting the Arikaras to attack. They did not disappoint him.

After supper several of the men, including Rose, went into the village without Ashley's permission. It had been a long time since they had left civilization, and if the fleshpots of the Rees were not so professional as the bagnios of St. Louis or so luxurious as those of New Orleans, neither were they so expensive.

Just before daylight Rose rushed into Ashley's cabin with the news that one of the men, Aaron Stephens, had got an arrow between his ribs and that the Rees would attack at dawn. Here again Rose gave the lie to the charge of treachery. He had already warned Ashley several times and as often been brushed aside, perhaps with some asperity, certainly with condescension. Under such circumstances, nobler men than Ed Rose have disavowed all further responsibility.

At last, and much too late, Ashley realized his danger and tried valiantly to initiate some sort of defensive action. But James Clyman, who was among those left on the beach overnight with the horses, said, "We had no military organization disciplin or Subordination"[5]— an indictment of Ashley's leadership seldom mentioned. * At the very edge of dawn, the Rees called out to Rose to take care of himself, a tribute to their respect for him, and then opened their attack on the beach party.

Inside the palisades, the squaws egged on their men or keened almost inaudibly while the children stared wide-eyed and silent. On the beach men moaned or cursed and listened to the thud of shot in the soft underbellies of screaming horses. Ashley said later that "about three fourth of them [Rees] are armed with London fusils that carry a ball with great accuracy and force, and which they use with as much expertness as any man I ever saw handle arms."[6]

The Indians were almost completely protected while the whites were as entirely without cover. The first volley killed the majority of the horses, but these then gave the tenders some protection. Whether the Rees actually crossfired from the sandbar is uncertain, but in any event the whites took terrible punishment for Ashley's dereliction.

The several reports of the fight are so divergent it is impossible to

---

* As with any other event involving several witnesses, the reports of the next few hours are not in agreement, either among those present or among later scribes. We offer one interpretation based on one or more reports for each detail, but readily admit that others may not agree.

separate fact from alibi. Ashley and his partisans tell the story this way. When he ordered the boats to rescue the men on the beach, the French voyageurs refused to expose themselves to any danger. After much pleading two skiffs, capable of holding a total of thirty men,[7] were manned and sent ashore, but the beleaguered men were so infuriated at the treachery of the Rees that they refused to leave; only the wounded and some half-dozen others returned, the rest preferring to stay and avenge their fellows. On a second attempt, the Indians killed one oarsman, and the other saved his life by tumbling to the bottom of the skiff and coasting out of range. Ashley ordered the remaining horses swum to the sandbar, but the Indians picked off both men and animals with such accuracy that they were ordered back to the beach. Yet that position was obviously untenable, and they were again ordered into the river, every man for himself. Cold water and the Rees took a steady toll, but some reached the boats and were pulled aboard and given what comfort the situation allowed.

Fifteen minutes after daybreak, Ashley raised the anchor of one keelboat and cut the cable on the other, and allowed both crafts to drop downstream.

Thirteen men were dead;* one would die in a matter of hours; eleven, including Hugh Glass, were wounded. And now bitter thoughts must have come to William Ashley, too, for he could not have avoided reflecting on how all this fortune lost, all these lives sacrificed, all this dissipation of white prestige might have been saved if only Ed Rose, or even Little Soldier, had been heeded. Later he claimed that if his orders had been obeyed, he would have lost no more than five men, but that is in the nature of an alibi to excuse his lack of caution and the failure of his leadership.

James Clyman, who survived the beach attack and who in later years put to paper his remembrance of the fight, gave a different version of the affair. He wrote that as soon as the firing started there were "many calls for the boats to come ashore and take us on board"; and that after the first volley, "Several men being wounded a skiff was brought ashore all rushed for the Skiff and came near sinking it but it went the boat full of men and water the shot still coming thicker and the aim better we making a brest work of our horses they nearly all being killed the skiffs having taken sevarl loads on Board...."[8]

---

* There are two or more lists of casualties and they do not agree.

There is a discrepancy here. Ashley left forty men on shore with the horses; the skiffs would carry thirty men. Thus if the men came "near sinking" the first skiff, and then the skiffs made several more trips, there must certainly have been no more men left on the beach, and Ashley must have erred in claiming he could not get the skiff manned. But since Ashley and Clyman refer to the men who had to swim for their lives, it would appear Ashley's report was the more accurate.

And Clyman himself said he despaired of geting to the boats by skiff and so left his hiding place behind a "dead hors," ran upstream to take advantage of the current, and tried to swim to the keelboats. He stuck his gun in his belt, but it was too long and hindered his swimming. He shifted it to several positions before finally discarding it.

Clyman misjudged the current, drifted beyond the range of the boats, and was just about to give up when Reed Gibson grabbed a drifting skiff and pulled Clyman to it. In the process, Gibson received a mortal wound, but the two men managed to get across to the east shore and Clyman clambered up the bank to see if the enemy were near.

They were.

Then Gibson crawled to Clyman's side, saw his own hopeless position, and urged Clyman to run for it, asking only that Clyman write the home folks and tell them how and when he died. Clyman refused to desert his companion in this manner, and yet the only real help he might give was to divert attention to himself while Gibson hid in some nearby bush. Clyman then openly fled across the prairies with the Indians yelping at his heels. This act of selflessness gave the dying Gibson a chance to be rescued by one of the keelboats.

Clyman outran the Rees and circled back to the river just in time to be picked up as Ashley was dropping downstream. Gibson, already on board, died a few hours later, "but before I had an opportunity of writeing to his friends I forgot his post office and so never have written," said Clyman.[9]

After the battle, Ashley ran down to the first stand of timber and tied up. He naturally wished to recoup his prestige with the Indians and with his own men, and early next morning he proposed they regroup their forces and make another attempt to pass the Arikaras. To his surprise and great chagrin, his men refused to do any such thing. They would not even talk about it unless he could furnish very considerable reinforcements—a provision both sides knew was impossible. It was with difficulty that Ashley prevailed upon them to agree to retreat only another twenty-five miles, go into temporary quarters, and await help.

Ashley was about to learn that his refusal to heed advice had cost him very dearly in terms of *esprit de corps,* for when the twenty-five miles had been covered, the men indicated they would desert unless a further retreat was accepted. For the moment Ashley gave up all pretense of commanding, and resignedly asked for volunteers to remain with him until he could send to Major Henry for help. Thirty volunteered, of whom five were voyageurs.

It has been a favorite role of writers of Missouri River history to indict Ashley's men for base cowardice. But there is another side to it. Granted that some of the Frenchmen were hardly Napoleonic heroes or Christian martyrs; why should they have been? They had been hired to pole boats, not fight Indians. They received no share in any profits; their hours of labor were long and brutally harsh at wages barely above slave status; their food was monotonous, often irregular, and sometimes nonexistent. That all these were customary at the time does not alter their truth. Clyman, whom no one ever dared call coward, said that the beach fight was more than he had bargained for and frankly admitted he wanted out of the situation.

General Ashley took his defeat manfully. He transferred his goods from the *Yellowstone Packet* to the *Rocky Mountains,* and arranged to dispatch the former to St. Louis with the wounded men and such others as refused to remain. On the way they would ask Colonel Henry Leavenworth at Fort Atkinson and Major Benjamin O'Fallon, Indian agent at Old Council Bluffs, for military aid.

These details settled, Ashley then asked for volunteers to go overland to Major Henry on the Yellowstone for reinforcements. Only Jedediah Strong Smith, perhaps the youngest member of Ashley's command, offered to risk his life. With difficulty Ashley coaxed one French Creole to accompany Smith.

The pair set out after dark and arrived at the Yellowstone post safely, a distance of approximately 250 miles. No details of this trip are known.

Henry, leaving twenty men to protect the property on the Yellowstone, loaded the season's pelts, and with Smith and the remainder of his men tried to slip down the Missouri and past the Rees unnoticed. They were detected and invited to land—a trap so obvious that Smith and Henry paddled hurriedly out of danger. They met Ashley, probably at the mouth of the Cheyenne River, on July 2.

The furs Henry and Smith brought down were far too few to satisfy Ashley's creditors, and it would be necessary to equip and dispatch a winter hunt into the mountains. With that in view, Ashley continued downriver, vainly seeking friendly Indians from whom to buy horses.[10] While doing this he received word that the federal military were prepared to aid him past the Rees and he hastily reversed his direction, reunited with Major Henry, from whom he had temporarily separated, and hurried into the next phase of his disaster.

But first he wrote his creditors of the present status of affairs, and sent that message and the few pelts brought by Henry and Smith to St. Louis under the command of Samuel M. Smith.* The letter and pelts arrived in St. Louis on August 15.

A considerable number of persons were involved, directly and indirectly, in Ashley and Rose's current adventure, and a brief dramatis personae is in order. Ashley was waiting for help downriver from the Ree villages; Samuel M. Smith was hurrying to St. Louis with dispatches and furs, and eventually arrived August 15, as we said; the *Yellowstone Packet* was also downriver seeking aid; Jed Smith and Henry, from the Yellowstone, were to meet Ashley July 2. The military chain of command began with John C. Calhoun, Secretary of War, who was responsible for all military acts touching the Indians; Major General Jacob Brown was general in chief in Washington; Major General E. P. Gaines commanded the whole western department from Louisville, Kentucky; Brigadier General Henry Atkinson commanded the so-called Right Wing at St. Louis; Colonel Henry Leavenworth commanded the 6th Regiment at Fort Atkinson, sixteen miles above the present Omaha; and Benjamin O'Fallon, at Fort Atkinson in Old Council Bluffs, was federal Indian agent for all the river tribes.

Obviously such a lengthy and complicated command structure

---

* Jedediah Strong Smith is sometimes erroneously credited with this mission (see Dale E. Morgan, *Jedediah Smith and the Opening of the West*, Indianapolis, Bobbs-Merrill Co., 1953, p. 66).

made any quick and resolute action impossible. Calhoun was a statesman, not a warrior, and had no capacity for his position beyond good
intentions. All the others were career men, intent on protecting their
rank and preferring always to sweep a problem under the rug than
risk disapprobation by taking action.

But there were times when action could not be avoided, and the
request for help from William Henry Ashley, lieutenant governor of
Missouri and general of the Missouri militia, was such a time.

When the request for aid reached O'Fallon and Leavenworth at
Fort Atkinson, the unfortunate Leavenworth was faced with a choice
of evils: it was impossible to wait for the chain of command to take
effect; it was impossible to ignore a lieutenant governor and brother
officer; it was dangerous to one's career to assume the initiative; it was
folly to allow the Rees to go unpunished.

What to do?

Leavenworth had an honorable career as a good, conservative
officer, taking orders cheerfully and executing them faithfully if not
brilliantly, and it was only natural that he should hesitate to risk a
criticism which might forever block further advancement. Yet he had
his pride, too, and he was no coward. So, after much soul-searching,
he decided to go to Ashley's aid without waiting for official permission,
and wrote a lengthy defense of his decision.

He quoted from Calhoun's previous orders to the border military
instructing them to protect American traders and repel foreign invaders; he noted that Calhoun had suggested that the Indian agent
should "associate . . . negotiation whenever it can . . . be done" (this
helped put the blame on O'Fallon); he told General Atkinson, "We
shall do all we can to support the honor of your regiment and hope,
with the blessings of Heaven, to meet the approbation of our superiors
and of our country"; he posted his own orders to the 6th Regiment
on June 18, 1823, "If any glory should be acquired, the regiment
generally will share it . . ."; and he told O'Fallon the Sioux wished to
help punish the Rees but that he was skeptical of "the continuance
of their ardor."[11]

All these were good, first-class military maneuvers designed to leave
his record clear in case of disaster. He was to need them.

While all this was going on, the *Yellowstone Packet* had been un-
loaded and rented to Leavenworth, who hired some of its crew, issued
the orders mentioned above, and in company with O'Fallon started

back up the river on June 23, 1823. He commanded 220 men, augmented with two six-pounders and several swivels. Three keelboats carried the supplies and some of the men while the remainder traveled overland.

Joshua Pilcher, only recently attacked by the Indians as noted above, faced ruin as well as Ashley, and he offered to join the military. Leavenworth accepted on the condition that Pilcher and his men would take orders from Leavenworth—a reasonable requirement if only Leavenworth had known what orders to give.

Exactly how the Sioux, Pilcher, Ashley, Jed Smith, Henry, and a few independent traders all got together just above Fort Kiowa in midmorning of July 19 is a bit uncertain, but they managed, and Leavenworth passed around the proper titles to all who pretended to any importance whatever. Pilcher was made a major and Indian subagent; Jed Smith was made a captain; and even Ed Rose, highly recommended as an interpreter by Ashley, was honored with an ensignship. Ashley, already a general, needed no special ranking.

Pilcher supplied two more boats and a 5½-inch howitzer, and rounded up four or five hundred Sioux. In all Leavenworth had close to 1,100 men.

Such an agglomeration needed a very special name (if for nothing more than to take the stigma from the 6th Regiment should plans go wrong), and "the Missouri Legion" sounded about right.

On to the Arikaras!

THE MISSOURI LEGION

1823

THE great Missouri was no respecter of titles. Before the Missouri Legion had gone far, one of the boats hit a snag, split in two, and sank, drowning seven soldiers; only the quick work of the crew saved any of the cargo.

On August 3 two small bands of natives invited the Legion to a feast as "they had killed a heap of dogs," said Leavenworth. He and Pilcher made a courtesy call but told Chief Fire Heart they had come to fight, not eat, and "he must excuse me."[1] This subterfuge surely amused Ed Rose, who had feasted many a time on spitted dog, but our sympathies must remain with Leavenworth.

And so the Missouri Legion worked its way up the river, but without any very authoritative sense of command. Leavenworth became "completely disgusted with my Indian allies" for not moving in approved army formations. There were no satisfactory advance scout patrols; Leavenworth was confused over the whereabouts, strength, and probable intentions of the Rees; there was a rumor that they intended to escape to the Mandans for sanctuary, and Leavenworth told O'Fallon that if so the Legion would advance on the Mandans, too, for "The honor of the American arms must be supported at all events."[2] Pilcher told O'Fallon he thought the rumor was idle talk and that the Rees would give battle.[3]

As for the manpower, defenses, and location of the Rees, either Pilcher's interpreter, Collin Campbell, or Ed Rose could have told Leavenworth that there were two towns on the west bank not far from the present state boundary of South and North Dakota, and that there were 600 to 800 warriors and a 3,000 to 4,000 population, of whom Ed Rose knew dozens by name. But Leavenworth disdained information from inferiors. Furthermore, he believed Campbell was telling the Sioux that Pilcher was the most important white chief in the Legion—a tale which annoyed the rank-conscious military and cast suspicion on all interpreters.

Some miles before the villages were in sight, the Sioux were getting anxious to have their fun, for war was a game to them. They urged Leavenworth to increase his speed, but "I took no notice of what they said."[4] Pilcher, too, asked Leavenworth to hurry his attack lest the Sioux get a bad impression of army enthusiasm.

But Leavenworth was not to be hurried. He went by the book. It had been a long time since a young George Washington had taught a haughty Braddock how to fight Indians, and Leavenworth had forgot that part of his lesson. When he finally reached the Arikara towns on August 9, 1823, the Sioux were already fighting the Rees, and Army prestige had suffered badly.

On seeing the Army, the Rees fled inside their stockade, but Leavenworth could not follow up this advantage because he had allowed part of his own force, the Sioux, to get between him and the enemy. In this predicament, he sat down to wait for Major A. R. Wooley to bring up the boats while the Army watched the Sioux perform their White Bear ritual.

A Sioux warrior wrapped a bearskin about his shoulders, got down on all fours, and pranced and circled about a fallen foe, smelling and licking the corpse and from time to time biting out and eating a piece of his dead enemy.

Another Sioux put a club in the hands of one of the women, and stood taunting the Rees for allowing a woman to mutilate their dead brother.

Both these were common tribal taunts and rituals, and the Sioux asked the whites not to ridicule them lest it spoil the "medicine if we did."

And Leavenworth sat and thought, and Pilcher fumed, and Ashley worried, and Ed Rose kept his dark thoughts to himself, and Major Wooley arrived at sundown with the artillery, and the Sioux gave it all up in disgust at the whites and withdrew to the Ree cornfields, and Leavenworth's command got what sleep they could.

Next morning the artillery occupied a hill above the towns and opened fire, but the guns could not be depressed enough to do any damage. They were moved to a lower location, after which they kept popping away until midafternoon, but still without much effect. Leavenworth thought of storming the works but a Mr. McDonald, who had once lived with the Rees, said the towns could not be taken except by sapping and mining.

And no one thought of asking Ed Rose what to do—he who was as familiar with the paths of the Rees as with the streets of St. Louis. But Leavenworth asked Pilcher to get the Sioux to help again, and Pilcher had to tell him that the Sioux would fight no more until they saw the whites in hand-to-hand combat also. Leavenworth debated using a trick to get inside the towns for information, when again all he had to do was ask Ed Rose to walk in. The artillery reported their shot almost gone and Leavenworth told them to hold their fire, only to find out later they had merely misplaced their supply, not exhausted it. And Leavenworth got hungry (as they were all entitled to be) and ordered the whole thing stopped and everybody into the cornfields for supper!

And this was the Battle of August 10, 1823!

Toward evening, as Pilcher and Leavenworth were trying to agree on some effective action, they observed several Sioux and Arikaras talking together. The interpreters and Pilcher knew what such a powwow meant, and it is doubtful whether Ashley misunderstood. But Leavenworth saw no ill omen. Inquiries revealed that the Rees were asking for peace, and Leavenworth readily agreed. Pilcher objected that the purpose of the expedition, the return of the goods Ashley had exchanged for horses he did not get, had in no wise been accomplished, and he at first refused to have any part of the proposal. This in turn convinced the Indians that Pilcher was indeed the most powerful white chief, and Leavenworth recognized that this prejudice in Pilcher's favor must be reckoned with. He begged Pilcher to cooperate, and the latter finally assented. In the conference that followed, the Rees agreed to leave five hostages with the Army and to return as much of Ashley's property as they could find.

For some reason not now clear, no action followed these promises, and Leavenworth ordered his men to entrench and then closed activities for the day. But Pilcher's interpreter, Collin Campbell, was so enraged at Leavenworth's actions, or rather inaction, that he threatened to start the battle all over again on his own initiative. Leavenworth quite properly commanded him to put his gun away and obey orders.

Next morning Little Soldier approached Leavenworth's staff with more talk of peace, claiming that the Rees had suffered intense losses and were completely humbled. He particularly wanted to know whether Pilcher would make peace. This was wormwood to Leavenworth, and he assured Little Soldier that Pilcher would do as he was told.

Leavenworth had much to learn.

At this juncture Collin Campbell came up again with a loaded gun, and was about to kill Little Soldier when Leavenworth ordered the interpreter put under guard, "where he continued until we left the place."[5] Such animosity did nothing to sooth the Leavenworth-Pilcher feelings, and their relationship steadily deteriorated.

Pilcher insisted there was no truth in Little Soldier's presentation of Ree conditions or intentions. The Sioux had killed only a handful of the 600 to 800 warriors; the artillery had not even succeeded in blasting a hole in the wooden palisade, let alone inflicting any damage on the earthen lodges on the inside; and the 6th Regiment had not fought at all. The Rees could not be very seriously hurt.

At this stage of affairs, Leavenworth's official report tenders Ed Rose the finest compliment of his controversial career. Said Leavenworth:

I had not found anyone willing to go into the villages except a man by the name of Rose, who holds the nominal rank of Ensign in Gen. Ashley's volunteers. He appeared to be a brave and enterprising man and was well acquainted with these Indians. He had resided for about three years with them. Understood their language and they were much attached to him. He was with Gen. Ashley when he was attacked. The Indians at that time called to him to take care of himself, before they fired upon Gen. Ashley's party. This was all that I knew of this man. Have heard since that he was not of good character. Everything he told us however was fully corroborated. He was perfectly willing to go into their villages and did go in, several times. He fully confirmed everything which the Indians had told us. He told us they had been severely whipped and were the most humble beings on earth, but that they were so much afraid of us, that they dared not come into our camp.[6]

It is difficult to reconcile two aspects of Rose's report with the facts. Little Soldier intimated that the artillery had done little damage, the

Indians merely lying on the ground below the level of the barrage, and the subsequent actions of the Rees were not commensurate with humbleness. Perhaps Rose wanted to spare his friends further punishment; perhaps he was interpreting "defeat" in terms of Indian war psychology, whereby a battle was won or lost on the basis more of noise and face than of deaths; perhaps he told Leavenworth what he thought the commander wanted to hear. It would not have been the first or last such case.

Little Soldier tried to induce Leavenworth to visit the villages, but he declined—a refusal in no way predicated on fear; it simply did not occur to him to go see things for himself. He sent Ed Rose, who brought back the opinion cited above, and one which time was to prove in error.

Leavenworth then sent Dr. John Gale, Lieutenant W. W. Morris, and Major Daniel Ketchum to make three independent surveys. *They agreed with Rose,* adding only that the Ree fortifications were very rudimentary and amounted to little more than a stout fence with a shallow ditch at the bottom.

What was Leavenworth trying to prove? Did he distrust Rose, or was he hoping that his own officers would bring a report of formidable defenses which would take the sting of defeat from his artillery? No one knows.

In the meantime the Rees brought food to the soldiers; Leavenworth paid for it and then sharply ordered them to send their important chiefs to talk. Two lesser ones did come, whereupon Pilcher pointed out that such men could not bind the Rees to anything. Leavenworth demanded others, and when new faces arrived he told Pilcher to draw up a treaty.

Pilcher refused point blank; another subagent refused; O'Fallon was not interested; Ashley declined. The unhappy Leavenworth was compelled to write it himself. Eleven Indians, six army officers, and a reluctant Ashley signed. Pilcher and the others refused.

Under the date of August 13, Pilcher wrote Leavenworth, "I still think it proper to inform you that neither of the principal Chiefs of the Arikara Nation have signed that paper and if I have been correct informed were not present at the meeting when the paper was signed."[7]

When the facts were all in, Pilcher was vindicated. Two principal chiefs were involved: Grey Eyes and Left Handed. The first round of artillery fire had killed Grey Eyes, and Left Handed was far too well known to have gone unrecognized had he attended the treaty rites. *

Leavenworth's treaty provided for the restoration of Ashley's property, unmolested traffic on the river, and the usual promises of "eternal friendship." Leavenworth was the only one who believed any of it. Rose made another trip into the towns and reported that the women were packing their belongings preparatory to a mass escape, taking Ashley's property with them, but Leavenworth did nothing to prevent it.

The Rees brought a token return of Ashley's property. Little Soldier came again, telling a pitiful tale of an exhausted and bankrupt people, and begged that Leavenworth not attack again until he could desert his tribesmen and bring his own family to the sanctuary of the white lines.

Leavenworth sat down to think.

Either he must reopen a genuine offensive or Ashley must go without his goods. But the day was spent, and even Pilcher agreed it was better to wait till the morrow before doing anything. But that held a problem too. Leavenworth's own men were restless and demanding action. Major Wooley favored attacking at once, and Captain (later General) Bennet Riley spoke bluntly for them all. Said he, "they had been laying at garrison . . . for 8 or 10 years doeing nothing but eating pumpkin and now a small chance for promotion occured and it was denied him and might not occur again for the next 10 yeares."[8] Colonel Leavenworth countered these arguments with "I . . . felt an unwillingness to recommense hostilities on account of the articles of property,"[9] a sentiment much to his credit and one not generally held by the military.

Ed Rose and Little Soldier went back into the towns to appeal for more Ashley goods, but with little success. On his return, Rose said the items he now brought had been literally taken off the backs of the Indians, and no more could be expected. He also reported their obvious plans to decamp overnight. Leavenworth then sent Rose with another message telling the Rees not to leave as they would not be fired upon during the night.

---

* It was Left Handed who had told Hunt in 1811 that the Rees could not supply the horses he needed, and it was Grey Eyes who had boasted, "We can easily steal more."

"He went to the villages with this message, and without my knowledge, or consent carried a piece of white cloth on a stick. He afterwards told me that it was a signal which he had promised to give them in case I determined not to attack them. Early in the morning of the 13th we discovered that the Indians had abandoned their villages and gone off during the night."[10] Only Grey Eyes' mother, a sad old woman much too feeble to travel, remained.

Not a very glorious feat of arms! Leavenworth tried to salvage something by spending the next two days searching for the Rees—a senseless and hopeless quest. On August 15 he made Grey Eyes' mother as comfortable as possible and ordered a return to Fort Atkinson. As the disgruntled Missouri Legion headed south, a solid mass of smoke arose from the Arikara towns. Their homes and Grey Eyes' mother were being sacrificed to white hate.

Leavenworth was properly outraged, and accused Pilcher of firing the towns. He denied any responsibility, but made no pretense of regret that the deed was done. At this, Leavenworth issued orders to the 6th Regiment forbidding any further contact with Pilcher's command, except for two individuals whom he seemed to consider worthy of trust. These two, on hearing they had been so honored, wrote a scathing note to Leavenworth saying they were "extremely mortified at having been selected as the object of his approbation and praise."[11]

It had not been a very happy campaign. Leavenworth tried to make it look as good as he could, and his official report speaks of the "galling fire" suffered by his men. But the record of losses will hardly sustain him. Casualties: seven drowned on the way up the river, two wounded in the battle. Rees killed according to Leavenworth's estimate: thirty. Positively known dead: thirteen, killed by the Sioux. General results: increased arrogance of the Arikaras and scorn from the Sioux. Expenses: $2,038.24.

"It is my sincere and candid opinion that the expedition agaist the Arikaras . . . will rather tend to increase, than diminish, the evil . . . ," wrote Pilcher to O'Fallon one week after the fight.[12] The whole campaign detracted credit from American arms, wrote Hiram Chittenden, historian of the mountain fur trade.

Leavenworth thought otherwise, and on August 29 posted the following for his men to read: "The Colonel Commanding is very happy to announce to his command that the objects of the late expedition . . . have been effected. The blood of our countrymen has been properly avenged, the Ricaras humbled, and in such manner as will teach them . . . to respect the American name and character."[13]

He added that other tribes would also take the lesson to heart. But events again proved Pilcher right, for less than two years later the federal government had to send the Atkinson-O'Fallon expedition, with Ed Rose, up the river again to quiet the Indians. But before that event took place, Rose was to help Jed Smith explore the West.

ED ROSE, CROW CHIEF

1824

WITH the defeat of Leavenworth, the Missouri Legion ceased to operate as a unit. The soldiers returned to Fort Atkinson; Pilcher took his trappers to Fort Lisa; Henry and twenty-five men went to their Yellowstone post; and Ashley and the remainder of his company returned to Fort Kiowa on August 27.[1]

Both Ashley and Pilcher faced bankruptcy. Only a spectacular harvest could save Ashley. Pilcher never recovered. He hung on for a few more seasons, but with the genius of Manuel Lisa gone, the odds were too great.

On the other hand, Ashley believed he could still amass a fortune if he abandoned the dangerous Missouri River route and struck directly west from Fort Kiowa for the valley of the Green River, reputedly alive with fur and reachable by a rumored southern pass. Who first proposed the departure from the Missouri is uncertain. Some partisans credit young Jed Smith; others believe Thomas Fitzpatrick thought of it; and Ashley has his supporters. Regardless of the authorship, Ashley ordered it and took the gamble.

No sizable party had ever crossed this area without meeting trouble; no one had more than a hazy idea of the general conditions prevailing.

Where were the Indians? Where and what was the food supply? North America has never been lavishly provided with wildlife foods, the American bison and the Barren Grounds caribou being unpredictable exceptions. In recorded times it has always been nip and tuck between the natural food supply and native starvation, with starvation frequently winning the race.

And where was the water? In an emergency men could and often did go a week without food, carrying their packs and covering their fifteen to thirty miles per day. It was not pleasant, but it could be done. Water was another matter.

Piled on top of all this was the eternal imponderable—weather. The mountain men had learned long ago that longitude, latitude, and elevation were only contributing factors to the whole climate, and Ashley had little real information on what climate to expect between Fort Kiowa and the mountains. Winter might come to one area weeks before it did in another, and a sudden snowfall, blotting out Indian trails and landmarks and eliminating forage, could mean death. Witness the Donner party many years after our present discussion.

It was as we say today a calculated risk, but Ashley had no difficulty finding men to take. Jed Smith was captain, and Thomas Fitzpatrick as second in command was ably supported by William L. Sublette, James Clyman, Thomas Eddie, and Ed Rose. Just how many others Smith had under him is uncertain. Ashley talked of a total of fifteen or sixteen, but Clyman, years later, could remember only eleven. It does not matter except to point up two items: the impossibility of being positive about the doings of mountain men, and the regularity with which Ed Rose was included in the important expeditions of the decade.

Smith borrowed enough horses for his immediate needs from the American Fur Company and hoped to acquire more from the Indians as he went along. By now it was late in September of 1823, and a less adventurous command would have waited until another season but Smith, Fitzpatrick, and Rose were not noted for caution. They headed west from Kiowa across modern South Dakota straight into the Bad Lands. Rose told Smith they would have to take water with them if they were to have any, but they had no canteens. Rather than delay, Smith ordered the advance without them, and so they entered a tree-less and arid waste without any means of carrying water.

It was close to calamitous. Winter rain and snow had not yet begun, and the first water hole was dry. Rose knew of another fifteen miles ahead and started for it alone while the others scattered at tangents in the hope of finding a different source sooner. James Clyman succeeded, but not before two men collapsed from thirst.

Smith thought of a possible way to save them. If water was where Rose said it was, some stronger member of the party might bring a minute amount to the exhausted men and rescue them. The problem was to keep them alive long enough to try this. Smith buried both men in the sand, excepting their heads, to reduce body evaporation to a minimum. Tradition has it that it was Smith himself who eventually staggered back with enough water to save them.

Water was the bane of Jed Smith's life, as it was of Charbonneau's, albeit in a different fashion; for one day in the future Jed Smith was to die while seeking it in the wastelands along the North Fork of the Cimarron.

At present, however, the revived and reunited party caught up with Rose the following morning, and he in turn made contact with a band of Sioux, from whom they got fresh horses. Rose then pointed out the Bad Lands and Black Hills, a safe and lovely vacation land in our day but a potential death trap a century and a half ago. Shortly he left the expedition and went on to the Crows with the idea of inducing them to help Smith reach the Green River country.

While Rose was gone, Smith got past the dangers of the Bad Lands, skirted the southern edge of the Black Hills, and ran smack into one of the most unbelievable adventures which make up the true history of the mountain men.

It was a beautiful, quiet fall day. There were no indications of unfriendly Indians; the men had food and water; they were on the right route, and Ed Rose had gone ahead to smooth their further trail. The men were walking single file along a brushy bottom, Smith in the lead. Coming around a clump of trees into an unexpected clearing, Smith almost literally stepped into the paws of a grizzly bear. These nasty-tempered beasts always preferred to fight rather than run, and before Smith could make any defensive move, the grizzly had delivered a savage mauling.

Grizzly did not hesitate a moment but sprung on the cap[t] taking him by the head first pitc[h]ing sprawling on the earth he gave him [Smith] a grab by the middle fortunately catc[h]ing by the ball pouch and Butcher K[n]ife which he broke by breaking several of his ribs and cutting his head badly . . . and laid the skull bare to near the crown of the head. . . . one of his ears was torn fom his head out to the outer rim.[2]

Smith was rescued as soon as possible, but by then it was a question of whether his life could be saved. To James Clyman fell the task of repairs. First-aid kits were unknown, whiskey (which Smith did not use) served as an anesthetic, a red-hot steel did a passing job of cautery, and a trade needle could be used for other things than sewing up moccasins.

"I got a pair of scissors and cut off his hair and then began my first Job of d[r]essing wounds."

Finally everything was back in place except the ear, which Clyman told Smith he did not believe could be saved.

"Oh you must try to stich up some way or other said he then I put my needle through and through and over and over laying the lacerated parts togather as nice as I could with my hands."[3]

A mile or two farther on, even the redoubtable Jed Smith called a halt to rest a few days.

Rose was still talking with the Crows. After recuperating, Smith moved on into the mountains, visited a Cheyenne village, bought more horses, picked up some survivors of the Jones-Immell massacre of the preceding May, and then tramped toward the Wind River Range and the Crows.

Clyman claimed that Rose and a dozen or more Crows had "been watching for two days . . . to assure themselves that no Shians were with us"—the Cheyennes being enemies of the Crows. When the trappers finally joined the Indians, the latter wished to move too fast for a trapping expedition, and Smith "gave them what they could pack sending Rose with them."[*][4]

After this separation, Smith trapped the Powder and Tongue rivers and then picked up Rose's trail again. The Rocky Mountain winter was fast closing in. Game was gone, trails were easily lost under constantly deeper snows, and Smith must either keep to Rose's route or starve. In desperation, but not panic, he hurried on to the base of Fremont's Peak, near which he found the Crow camp and Ed Rose.

For two months they sat about Crow fires, telling tales, stuffing on Indian rations, and dreaming of the wealth of the Green River beaver ponds. Smith endlessly asked questions which Rose rephrased and posed to the Crows.

The cold weeks of the winter encampment on Wind River were one of the great epochs in Ed Rose's life, for he alone among the whites could understand the Crow tongue, and from his exploit of five scalps the Crows

---

[*] It is sometimes said that Rose deserted Smith at this juncture, but Clyman's statement indicates otherwise.

were disposed to regard him as the greatest man alive. . . . the Crows would do nothing without him. He was consulted on all occasions; his word was law, and none knew better how to give an elevated tone, meanwhile handing out Jedediah's goods with a lavish hand. By the time the winter camp broke up, Jedediah was well satisfied to leave Rose among a people who held him in such high esteem.[5]

Late in February of 1824, Smith took leave of Rose and made the usual farewell rituals with the Crows. Disregarding the still intense cold, he headed south for the Sweetwater, turned west, crossed South Pass, and plunged down the western slope to the Green in March, 1824.

Smith's route marked the effective discovery of South Pass, although Colter may have stumbled through it and Robert Stuart probably used it on his return from Astoria.

On the Green the Smith expedition divided, trapped, and garnered a fortune to take to St. Louis. Then Ashley himself visited the Green, instituted the great mountain trade fairs, returned to St. Louis, paid his debts, and had the munificent sum of $80,000 left over. Smith, under a new business organization, went on to new adventures and greater honors, but these had nothing to do with Ed Rose.

The mulatto had found his people. From then until his death, he was never very far from the Crows.

31

THE LAST DECADE

1823–1833

THE War of 1812 had stirred the Indians to a high pitch of restlessness, and the Arikara campaign of 1823 had only made matters worse. President Monroe, backed by Congressional approval and funds, determined to send General Henry Atkinson and Major O'Fallon to make a new show of force along the river. They were to go to the headwaters of the Missouri with 500 men, eight keelboats, and a cavalry escort under a Captain Armstrong.

Atkinson left St. Louis the latter part of March, 1825, and picked up Ed Rose at Council Bluffs. Rose and Armstrong then pushed on to the Ponca village two weeks ahead of Atkinson and O'Fallon. The subsequent wait was a pleasure for Rose. There were always old acquaintances, generally a good fire with food, and perhaps a cup of rum or a new girl. Better yet—perhaps a good fight.

This was a military expedition but not a war party, and Rose's chief service was to keep ahead of the command and gather the Indians to places where Atkinson and O'Fallon could display their military might, make speeches, sign treaties, and hunt buffalo. It was all really quite a lot of fun. They would pass among the Sioux, the Cheyennes, the Ogallalahs, the Rees, and the peaceful Mandans, spending their energies on fast horses, Indian games, colorful costumes, and tall tales—especially the last.

And sometimes they made good their boasts.

One day the Army and Indians were off on a buffalo hunt and Rose decided to flaunt his prowess. He seized an armful of brush, rammed it over his head and around his shoulders, crawled into the very midst of eleven old bulls, and killed six of them before they could escape. It was an amazing display of speed and accuracy, but Ed Rose was an amazing man.

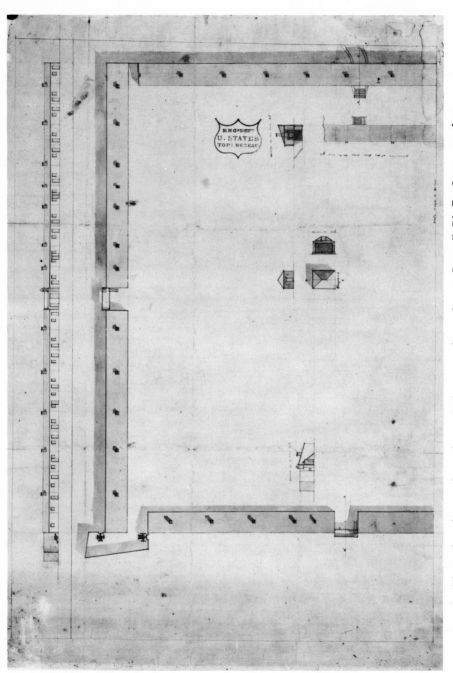

Plan, elevation, and sections of the army barracks at Council Bluffs, Iowa, as they appeared during the fur trade era, 1820. *The National Archives, Record Group #77, Dr. 131-18.*

Early in July he brought in a small band of Crows who happened to hold two Iroquois prisoners. Atkinson demanded the captives be released. The Crows, not in the least understanding why they should, retaliated a little later by trying to seize the presents which would normally be theirs only after the powwow. At this, O'Fallon, contrary to his usual good sense, clubbed a Crow with his pistol butt. An uproar followed.

Atkinson, returning from his dinner, immediately ordered his troops under arms. But the Crows had outplayed him by having already plugged the touchholes of his cannon with earth.

This was the sort of first-quality row that Ed Rose loved. He did not wait for Atkinson to act. He had seen Colonel Leavenworth hesitate and lose a whole campaign, and he did not intend to see things happen that way again. He grabbed his fusee, broke the stock over the head of one of his own Crows, and then, using the barrel as a club, laid to with such abandon and delight that the entire gang of troublemakers fled.

Nor did the Crows resent this show. It only went to prove that Ed Rose was indeed a mighty chief.

Eventually Atkinson and O'Fallon reached the Mandans, whence they went to the Yellowstone, where they met Ashley and Smith coming down with a cargo of furs. The meeting may have been prearranged. In any event, Ashley gladly accepted Atkinson's offer of safe-conduct to St. Louis.

There were many other Indians in the area, but they were too scattered for the military force to make contact with them, and Atkinson believed he had fulfilled his instructions. When Ashley and Smith were ready, he turned about and headed for St. Louis, where he arrived in October of 1825.

Ed Rose had been of "great use to the commissioners,"[1] and is credited with turning the Crows into sturdy friends of the whites,[2] but it is unlikely that he continued to St. Louis with the Army. He rarely remained with an undertaking after the adventure wore off, and he could certainly find more of that with the Crows or Blackfeet than with Atkinson or Armstrong plodding toward civilization.

After 1825 the tales about Ed Rose are scanty or unreliable. He left no written record, and those who kept journals often failed to name their interpreter-guides. Most confusing, James P. Beckwourth, another mulatto, became prominent. Both Rose and Beckwourth knew the Missouri and the fur business; both lived with and became chiefs among the Crows; and confusion is further augmented by such volumes as the *Narrative of the Adventures of Zenas Leonard* and Coyner's *Lost Trappers,* * both of which have Rose and Beckwourth confused at least part of the time.

Coyner had best be regarded as unreliable, but Leonard commands some attention. He was a free trapper from Clearfield, Pennsylvania, who went to the mountains about 1831 to seek his fortune. Later he was employed by Captain Benjamin Bonneville, the West Pointer who took leave from the Army and, backed by New York capital, explored and trapped the West for three years and was immortalized by Washington Irving.

Although Leonard's *Narrative* has merit, he abets the confusion between Rose and Beckwourth. He says that while trapping the headwaters of the Colorado River about January of 1833, he was visited by a party of Crows looking for the Snakes. The Crows professed friendship (and probably meant it in their own way), but they stole five of Leonard's horses anyhow. He and his men went in hot pursuit:

We steered across the mountains towards the Southern headwaters of the Missouri river . . . [and came to a Crow village where] we found a nagro man, who informed us he first came to this country with Lewis and Clark . . . [and had been with the Crows] about ten or twelve years. . . . He has rose to be quite a considerable character, or chief, in their village; at least he assumes the dignities of a chief, for he has four wives with whom he lives alternatively. This is the custom of many of the chiefs. [3]

Leonard found his horses in this camp. Rose explained that since Leonard had been found in enemy territory, he presumably might give help to the Snakes; therefore, it was only fair he should lose his horses—a rationalization not too far from our present-day theory of "preventive war."

For a few trinkets, Rose arranged for Leonard's horses to be sold back to him.

A little later Leonard hired out to Bonneville, and under the com-

---

* David H. Coyner's *Lost Trappers* purports to detail the adventures of a lost party sent by Manuel Lisa to trade with the Arapahoes. The volume first appeared in 1847.

mand of Joseph Reddeford Walker, another associate of Bonneville, went to California and back. In 1834 Leonard again visited the Crows, and found Rose "as great advantage to us as on former occasions . . . and considered a great value by the Indians. He enjoys perfect peace and satisfaction, and has every thing he desires at his command."[4]

There are discrepancies in Leonard's narrative: He identifies Rose as much by implication as by name; Rose was not with Lewis and Clark, nor was Beckwourth; and Leonard claims he talked to Rose in 1834 months after his accepted death date.[5]

Despite these conflicts, it is generally believed that Leonard's "nagro" was Ed Rose.

On the occasion of Leonard's second visit to the Crows, he implies he witnessed the most famous of all the stories told about Rose. A small band of Blackfeet had come into Crow country and fortified a nearby hill with an effective breastwork. The Crows went through the usual war-speech routines and even made a few halfhearted charges up the hill, but without any damage whatsoever to the Blackfeet.

Ed Rose watched this fiasco as long as he could, and then:

He told them they had been making a great deal of noise, as if they could kill the enemy by it—that they had talked long and loud about going into the fort, and that the white man would say that the Indian had a crooked tongue, when talking about his war exploits. He told them that their hearts were small, and that they were cowardly—that they acted more like squaws than men, and were not fit to defend their hunting ground. He told them that the white men were ashamed of them and would refuse to trade with such a nation of cowards—that Blackfeet would go home and tell their people that three thousand Crows could not take a handful of them,—that they would be laughed at, scorned, and treated with contempt by all the nations wherever known—that no tribe would degrade themselves hereafter by waging war with them, and that the whole Crow nation, once so powerful, would forever be treated as a nation of squaws. The old negro continued in this strain until they became greatly animated, & told them that if the red men were afraid to go amongst his enemy, he would show them that a black man was not, and he leaped from the rock on which he had been standing, and, looking neither to the right or left, made for the fort as fast as he could run. The Indians guessing his purpose, and inspired by his words and fearless example, followed close to his heels, and were in the fort dealing destruction to the right and left nearly as soon as the old man.[6]

There are those who think it was Beckwourth who taught the Crows how to fight that day,[7] but others say the story was told about Rose long before Beckwourth came to the land.[8] And the adventure is very much like Ed Rose. From river piracy to buffalo bulls to Blackfeet— it was all of a pattern, and legend has it that a few years later Rose was to die as he had lived.

In the winter of 1832–1833, Rose, Hugh Glass, and some Indian friends were hunting on "the frozen Yellowstone below the Big Horn" near Fort Cass[9] when they were surprised and surrounded by a party of Rees. The Rees set the prairie grass afire and stood waiting for their victims to rush screaming from the flames.

Instead they heard a mighty roar. Ed Rose had exploded an enormous charge of gunpowder. He would choose his own way to die.

But even the manner of the great mulatto's going was to have many versions: a "licentious life" caused death; he was murdered in a Crow feud; he committed suicide by gunpowder.[10]

And indeed Fort Cass may not have been the scene of Ed Rose's last fight, for early steamboat itineraries have "Rose's Grave" opposite the mouth of Milk River, a considerable distance from Fort Cass. And frontier bodies were never moved far from the place of death. The conflict does not really matter, for it is entirely fitting that a life which began with a legend of piracy and the City of Sin should close with a legend of suicide in the heart of Crow land.

PART IV

MOUNTAIN MAN
STORYTELLER

LONG before man had a memory, he who could tell stories owned a special niche—whether it was in the prehistoric caves of France, or around the savage fires of Patagonia, or in senatorial baths of Rome, it made no difference. It was demanded not that these tales be true but that they be exciting, polished, and perfected until they became the mirror for the culture of their age. The great storyteller appropriated to himself any adventure that had ever happened to anyone—tales of the gods and the first man, the Flood and the sacrifice of sons; tales of war and the hunt and flaming passions. And because his own adventures were unsurpassed, and his tales of wild horses and bloody scalps and Indian nymphs placed him with the greatest storiers of the New World, Jim Beckwith, son of a Virginia planter and a quadroon slave, deserves his special chapter among the mighty breeds and half-breeds.

JAMES P. BECKWOURTH

1798?–1824

RUMORS had drifted into the remote mining camp that a book could be had retelling the adventures of Jim Beckwith. An illiterate miner was sent to buy a copy. The general store had no such volume, but not wishing to miss a profit, sold a Bible to the unlettered customer. That evening a partially literate comrade opened the Book at random and read:

And Sampson went and caught three hundred foxes, and took firebrands, and turned tail to tail and put a firebrand in the midst between two tails.

And when he had set the brands on fire, he let them go into the standing corn of the Philistines, and burnt up both the shocks, and also the standing corn, with the vineyards and olives.[1]

"Thar, that'll do," broke in a disgusted old-timer. "I'd know that for one of Jim Beckwith's damned lies anywhere."

He was indeed, said Hiram Chittenden, a redoubtable prevaricator,[2] and Francis Parkman called him "Jim Beckworth, . . . a mongrel of French, American and negro blood. . . . He is a ruffian of the worst stamp; bloody and treacherous, without honor or honesty; such at least is the character he bears upon the prairie. Yet in his case the standard rule of character fails, for although he will stab a man in his sleep, he will also perform most desperate acts of daring."[3]

And so Jim Beckwith was a legend in his own years—a legend long before the bloodstream slowed in his mighty arms or the ashes of old passions dimmed his black-brown eyes.

Strictly speaking, the story of Jim Beckwith, or James P. Beckwourth as he liked to be called, has no place in the annals of the interpreter-guides, for he was more squaw man than interpreter, more

Jim Beckwith (James P. Beckwourth), interpreter-guide and master storyteller. *Denver Public Library Western Collection.*

Indian fighter than guide. Yet he cannot be left out of any tale of the great half-breeds; he too managed to be associated with the most exciting events of his time, and then to collect and retell the heroic stories of the West in such a manner that to ignore him would be to leave any record of the half-breeds more than merely incomplete.

If one repudiates his dictated autobiography and accepts only the evidence of others, Jim Beckwith's life was a wild and incredible threescore years. If we accept his own embellishments of those years, they become superb fiction and rank him without peer in the American West.

As Bernard DeVoto said, much of Beckwith's life is "impossible to check, impossible to believe,"[4] and, we might add, impossible to forget.

Jim Beckwith deserves his substantial niche among the breeds and half-breeds—not as interpreter-guide, though he was above average in that role too, but because he was unsurpassed in telling the tales of the mountains, the grizzlies, the massacres, the horse-stealings, and the conquests of Indian virgins.

It is as a great storyteller that Jim Beckwith should be read and remembered. Into his sensitive memory was etched almost every adventure that had ever happened to anyone west of the Missouri and north of the Rio Grande. And he appropriated each adventure for his own, and emerged standing quite alone against the western sky, gigantic and heroic.

That his thousands of Indian warriors were in truth but hundreds lessened none of the peril of battle. That his scores of dripping scalps were in fact but two or three sagging from his war lance in no way wiped out the fact that both savage and Christian collected the bloody trophies and retold the glories of their conquest during the long winter fires.

Perhaps Jim Beckwith should be equated with history only insofar as he told better than anyone else of the great deeds which were as much a part of the American West as John Alden and Priscilla are of New England—but not nearly so dull.

Jim left no journal to authenticate his claim to four years of schooling in St. Louis, but sometime after 1850 he dictated his autobiography to one T. D. Bonner, probably a San Francisco newspaperman.[5] Bonner put the known facts of Jim's life plus a considerable store of frontier fiction into a volume in which it is impossible not only to sort fact from fancy but sometimes to separate Bonner from Beckwith.

Perhaps there is no reason why we should. Here was a master storyteller who placed his hero, generally himself, against the factual background of the mountains, beaver streams, war parties, blizzards, starvation, and homeless fires—and the authentic record of the mountain fur trade.

Jim Beckwith seldom if ever told a tale that *couldn't* happen, and most of his events, or ones exactly like them, almost certainly happened to someone, said DeVoto.[6]

Let us then get on with Jim's "life" as he himself told it, verifying a deed here, a date there, but never forgetting that we are reading western historical lore. Indeed, today we might call Jim a historical novelist. But he had to compete with the starched respectability of Irving's *Astoria* and Parkman's *Oregon Trail,* and he emerged from the contest a "ruffian . . . bloody and treacherous, without honor or honesty."

The elder Beckwith, according to Jim, was a Virginia planter of moderate means who served as a major in the Continental Army during the American Revolution. This meant, of course, that he was a white man who owned slaves. Not many, perhaps, but enough to give him prestige.

And among these few was a lovely quadroon.

Jim often mentioned his twelve brothers and sisters and implied they had a common parentage. While unlikely, it could have been true. For although miscegenation was damned from the pulpits and denied in the drawing rooms, the slave quarters knew better, and an ever-growing number of mulattoes, quadroons, and octoroons spread from New Orleans to Puritan New England.

Young Jim, then, was the son of a white planter and a quadroon slave.* He was born in Fredericksburg, Virginia, probably in the spring of 1798, and was the third child in the family, one brother and one sister being older. Nine other slaves completed the Beckwith ménage.

Shortly after the return of Lewis and Clark from the Pacific, the

---

* Horace S. Lyman says Beckwith's mother was a Negro slave (*History of Oregon,* 4 vols., New York, North Pacific Publishing Society, 1903, III, 60).

senior Beckwith and his slaves moved near the raw Spanish-French town, St. Louis, and took up land twelve miles below St. Charles.

Jim could soon tell his first tale of Indian war. At the crossroads two miles away was a small gristmill to which he was sent with a sack of corn to be reduced to meal. On the way there one day it struck his fancy to visit another little slave boy with whom he was sometimes allowed to play:

I rode joyously up to the little fence which separated the house from the road. What was my horror at discovering all the children, eight in number, from one to fourteen years of age, lying . . . with their throats cut, their scalps torn off, and the warm life blood still oozing from their gaping wounds! In the door way lay their father, and near him their mother, in the same condition; they had all shared the same fate.

Young Jim, forgetting all about his corn, raced home and told his father. The infuriated settlers rose to a man, hunted down the guilty Indians—or at least some Indians—and "in two days returned, bringing with them eighteen scalps."[7]

And so a career was launched. Jim Beckwith, the half-breed slave, became James P. Beckwourth, famous Indian fighter and storyteller.

Following his alleged four years of schooling, Jim was apprenticed to a blacksmith in St. Louis, one Casner, but they threw hammers at each other and the apprenticeship was never completed. Then, when he was nineteen, Jim's passion surmounted the defenses of a young female and he thought it best to go off to the mines near Galena, where Casner tracked him down and demanded his pound of flesh.

Jim refused to return.

Father Beckwith sided with Casner. Jim refused them both. Father was getting worried. The boy was willful, passionate, and very, very strong.

But he was more. He effused character. His eyes held the deep twinkle of the joyous adventurer; his mind was sharp and challenging; he feared no man but held a proper respect for ability and authority in others. Forty years later William N. Byers, editor of the Denver *Rocky Mountain News,* wrote:

We recently were honored by a visit from this justly celebrated mountaineer and adventurer. . . . We had formed the opinion, as has, we presume, al-

most every one, that Capt. Beckwourth was a rough, illiterate backwoods-
man, but were most agreeably surprised to find him a polished gentleman,
possessing a fund of general information which few can boast. He is now
sixty-two years of age, but looks scarcely fifty, hale, hearty, and straight
as an arrow. [8]

With all these attributes, thought Father Beckwith, maybe a
business of his own would— The sentence was answered before it
was complete.

"No," said Jim. He was going to travel.

Now, these were the years of the great frontier religious revivals.
Thousands went to sultry summer camps and boasted of their sins as
they crawled down a sawdust trail to redemption. And it was a sincere
and serious frenzy, make no error about that. Beckwith senior may
well have been caught in the mighty web. Certainly he could not
have escaped the general mass sense of sinfulness.

Twenty years before, he too had sinned; now his bastard Jim had
committed the same grievous fault, and it was very difficult indeed to
pretend the sins had not been. Jim was very real.

Perhaps travel *was* the best way. Would $500, a good horse, and
other suitable equipment be enough to guarantee distance and reasonable oblivion?

Jim took the next boat to Galena.

There an Army detachment was about ready to start on a treaty-
making mission to the Sacs and Foxes, and Jim hired on as a hunter.
Twenty days later he had tasted Indian life on the Illinois side of the
Mississippi River. Another eighteen months and he knew their secret
hunting grounds, had reveled in their iniquities and, by working part
time in the mines, had accumulated $700, with which fortune he was
willing to risk a return to St. Louis.

A short visit with his father and the sprawling family was enough.
The incurable wanderlust was already flowing rampant, and Jim
Beckwith never again remained long in one place.

He went to New Orleans, stayed ten days, got yellow fever, came
home to recuperate, and immediately he could half-hold his own in
the frontier world joined William Henry Ashley's overland trading
expedition to the Rockies.

BECKWITH JOINS ASHLEY

1824

IN our delight over the very real accomplishments of Lewis and Clark, we tend to forget that they failed to report a true picture of the potentialities of the great central plains or the wealth of furs to be taken from the Rocky Mountains; at least, they failed to do so in a manner that reached and convinced the man in the street. Even John Jacob Astor, who had already made a fortune in furs, does not appear to have had any very solid plans for exploiting the Rockies.

But his rival, Manuel Lisa, was not so remiss. He pushed his men farther and farther up the Missouri, and in the process, despite certain failures, was very near being the most important man in the business when he died in 1820.

Lisa's death and Astor's failure at Astoria, along with Indian unrest during and after the War of 1812, left the empire of furs in some confusion. The rich plum lay ready to be plucked by anyone with capital enough to stand temporary losses and raw courage enough to challenge a combination of untamed wilderness, unpredictable tribes, and a sum total of considerable and ruthless competition.

It was by no means a clear field. Joshua Pilcher was bidding for Lisa's mantle; the Spaniards had visited the lush Green River Valley in Wyoming; the Chouteau family was very much involved all the way from Taos to the Canadians; the Hudson's Bay Company kept up a steady pressure southward; Astor and his American Fur Company were at St. Louis; and an indefinite number of individual traders with substantial funds and various-sized crews were scouring the fringes of the far western trade.

William Henry Ashley, lieutenant governor of Missouri, believed he could challenge the odds. We have seen how he started for the source of the Missouri in 1822; how Major Andrew Henry, his field commander, got only as far as the Yellowstone; how Indian depredations and losses forced Ashley to recruit more men and money, only to meet serious defeat at the hands of the Arikaras and be laughed off the Missouri by the comic opera campaign under Colonel Leavenworth; and how Ashley then embraced the idea of leaving the river below the unruly Indians and going overland with pack animals.

As we have said, no one knows who first suggested the overland attempt, but Jim Beckwith claimed in later years that Ashley personally headed one abortive overland jaunt which was stopped when Indians stole all his horses.[1]

About the end of September, 1823, Ashley ordered the Smith-Clyman-Fitzpatrick-Sublette-Rose brigade, supported by six to ten others, west from Fort Kiowa. We have followed them around the Black Hills into Crow country, over the Big Horn Mountains to the Big Horn River at the juncture of the Wind River and the Popo Agie, and up the Wind River to the winter camp of the Crows; and the following February we saw them leave Ed Rose with the Crows to start south to the Sweetwater, and then travel over South Pass and down the Green River late in March, 1824.[2]

After a good season caches were dug, and Fitzpatrick, with great difficulty, got to Fort Atkinson in late summer, and sent a report to Ashley. In September Fitzpatrick, with Robert Campbell and Jim Beckwith, "turned back to . . . recover his furs and bring in the men he had left behind."[3] They returned to Fort Atkinson with the men and pelts in October.

Five days before Fitzpatrick got to Fort Atkinson, Ashley arrived from St. Louis. In the meantime Major Henry, who had returned to the mountains after the Arikara fight, also brought in his furs. It was the first good news Ashley had had in a long time, and he was properly excited. His faith in the overland venture grew, and he immediately ordered Fitzpatrick west with a hastily equipped party.

Then, on November 3, 1824, Ashley set out with Jim Beckwith to catch Fitzpatrick. Two days later, "I overtook my party. . . ."[4]

It was sometime during the preceding year of 1823 that Beckwith had come to the attention of Ashley and been hired in one or more capacities: body servant, horse wrangler, or blacksmith—perhaps all three.[5] Jim probably enlisted with Ashley shortly after the Arikara

Independence Rock on the Sweetwater River, Central Wyoming. The name probably dates from 1824 when the Smith-Fitzpatrick party cached their furs nearby about July 4. The rock later became a landmark on the Oregon Trail. *Wyoming Travel Commission.*

Fort Atkinson, ground plan and inset elevation, 1842. *The National Archives, Record Group #77, Dr. 131-19.*

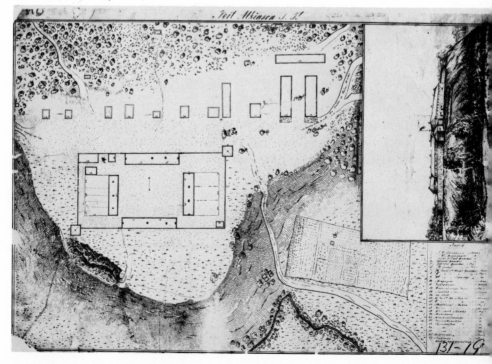

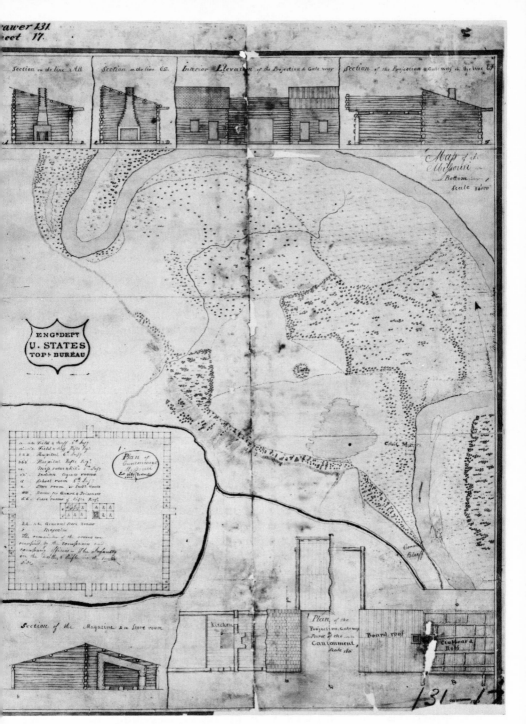

Plan of Cantonment Missouri (insets) and map of the river bottom land above
Council Bluffs, Iowa. Undated. *The National Archives, Record Group #77,
131–17.*

defeat, was sent to purchase horses from the Pawnees, and was kept "at this employment through the remainder of 1823 and most of 1824."[6] However, he is also believed to have been with Jed Smith in the mountains in the spring of 1824, and to have attended the rendezvous on the Sweetwater in June.[7] Following this he is reported as being with Fitzpatrick when the latter arrived from the mountains after the rendezvous, and as returning with him to the caches and being still in Fitzpatrick's company when he delivered the furs to Council Bluffs just above Fort Atkinson in October, 1824.[8]

Jim himself said that early in his employment by Ashley, he was sent to the Pawnees on the horse-buying errand in company with Black Harris, a mountain man of "great leg" who had the reputation of making high speed on the trail but of abandoning anyone unable to keep up with him. After an adventure in which Beckwith claimed he outwalked Harris and reduced him to begging not to be left behind, they found the trail bereft of game, and Harris collapsed from starvation. He was saved by the dauntless Jim, who then located a friendly Indian camp where both men were restored to health on Indian gruel and set safely on the trail to a Kansas River trading post.

By this time it was too late in the season to return to Ashley, and Jim hired out to "G. Chouteau [who] engaged me to assist in packing peltries during the winter, at twenty-five dollars per month."[9] When spring came Jim and Harris, presumably with the horses they had been commissioned to buy, rejoined Ashley's command. Jim resumed his duties as wrangler and blacksmith, and apparently went to the mountains with Jed Smith as noted above.[10]

Despite these clear discrepancies, Beckwith was certainly with Ashley's company when it left Fort Atkinson in November of 1824.

The risk Ashley took that fall morning was no less than the challenge faced by the Fitzpatrick group ten months earlier. Not only was his pace retarded by the first attempt to use a loaded wagon (speedily abandoned), but it was the first winter crossing essayed in those latitudes. The enormity of his peril was soon apparent.

The Indians were gone to their winter grounds and could give Ashley no help; and his main force, two days ahead on the route, were even then on short rations. When he joined them "without any provisions, they were greatly disappointed," said Jim.[11]

Always hoping that game would be found the next day, the united party moved up the long slopes of the western plains. "Our allowance was half a pint of flour a day per man, which we made into a kind of gruel; if we happened to kill a duck or goose, it was shared as fairly as possible."

When the cold November dawns arrived, the men crawled stiffly from their single blanket each and set about getting the expedition on the trail. But there were "No jokes, no fire side stories, no fun; each man rose in the morning with the gloom of the preceding night filling his mind; we built our fires and partook of our scanty repast without saying a word," said Beckwith.[12]

The trail was up the Loup River, south to the Platte, where game became plentiful for the moment and the horses could eat the river rushes, then up the Platte for 100 miles until December 3, when a Grand Pawnee camp was sighted.

Route of the U.S. Rangers from Fort Leavenworth up the Platte River in 1835. Chimney Rock is the black smudge just west of the Black Hills. *The National Archives, Record Group #77, Q 14.*

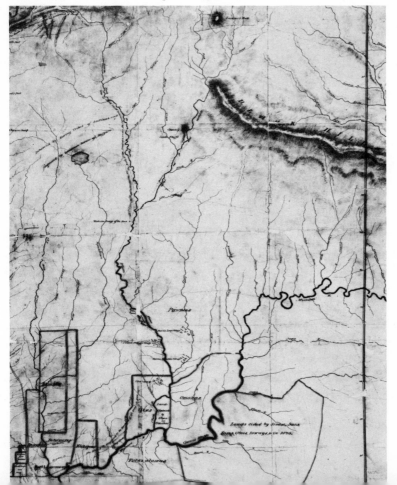

The Pawnees added to Ashley's gloom. There was no hope of game in the miles ahead and no forage for the horses except at the forks of the Platte, where the Indians suggested Ashley spend the winter. But the General was in too much of a hurry to take a safe trail, and his crew were not men to seek security if adventure or wealth beckoned. Eight miles farther on Ashley met a band of Loup Pawnees, traveled with them to the forks of the Platte, bought twenty-three horses, some dried meat, and beans, and headed up the South Platte.

For 200 miles beyond the forks there was little fuel; the day after Christmas, 1824, a screaming blizzard stifled conversation, killed four horses, and endangered all human life; the Crows raided the horses; and only old buffalo trails made it possible to travel at all.

New Year's Day, 1825, Ashley arrived at an island in the South Platte where game and cottonwood trees offered food, forage, fuel, and some protection against weather and hostile Indians, should they appear. After a ten-day rest he continued up the river, and a month later, on February 4, reached the base of the Rockies. There he camped three weeks on Cache la Poudre, surrounded by a solid mass of ice and snow.

Nevertheless, trapping was good, and an encouraging pile of prime pelts was in the making.

Ashley stayed on Cache la Poudre until the last of February, 1825, when he started across the mountains. His situation "required violent effort. . . . things were made ready, and on the 26th we commenced the doubtful undertaking," said Ashley.

Three days later he reached the Laramie plains and hobbled his tired animals to feed on the rich bunch grass, so dry-looking but so nutritious. "My horses retained their strength and spirits in a remarkable degree," said the General.[13]

Crossing the low front range to the Laramie plains was one thing; challenging the Medicine Bow Mountains with five feet of frozen snow was quite another. In fact, it was impossible, and the expedition turned north. Great herds of "Buffaloe, Antelope and Mountain sheep" appeared, heralding the advent of spring. Late in March they found the modern Bridgers Pass, and on the other side the upper valley of the North Platte with the Wind River Mountains shining bright and clear off to the north and west.

At least two of Ashley's men, Clyman and Fitzpatrick, had seen the Wind River Mountains before; but they did not recognize them

Chimney Rock and Scott's Bluff National Monument, Nebraska, 1936. *WPA Photo 69-n-2606-c, The National Archives.*

Indians attacking a wagon train at Chimney Rock on the North Platte, by W. H. Jackson. *U.S. Bureau of Public Roads, Photo 30-n-38772, The National Archives.*

from their present angle, and so at the moment Ashley was lost. He climbed a nearby butte where he was seen by Crow horse thieves, who trailed him to camp and stole seventeen of his best animals.

There was only one thing to do: load the men with the freight while Ashley with one companion went after the Crows. However, Ashley thought he was chasing Snakes, because the wily Crows had dropped a Snake arrow where they knew Ashley would find it. Ashley ordered a hot pursuit. In doing so the two men came upon the "Sweetwater and found that they [the horses] had been taken by a party of Crows. . . ."[14]

Ashley lost his horses, but he found out where he was: the Wind River Mountains, the Sweetwater, and the valley of the Green.

The first winter overland expedition into the Rockies had been accomplished, and Jim Beckwith had, according to his boasts, saved the venture from disaster on at least one occasion. Never again would weary muscles have to pull a laden pirogue against the current of the Missouri. Never again would fearful voyageurs have to face the deadly Sioux or Rees. That is, not unless they thought it would be more profitable to do both, in which case sweat and fear would have to be borne.

34

THE FIRST MOUNTAIN FAIR

1825

APRIL 19, 1825, General Ashley, Jim Beckwith, and his two dozen comrades camped on the Green River. The General arranged for a rendezvous for the first week in July, and fifteen miles above the Sandy divided and sent his men on four trapping-exploring parties: Zacharias Ham and five men went straight west as far as the present Ham's Fork; Fitzpatrick with six companions turned south looking for a river along the east base of the Uinta Mountains, and by so doing found and trapped Henry's Fork of the Green; Jim Clyman with Jim Beckwith* and five others trapped the several tributaries of the Green; while the General with seven men explored the "great canyons and dangerous rapids of the lower Green"[1] in a seven- by sixteen-foot bullboat.

Ashley went to the mouth of the Uinta, dared Desolation Canyon, returned to the Uinta, bought horses from the Utes, ascended the Uinta to the Duchesne, crossed the Uinta Mountains to the Weber watershed, and followed the Weber to Kamas Prairie, the modern Park City, Utah. From the Prairie he returned to the rendezvous at Henry's Fork, half a mile above the "Suck," the Flaming Gorge Canyon of tourist attraction.[2] He had passed the mouth of Henry's Fork on his way, of course, and "finding this a more suitable place for a Randavouse I have made marks indicative of my intention to randavouse here. . . ."[3]

Jim Beckwith believed Ashley's journey ought to be recorded as a dangerous one, which it was, and himself as hero, which he was not:

---

* LeRoy R. Hafen and W. J. Ghent state that Beckwith was with Ashley's group (*Broken Hand,* Denver, Old West Publishing Co., 1931, p. 52).

One of our boats being finished and launched, the general sprang into it to test its capacity. The boat was made fast by a slender string, which snapping with the sudden jerk, the boat was drawn into the current and drifted away, general and all, in the direction of the opposite shore.

His frail bark having reached the opposite shore, encountered a ledge of rocks, and having hardly touched, when, by the action of the rolling current, it was capsized, and he thrown struggling into the water. As providence would have it, he reached the bluff on the opposite side, and holding on to the crevices in the high and perpendicular cliff, sung out lustily for assistance. Not a moment was to be lost. Some one must attempt to save him, for he could not hold his present position, in such cold water, long. I saw that no one cared to risk his life amid such imminent peril, so, calling to a Frenchman of the name of Dorway, whom I knew to be one of the best swimmers, to come to the rescue I threw off my leggings and plunged in, supposing he would follow. I swam under the water as far as I could, to avail myself of the under current (this mode is always practiced by the Indians in crossing a rapid stream). I struck the bluff a few feet above the general. After taking breath for a moment or two, I said to him (by the way, he is no swimmer), "There is only one way I can possibly save you, and I may fail in that; but you must follow my directions in the most minute degree, or we are certainly both lost."

"Anything you say, James, I will follow," said he.

"Then," I continued, "when I float down to you, place your hands on my shoulder, and do not take hold of my neck. Then, when I give you the word, kick out with all your might, and we may possibly get across."

I then let myself down to the general, who was clinging to the rocks like a swallow. He did as I had directed, and I started, he kicking in my rear like the stern wheel of a propeller, until I was obliged to bid him desist; for, with such a double propelling power as we produced, I could not keep my mouth out of the water. We swam to within a few yards of the opposite shore, where the main suck caught us, and, my strength becoming exhausted, we began slowly to recede from the shore toward inevitable death. At this moment Fitzpatrick thrust a long pole to us, to the end of which he attached a rope which the party on shore retained possession of. I seized the pole with a death grip, and we were hauled out of our perilous situation; a moments delay, and the world had seen the last of us.

"That Beckwourth is surely one of the most singular men I ever met," said Ashley to Fitzpatrick (according to Beckwith). "I do not know what to think of him; he never speaks to me except when absolutely unavoidable; still, he is the first and only man to encounter peril on my behalf. Three times he has now saved my life when not another man attempted to succor me. He is a problem I cannot possibly solve."[4]

Ashley was properly appreciative, and asked Jim to forgive him for a row in which the two had had words over Jim's cruelty to a pack animal. Ashley offered Jim the command of one of the trapping crews, but he modestly declined on the grounds of youth and inexperience.[5]

Only one thing was wrong: excepting the statement that Ashley could not swim, probably none of the story is true. It is argued that "In small parties the Ashley men had been scattered over territory west of the mountains from perhaps the thirty-eighth to the forty-fourth degree of latitude," and that Jim, attached to Clyman's party, instead of rescuing Ashley was trapping the tributaries of the Green more than a "hundred fifty miles away, on the other side of the Uinta Mountains."[6]

And yet there is a strange contradiction here, for Jim does not pretend that he was with Ashley on the Green exploration. He specifically places the adventure before the command split into four sections.[7]

But who cared, then or now? Jim Beckwith knew how to tell a tale, and this was all that mattered around the winter fires. The only adventure which actually overtook Clyman's crew, and therefore Jim, was rather prosaic as mountain adventures went. Said Clyman:

... one day 17 Indians came to us and stayed 3 or 4 days. At last, one night the Indians crept up and killed the man on guard with an ax, and charged on us with two guns a ball passed through my caput that answered for a pillow, but did not touch me. We all sprang up. The Indians flew into the brush, we crawled out into the open ground and made a little breastwork or fort of stone, just about daylight. They tried to get us out from behind it, but didn't succeed. We fired on them, and I think I killed one. We were very discouraged—being only 3 men in a country full of Indians, and concluded to take Fitzpatrick's trail and join him.[8]

Following this attack, Jim says, Clyman wished to make a dash for

Mountain Rendezvous, painted by A. J. Miller. *The Walters Art Gallery.*

New Mexico; but when they met a party of their comrades quite by chance, the plan was quickly changed, and all set out for the site chosen for the first Rocky Mountain fair, July 1, 1825.

And it was a fabulous gathering:[9] Jed Smith, with his Bible and his gun and twenty-four deserters from the Hudson's Bay Company, down from his 1824 trip into Company territory around Flathead Lake, Montana; Peter Skene Ogden, Hudson's Bay Company factor, and his party of trappers; Etienne Provost, former Ashley man; independents from Taos and Santa Fe; 800 Indians, including women and children—a total of nearly a thousand untamed humans, thirsty for adventure, profit, and whiskey. *

There were to be sixteen of these great mountain fairs, unique in the history of world trade. Only the ancient fairs at Khiva or Nizhni Novgorod (modern Gorki) rivaled their color and excitement.

Gathered there were savages of all degrees; naked children playing their everlasting game of war; skulking dogs; half-wild horses and mules tethered to stakes; traders from every sort of company and from no company; . . . half-breeds with their native squaws; educated gentlemen out to see the west at first hand; traders who, gamblers at heart, prided themselves on spending a year's earnings in an evening's play; frontiersmen who had throttled the throats of savages; partners with such deep mutual faith that, as they rushed into battle with the Indians, they had been known to shout their wills to each other, well aware that the survivor would execute them as faithfully as if they were written in legal phrase.

They drank and gambled, raced their horses, slept little, ate much, talked long and boastfully, fought, swaggered, lied, cheated the Indians, their own people, and each other. When the occasion finally spent itself, and all the beads and baubles had been exchanged for hides and pelts, each trader went his way to labor and fight for another year, so that for a few days he could live again through these wild scenes. Yet with all their debauchery and even filth, these mountain rendezvous were brilliant pages in the story of the American fur trade.[10]

---

* There was no question about the thirst—only about whether it was satisfied. Dale E. Morgan says there was no rum at this first fair (*Jedediah Smith and the Opening of the West*, Indianapolis, Bobbs-Merrill Co., 1953, pp. 171–172). W. J. Ghent says "whiskey flowed like water" (*The Early Far West*, New York, Tudor Publishing Co., 1936, p. 214).

And the likes of Ed Rose and Jim Beckwith added more than their portion to this brilliance.

Strangely enough, sin apparently played a relatively minor part in this first mountain fair. Jim, who was certainly no bluenose, doesn't mention it, and others either omit all reference or give it only passing attention—all quite contrary to the accounts of vice along the Missouri or the reports from Lewis and Clark at Fort Clatsop.

The first Rocky Mountain fair was over in a day's trading. Ashley made a fortune estimated at $80,000 (as noted in Chapter 30) and withdrew personally from the mountain trade. He turned his field command over to Jed Smith, whom he took as a partner, and started for St. Louis via the Big Horn, Yellowstone, and Missouri rivers. He was accompanied by Smith, Jim Beckwith, and about fifty other men. After reaching the Big Horn, he planned to send half his men and all the animals, some of them borrowed, back to the mountains while he and the remainder of the crew continued to St. Louis. Ashley wrote to General Atkinson:

I had forty packs of Beaver cached a few miles east of our direct route. I took with me 20 men, passed by the place, raised the cache and proceeded in a direction to join the other party, but previous to joining them I was twice attacked by Indians, first by a party of Black-feet about sixty in number—they made their appearance at the break of day, yelling in the most hideous manner & using every means in their power to alarm our horses which they so effectively did that the horses although closely hobbled broke by the guard and ran off. A part of the Indians being mounted they succeeded in getting all the horses except two, and wounded one man. An attempt was also made to take our camp, but in that they failed. The following night I sent an express to secure horses from the party of our men who had taken a direct route, in two days there after I received the desired aid, and again proceeded, on my way, made about ten miles, and encamped upon an eligible situation that night, about 12 o'clock we were again attacked by a party of Crow Indians which resulted in the loss of one of the Indians killed and another shot through the body, without any injury to us. The next day I joined my other party and proceeded direct to my place of embarkation just below the Big Horn mountain where I arrived on the 7th day of August.[11]

Now, Jim was not going to let a real Indian attack go unembellished. For him there were prowling savages shot by his vigilant self and praise from the General, who said, "Very good; whenever you see an Indian about camp at night, . . . shoot him"; there were lovely buckskin leggings and a glossy scalp to take from a fallen foe; there were Crows who asked embarrassing questions and the pretty leggings and scalp must be hastily buried, "knowing they belonged to a Crow," which made Jim fair prey for vengeance;[12] there was the "almost naked" old mother "covered with blood, and, crying in the most piteous tones" to the Crow chief, "These are the men that killed my son . . . will you not avenge his death?"; there were grizzly attacks upon frightened trappers and miraculous rescues by a single shot through the heart of Bruin—all by Jim.

It was wonderful fiction.

But in truth, Ashley did get safely to the Big Horn, build boats, coast down to the mouth of the Yellowstone, and on August 19 meet General Atkinson, who was on the treaty-making mission already discussed.

Ed Rose was with Atkinson, and Beckwith refers to him as "one of the best interpreters ever known in the whole Indian country."[13] Since Atkinson and Ashley were camped close by and traveled to St. Louis together, the two greatest mulattoes in American frontier history must have been together again at least for visits at their respective camps.

What tales! No wonder it is often impossible to tell which interpreter was involved in an episode.

Ashley arrived in St. Louis October 4, 1825. Jim has it that they were met at the dock by a cannon salute and most of the town, including his father; that Ashley paid off all of the crew except Jim and two others, whom he told to enjoy themselves at his expense until he contacted them; and that thereupon for three days they lived in high estate at the best hotel, eating and drinking and taking carriage rides with "a good share of the lasses and mountaineers,"[14] after which Ashley gave them each a bonus of $300 in consideration for their faithful services and for saving his life on numerous occasions.

Perhaps!

Jim also has it that somewhere upriver a grizzly bear had been captured and chained on Ashley's boat to be given to Major Biddle, prominent St. Louis citizen, as a present from Joshua Pilcher.

"James, how under the sun, are we to get that animal off the boat?" said Ashley.

Jim, admitting that he had had several glasses of "artificial courage," picked up a light club, looked the bear in the eye, unhooked his chain, spoke sharply to him, and led the now meek creature to Biddle's home, where he fastened him to a tree. While the Major was inspecting his new pet, a young pig sauntered by. "Grizzly dealt him such a blow with his paw that he left not a whole bone in his body, and piggy fell dead out of the bear's reach."[15]

Obviously, this yarn was not in the best Beckwith tradition, but it was a part of his repertoire and could be used as an encore if his audience was not too critical.

Jim stayed in St. Louis only a few days. He says little or nothing about his family except that it was the last time he saw his "aged father."

There was, however, "Eliza"—no family name mentioned—who was heartbroken when Jim told her their wedding would have to be postponed: Ashley had suddenly offered him $1,000 to deliver special dispatches to William Sublette, who had remained in the mountains when Ashley brought the 1825 catch to market. Jim pretended to be crushed, too; but since he had not dwelt on Eliza at any previous time and made no effective effort ever to return to her, we may reasonably assume either that such a girl never existed or that she was one of the "lasses" who shared the three-day spree paid for by Ashley—if there was any truth in *that*.

Even the authorities cannot sort fact from fancy here except to agree that perhaps Ashley did send Jim on some kind of mission somewhere, sometime.[16] And this seems not unlikely, for by now Beckwith had been accepted as a valuable man. What more natural than that he should be sent to run a routine errand?

Anyway, Jim did return to the mountains in the autumn of 1825 with Jed Smith, who was commanding sixty or seventy trappers and 160 horses and mules, and carrying goods worth $20,000 or more.

Little or nothing is known of this trip. Smith and Jim probably went up the North Platte, over to the Green, northwest to the Hoback, down to Jackson's Hole, over the Tetons to Henry's Fork of the Snake, down it and the Snake to the Salt, up the Salt to headwaters, down Smith's Fork to the Bear, and on to Cache Valley.[17] At Cache Valley William Sublette, who seems to have been in charge at the moment, ordered a removal to a new rendezvous near the present Ogden, Utah.*

If the above journey is correct, "it was a tremendous, even incredible journey to make in late fall,"[18] especially as the snow was or soon would be eight feet deep in Cache Valley. This fact compelled the removal to the Salt Lake basin, where buffalo were plentiful and the ground bare.

---

* If Ashley placed Sublette in charge of the mountain crew during the latter months of 1825, then Jim's tale of delivering an important message to Sublette may be true, although the pretended fee of $1,000 certainly may be questioned.

35

JIM BECKWITH

BECOMES A CROW

1825–1829

IT was on this late fall trip of 1825 that Jed Smith organized the system of travel which put an end to successful Indian forays against the overland pack units.

A commander and assistants were divided into messes of eight or ten men each, and all animals, equipment, and goods were given into the care of individuals who were held responsible for them. Camps were laid out in a hollow square, with the fourth side on a river or lake when possible. Grazing sites were assigned inside the square. Night sentries were posted but were not permitted to move about, which made them difficult for the Indians to see in the long shadows of the dark.

At daybreak two men would scout the area before the messes lined up. The messes took their places in the order of "first ready, first in line," which put a premium on efficiency; for it was no joke to "eat dust" behind fifty or a hundred pack animals, nor was it any pleasanter to be at the wrong end of the line when a northerner was blowing across the western prairies.

Under this system Smith delivered his men and goods to Cache Valley and Salt Lake, where they were divided into two camps: one was at the mouth of the Weber River, while Smith, with Jim and the other half of the outfit, located northward at the mouth of the Bear.

The severe winter had driven the Indians to the Salt Lake Valley also, and there was a total of 600 to 800 men, women, and children living in a sort of winter fair. Not many days passed but what some event livened the drudgery of working the traplines. Old chiefs, jealous of their prerogatives, must put some young upstarts in their place; white men, jealous of their assumed superiority, must try to prove it by some feat of derring-do; husbands and young bloods, jealous of their women, must defend their beds against the not always uninvited guests.

And there were always the horse raids. This source of constant friction was caused by the fact that the Indian and white man looked upon horse-stealing from opposite poles. The frontiersman seldom had a surplus of animals, and the theft of a horse might mean the difference between wealth and bankruptcy, life or death. A horse was the Indian's war companion and beast of burden, too, but it was also his token of wealth, his status item. To lose one or many constituted little more than a loss of prestige which could readily be repaired by stealing them (or others) back—all of which was prime fun.

In short, to the white man horse-stealing deserved death; to the Indian it was a war sport, deserving only the boos of defeat or the cheers of success. These irreconcilable views fathered much of the white man's hate for the Indian.

As the winter of 1825–1826 wore on and the short days and long nights mounted to boredom, a band of Bannocks slipped into Sublette's camp and stole eighty horses.

Sublette yelled for Fitzpatrick and Jim Bridger, and then roused forty others from their blankets and sent them charging after the thieves.

Of course Jim Beckwith went. Despite his tall yarns, dull history verifies that Beckwith actually did take part in many of the happenings about which he wove his stories, albeit perhaps in a less heroic role than he pretended. In the present case he *was* with Bridger.

Since it is impossible to cover a trail left by eighty horses, it was no trouble to find them. Bridger and Jim were detailed to stampede the animals while Fitzpatrick and his crew kept the Indians busy: "we succeeded in getting off with the number of our own missing, and forty head besides. In the engagement, six of the enemy were killed and scalped, while not one of our party received a scratch." [*][1]

---

[*] Peter Skene Ogden says that the Indians made good their escape (*Snake Country Journals,* London, Hudson's Bay Record Society, 1950, pp. 173, 180). Harrison Clifford Dale and Dale E. Morgan both appear to credit Jim's story even while noting Ogden's denial (Dale, *The Ashley-Smith Explorations and*

Following the above diversion, a band of several hundred Snakes moved in with the Americans, and Jim Beckwith's future pattern of life began to emerge. He had an affinity for the red man, and little by little he was becoming like an Indian. But he was not yet quite ready openly to forswear allegiance to civilization. There were to be a few more months of routine work and adventure with the mountain men before he deserted them for his life with the Crows. Throughout the winter he did his share of trapping and more than his share of story-telling.

After the winter catch, the whole colony, whites and Indians, returned to Cache Valley, where an episode took place that points up the mountain man's grim sense of humor coupled with practical operations.

As the deep hole was being dug to cache the pelts until they could be moved to market, one of the hands, named Marshall, was buried alive by a sudden cave-in. No effort was made to rescue him. They *"Believed* [him] to have been instantly killed, *knew* him to be well buried. . . . cache destroyed. . . . therefore left him 'Unknelled, uncoffined, ne'er to rise, Till Gabriel's trumpet shakes the skies'."[2]

About now, Jim renewed his contract with the Ashley-Smith Company for another year at $500† plus the right to acquire the widow of the "uncoffined" Marshall. She was, said Jim, "light complexioned, smart, trim and active. . . . I had never had a servant before, and I found her of great service in keeping my clothes in repair, making my bed, and taking care of my weapons."[3]

A rendezvous was set for June of 1826 in the Ogden Valley, and

---

the Discovery of a Central Route to the Pacific, Cleveland, Arthur H. Clark Co., 1918, pp. 166–167; Morgan, *Jedediah Smith and the Opening of the West,* Indianapolis, Bobbs-Merrill Co., 1953, p. 180). Indian "battles" often resulted in extremely light casualties: "Mr. Finan McDonald fired forty five shots, killed two men and wounded one, the other two each fired forty three balls, and each wounded one man . . . ," said the report of one such frontier battle (see David Thompson, *David Thompson's Narrative of His Explorations in Western America, 1784–1812,* ed. J. B. Tyrrell, Toronto, Champlain Society, 1916, p. 425).

† Three hundred dollars a year was considered good wages, but considerably more was sometimes paid. The Sublette-Campbell Company gave their interpreters $500 to $600, and the American Fur Company was reported to have paid Beckwith $800. (See Hiram Martin Chittenden, *The American Fur Trade of the Far West,* 2 vols., Stanford, Academic Reprints, 1954, I, 351; II, 691.)

the trappers again divided into four parties. One set out to explore the shores of Great Salt Lake. Fitzpatrick, Jim, and a small crew went off to trap the Bear and its tributaries. Jed Smith headed for the wilds north and west of Great Salt Lake, into the Salt Desert, to Salmon Falls Creek, down the south branch of the Snake, north to Boise River and Payette Lake, back to Boise River, and thence to the Malade (Big Wood), Henry's Fork of the Snake, the Tetons, Jackson Hole, and Cache Valley. The itinerary of the remaining trappers may be generalized by saying that one or another of the crews worked the Interior Basin, the tributaries of the Snake, the Snake itself, and the Portneuf.

Early in the spring the Americans fell in with Peter Skene Ogden's men from the Flathead Lake area where the Hudson's Bay Company had a post, and by mutual agreement the Americans worked up the Portneuf and the Britishers downstream.

Later, when a courier arrived with the news that Ashley himself was near, both Americans and Englishmen moved back to Great Salt Lake. There Ashley eventually sold out to the Smith-Jackson-Sublette combination and retired from the mountain fur trade, except for an agreement to supply his successors with their supplies.

Sublette made an extensive run into Blackfoot country: North Fork of the Snake, Henry's Fork, around the Tetons, Jackson Hole, the sources of the Snake, over the divide to Yellowstone Lake, and back to Cache Valley.

Sublette and Black Harris then left for St. Louis, on January 1, 1827. They arrived the first week in March only to find that Ashley was organizing a new company to compete with his late partners, although they believed he had agreed to supply no one but themselves with mountain goods. It was very near a doublecross, and it did not sit well with men who believed in firm, uncomplicated human relations. Although the deal eventually fell through because Ashley said he had no intentions to reenter the mountains personally, the affair left an uneasy note in St. Louis and unpleasant questions of business integrity for historians either to resolve or to ignore.

The rendezvous of 1827 was at Bear Lake, Utah, and Jim Beckwith was on hand.[4] To the benefit of his later storytelling, trouble was not long aborning.

Many hundreds of Indians were encamped at the mountain fair, and three Snakes and two squaws were out digging roots a short distance from camp when they were surprised and scalped by a party of Blackfeet.

The Battle of Bear Lake was on.

Daniel Potts, one of the mountain men, recorded his version of the battle in a letter published in the *Philadelphia Gazette and Daily Advertizer* on July 8, 1827:

... a party of 120 Blckfeet approached the camp and killed a Snake Indian and his squaw. The alarm was immediately given and the Snakes, Utaws and whites sallied forth for battle. . . . the enemy fled to a small concavity thickly grown with small timber surrounded by open ground. In this engagement the squaws were busily engaged in throwing up batteries and dragging off the dead. There were only six whites engaged in this battle, who immediately advanced within pistol shot and you may be assured that almost every shot counted one. The loss to the Snakes was three killed and the same number wounded; that of the whites, one wounded and two narrowly made their escape; that of the Utaws was none, though they gained great applause for their bravery. The loss of the enemy is not known—six were found dead on the ground. a great number besides were carried off on horses.

Jim's description, of course, had a more lurid flavor:

One Indian issuing from their position was shot through the back bone, thus depriving his legs of all power of motion. . . . Sublette said to me, "Jim, let us go and haul him away, and get his scalp before the Indians draw him in." We went, and, seizing each a leg, started toward our lines with him: the wounded Indian grasping the grass with both hands, we had to haul with all our strength. An Indian suddenly springing over their breastwork, struck me a heavy blow in the back with his gun, causing me to lose hold of my leg and run. Both I and my companion were unarmed; and I, not knowing how many blows were to follow, deemed discretion . . . the better part of valor. Sublette made a strong demonstration against my assailant with his fists, at the same time calling me back and cursing me for running. I returned, and, together, we dragged the Indian to one of our men, also wounded, for him to dispatch. But the poor fellow had not sufficient strength to perforate the Indian's skin with his knife, and we were obliged to perform the job ourselves. [5]

The battle raged for six hours, said Jim, after which everyone got hungry and went to camp to eat! Sublette asked his Indian allies, the Snakes, to keep the pressure on the Blackfeet until the Americans could return, but for some reason the Snakes were hungry too and joined the trappers at the camp. After supper everyone returned to the fun but the Blackfeet had gone.

Perhaps they were hungry.

Jim's score: 173 scalps; quantities of quivers, war clubs, battle-axes, lances, and horses killed; seven or eight whites wounded, none seriously; and eleven Snakes dead, plus the five who started it all!

Such a victory demanded a rousing scalp dance.

In the late summer of 1827, the Blackfeet indicated they would accept a trading party. The following spring Sublette, Beckwith, and probably several former Hudson's Bay Company men started for the headwaters of the Missouri. On arrival there was some friction, but twenty days later Sublette was back at Bear River with thirty-nine packs of prime fur and not a few good horses.[6]

Referring to this trip, Jim said, "I soon rose to be a great man among them, and the chief offered me his daughter as a wife. . . . I accepted his offer, and, without any superfluous ceremony, became son-in-law to As-as-to, the head chief of all the Blackfeet."[7]

Very rapidly now Jim Beckwith was loosening his few remaining ties with the white world. Still, he returned with Sublette to the Salt Lake basin, and was on hand in the spring of 1828 when Robert Campbell and eighteen men with their squaws and children returned from their own successful cruise into Blackfoot territory. When news of Campbell's approach reached camp, Jim, Provost, and one Jarvey rode out to meet him. The parties camped overnight together, and were riding leisurely toward the main camp when they heard voices to their rear.

"Approaching within a short distance, to our horror and surprise we discovered they were Blackfeet, a tribe who prize white scalps very highly," said Jim.[8]

Campbell hastily ordered his women and children to a grove of willows a few miles ahead.

By this time the Indians had commenced charging upon us. . . . Situated as we were it was impossible for them to surround us, for we had a lake on one side and a mountain on the other. They knew, however, that we must emerge into the open country, where their chance of attack would be improved.

The firing continued between both parties during the whole time of our retreat to the willows; in fact, it was a running fight through the whole six miles. On the way we lost one man, quite old. He might have saved himself by riding to the front and I repeatedly urged him to do so, telling him that he could not assist us; but he refused even to spur on his horse when the Indians made their charges. I tarried with him, urging him on, until I found it would be certain death to delay longer. My horse had scarcely made three leaps in advance when I heard him cry, "Oh God, I am wounded!" Wheeling my horse, I called upon my companions to save him. I returned to him, and found an arrow trembling in his back. I jerked it out, and gave his horse several blows to quicken his pace; but the poor old man reeled and fell from his steed, and the Indians were upon him in a moment to tear off his scalp. This delay nearly cost us two more lives for myself and Jarvey were surrounded with Blackfeet, and their triumphant yells told us they felt certain of their prey. Our only chance of escape was to leap a slough fifteen feet from bank to bank, which we vaulted at full speed. One Indian followed us, but he was shot in the back directly upon reaching the bank, and back he rolled into the ditch. We passed around the slough in order to rejoin our companions, but in doing so we were compelled to charge through a solid rank of Indians. We passed with the rapidity of pigeons, escaping without damage . . . although a shower of arrows and bullets whistled all around us. As we progressed their charges became more frequent and daring; our ammunition now grew very short, and we never used a charge without we were sure of its paying for itself.

At length we gained the willows. . . . Eroquey proposed one bold charge for the sake of the women and children. . . . "If we are to die, let us fall in protecting the defenseless." . . .

Sixteen of us mounted our horses, leaving the remainder to hold out to the last. Eroquey led the charge. . . . We broke through two ranks of mounted Indians, killing . . . everything in our way. . . . My beautiful horse was killed in his tracks . . . leaving me alone among a throng of Indians. I was wounded with an arrow in the head. . . . My boy Baptiste, seeing my danger, called upon his comrades to assist him to save his brother. They charged a second time. . . . Baptiste rode up to me; I sprang on the saddle behind him, and retreated in safety to the willows. . . .

To hold out much longer was impossible. Immediate assistance must be had, and it could come from no other place than our camp. To risk a message there seemed to subject the messenger to inevitable death. . . . "Who will go?" . . . I was wounded, but not severely; and, at a time so pressing, I hardly knew I was wounded at all. "Give me a swift horse, and I will try to force my way. Do not think I am anxious to leave you in your perilous position."

"You will run the greatest risk. . . . take the best horse."

Campbell said that two had better go, for there might be a better chance of one living to reach camp. Calhoun volunteered . . . if he had his choice of horses, to which no one raised any objection. Disrobing ourselves . . . to the Indian costume . . . we mounted our horses fleet as the wind, and bade the little band adieu.

. . . we dashed through the ranks of the foe before they had time to comprehend our movement. The balls and arrows flew around us like hail, but we escaped uninjured. . . . When about five miles from camp we saw a party of our own men approaching. . . . We . . . signaled to them . . . for haste, and then that it was a fight. . . . one man wheeled and returned to the camp. . . . soon the road was lined with men, all hurrying along with the utmost speed of the animals they bestrode. My companion and I returned . . . and, breaking once more through the enemy's line, rode back into the willows, amid the cheers of our companions. . . . The Indians were surprized at seeing a re-inforcement. . . . They instantly gave up the battle and commenced a retreat. . . .

On our side we lost four men killed and seven wounded. Not a woman or child was injured. From the enemy we took seventeen scalps, most of them near the willows; those that we killed on the road we could not stop for. We were satisfied that they had more than a hundred slain. . . .

After attending our wounded, we all proceeded to camp, where the scalp dance was performed by all the half-breeds and women, many of the mountaineers taking part in the dance.[9]

During the season of 1828–1829, Campbell led another brigade northward, this time to the Crows. There were thirty-one men including Jim Beckwith and Caleb Greenwood—a not inconsiderable liar in his own right, as we shall see.

It was to be Beckwith's last journey for several years as a civilized mountain man.

It is easy for us now to forget that if Beckwith had returned to St. Louis, he could never have hoped to be anything but what he was, a mulatto ex-slave. The Civil War with its promise of freedom for all men, white and black, was many years in the future, and when it came it would bring precious little boon for the like of Jim Beckwith.

No wonder, then, that when Caleb Greenwood thought to have some fun by telling a band of Crows that Jim was the son of a Crow chief stolen from his tribe by the Cheyennes and later acquired and raised by the whites, among whom he was now a great chief—no wonder that Jim explored quite seriously the advantages he would derive by not denying the silly story.

"I said to myself, I can trap in their streams unmolested, and derive more profit under their protection than if among my own men, exposed incessantly to assassination and alarm. I therefore resolved to abide with them, to guard my secret, to do my best in their company, and in assisting them to subdue their enemies."[10]

Whether Jim ever discussed these thoughts with his trail mates is unknown, but we do know that on January 6, 1829, he signed, with his mark, a promissory note as follows:

"On settlement of all accounts up to this date with Smith-Jackson-Sublette there appears a Balance due by me to them of Two hundred and Seventy five Dollars 17½¢ which I promise to pay in good merchantable Beaver Furr at Three Dollars per pound for value received."*[11]

Jim's version of his entry into Crow life is that he was on a trapping excursion with Jim Bridger when he stumbled into a band of Crow horses and was seized by the horse guards. Bridger, not knowing the guards were Crows or that Beckwith would acquiesce in the Caleb Greenwood swindle, reported Beckwith as captured and presumably killed.

That evening the white camp celebrated Jim's demise with appropriate remarks of affection.

In the meantime, he later said, he was actually being marched

---

* There is an apparent conflict in dates here. The promissory note of 1829 seems to imply that Beckwith was just then leaving his association with his white comrades, and Dale E. Morgan evidently accepts that interpretation: he places Beckwith at the Battle of Bear Lake in 1827, with Sublette on a trip to the Blackfeet in the spring of 1828, and with Robert Campbell on a tour of the Crows in 1828–1829 (*Jedediah Smith and the Opening of the West*, Indianapolis, Bobbs-Merrill Co., 1953, pp. 228, 234, 291, 301, 306). On the other hand, Bernard DeVoto places Beckwith's adoption by the Crows in 1826 (Introduction, in T. D. Bonner, *The Life and Adventures of James P. Beckwourth*, New York, Alfred A. Knopf, 1931, p. xxiv; Bonner, p. 392). So many possible explanations of these seeming contradictions are at hand that it is feasible only to note they exist.

before Crow chiefs, where he was proclaimed the very man Greenwood had told them about. An old woman shuffled up to Jim, peered intently at his face, and remarked, "If this is my son, he has a mole just over one of his eyes."

". . . sure enough, she discovered a mole . . . over my left eye!"[12]

Now there was a great to-do. Jim was hustled off to the lodge of his "father." His "brothers," "sisters," "aunts," "uncles," and others of every possible degree of relationship jammed into the lodge, and "my face positively burned with the enraptured kisses of my numerous fair sisters. . . ." These ladies immediately stripped Jim of his soiled clothing, outfitted him in their best needlework, built him a high bed as a token of their esteem and his new position, and again trotted him before his "father," who inquired if he would like a wife.

"I assented, of course."

Three beautiful sisters, daughters of a great brave, were presented for Jim's choice. He chose Still Water, the eldest.

The marriage ceremony was complete.

Jim's "brothers" supplied him with horses; he went with a war party; he drew first blood; he counted coups;* he joined the scalp dances and was accepted into the secret military clique, the Dog Soldiers.[13]

Jim Beckwith was a Crow.

---

* Counting coups involved a semisocial, semiserious talk fest or bull session, at which the main purpose was to boast of past deeds of valor. The hunt and particularly the collecting of scalps were invariably featured. These sessions were often preliminary to a horse raid, a buffalo hunt, or a war party. And of course the brave who could count the most coups when he got back was the biggest hero—something like an aviator or submarine commander boasting of "kills" and "near misses."

ABSAROKA,
HOME OF THE CROWS

Circa 1830

ABSAROKA, home of the Sparrowhawk People—Crow land, lying high and serene along the Yellowstone, the Powder, the Rosebud, and the Big Horn.

It was and is an untamed and enchanted land, this Absaroka, where the Sparrowhawks gave their war cries, chanted their death songs, and fought their inveterate foes, the Blackfeet. This land, on whose far edge the Morning Glory pool shimmers and Old Faithful booms; where over the southwest shoulder the Tetons climb, jagged and magnificent, and Jackson Hole once served as the crossroads for all the mountain trade; where eastward lie the Black Hills and Sturgis, Lead, Spearfish, and Deadwood, which one day built museums to preserve the flavor of their past, and where modern pilgrims may watch, on summer nights, the Passion Play retell the story of the crucifixion; where eastward, too, old layers of mud and sand and gravel, sandstone and clay, iron oxide and fossils bespeak the burial ground of climates and animals and rivers long gone, and time and the winds have chiseled the Mauvaises Terres of the French voyageur, the Mako Sico of the Dakotas—the Bad Lands of the white man. This land, where the Crows hunted wild stallions down Shoshone Canyon and the western sun still floods the crags with every color; where quiet lakes and rushing rivers and unclimbed mountains and soft meadows and mighty quakes dwarfed both red man and white, but made them fiercely jealous of this Absaroka, this home of the Crows.

They were a friendly and tolerant lot, these Indians of Siouan stock, and their love of horseflesh approached a passion. But for all these softer virtues, the Crows were noble warriors, good hunters, and fine craftsmen in the military arts. They tempered an intricate ceremonial system with a penchant for earthy humor; and their women were superb artists with leather and beads, and sometimes planted corn, although they usually left nature to finish the task, for they were a restless and nomadic tribe.

Absaroka and such people exactly suited the young, fiery, turbulent Jim Beckwith.

Very shortly after moving to Absaroka, Beckwith was marking "J.B." on his own pelts and receiving an invitation to visit James Kipp in charge of Fort Clark, Indian trading post among the Mandans and Gros Ventres. This meeting initiated a long and generally harmonious connection with Kipp and his company. Beckwith became their secret agent among his Crows, maintaining a relationship of dual loyalties which the Indians never fully understood.

Even here, however, Jim could not refrain from embellishing the facts. He stated that Kenneth McKenzie, Astor's factor at Fort Union at the mouth of the Yellowstone, had heard of the "Enemy of Horses" and commissioned him to establish Fort Cass, or Tullock's Fort, as it was often called, three miles below the mouth of the Big Horn— which pretense by Jim is pure balderdash, of course. He had nothing to do with the founding of Fort Cass, and Samuel Tullock, who did, was never under Jim's orders in the slightest degree. Tullock took his orders from the Astor-Chouteau Company.*

Actually, Jim had all he could do to serve effectively as silent agent among the Crows. For a few weeks at a time he could keep his Indians tending traps; but before long the excitement of war and their love of horses would overcome all good resolves, and one by one the braves would steal out at night in search of new adventure. In truth, Jim often led these forays, partly to maintain his prestige and partly because he too could not remain quiet.

It was from one such excursion that he returned to the Laramie Forks and told what may have been a version of Abraham's sacrifice of Isaac. But somehow Jim twisted it about until he was the hero and arrived with fourteen scalps, earning the sobriquet "the Bloody Arm."

---

* Tullock was a subleader for the Smith-Jackson-Sublette Company in 1828. (See Frederick Merk, *Fur Trade and Empire*, Cambridge, Mass., Harvard University Press, 1931, p. 299.)

Only a few of the many adventures claimed by Beckwith during his life with the Crows can be outlined here. We must pass quickly over the valiant rescues, the horse raids, and the war parties—each of which brought him a new tribal name: the Morning Star, Antelope, Big Bowl, or the Enemy of Horses. We can note only in passing his conquest of Red Cherry, wife of Big Rain, and the floggings, decreed by Crow laws, until his Dog Soldiers stopped the lash and said that since Jim would not desist in his seductions and Red Cherry appeared so willing, Big Rain would just have to yield to a better man; or the little girl who begged him to take her to wife so she could paint her face as the big girls did, and the "little innocent used such powerful appeals that, notwithstanding I had already seven wives—I told her she might be my wife"[1]—after she outgrew her childhood.

Despite such boastful nonsense, it was a pleasure listening to Jim Beckwith lie, for he could take an authentic event and embellish it with his own details until it became a "new" story. Three of his most famous efforts in this respect were his versions of the death of Ed Rose, John Colter's escape from the Blackfeet, and the storming of the Blackfoot fortress by a mulatto chief among the Crows. The first and last of these tales bear partial repetition here.

How Ed Rose, Hugh Glass, and one or two companions died by suicide in a gigantic blast of gunpowder set off by Rose himself has been told elsewhere.

Shortly thereafter Johnson Gardner, a free trapper, in company with some twenty other men, ran into the band of Arikaras who had ambushed the Rose-Glass party. The Rees pretended to be Minnetarees, but Gardner was suspicious. Just as the Indians were about to stampede the Gardner horses, he seized three of them and found Glass's gun and hunting knife in their possession. They were shot without qualm.

But Jim could easily improve on such simple facts. Laying the usual improbable background of personal involvement, Jim gets into full stride as he approaches Gardner's camp and cries out, "Hallo the camp! Dont shoot boys! I am Jim Beckwourth." Riding forward, he finds Gardner with three Rees bound in trap chains and a great log fire in full blaze.

"They opened the logs on top of the fire, and, swinging the . . . victims into the flames, rolled back the burning logs. There was a terrible struggle for a moment; then all was still. A blue flame towered high above the pile, and quickly subsided."[2]

Ed Rose and Hugh Glass were avenged according to the gospel of Jim Beckwith.

Regarding the second incident, it is unlikely that anyone will ever know positively whether it was Ed Rose or Jim Beckwith who stood one day watching the Crows try to dislodge the Blackfeet from their fortress with so little success that they were about to give up in disgust. Each mulatto has his partisans among historians of the Old West, who are agreed only that the story is probably based on fact, is dramatic, and is in the full flavor of either man.

As Jim told the story, it was he who heard Long Hair, the Crow chief, recommend that his warriors retreat since the Blackfeet had found an impregnable position.

Said Jim, "I replied, 'No! Hold! Warriors listen! If these old man cannot fight let them retire with the women and children.'"

The Great Spirit, said he, had sent the Blackfeet to them, and He would be offended if the Crows failed to slaughter them.

"Enemy of Horses, lead us, and we will follow you to the spirit land," replied the braves.

Deploying part of his warriors to divert the Blackfeet while he scaled the rocky walls with his chosen few, Jim led the attack:

When I sprang for the summit of the wall, I found that my women were holding my belt; I cut it loose with my knife and left it in their hands. I was the first on the wall, but was immediately followed by scores of warriors. . . . The carnage for some minutes was fearful, and the Blackfeet fought with desperation, knowing their inevitable doom if taken. The clash of battle-axes, and the yells of the opposing combatants were truly appalling. Many leaped to the wall only to meet their certain doom below, where hundreds of battle-axes and lances were ready to drink their blood as soon as they touched the ground. The interior surface of this huge rock was concave, and the blood all ran to the center, where it formed a pool, which emitted a sickening smell as the warm vapor ascended to our nostrils. It was the work of great difficulty to keep one's feet, as the mingled gore and brains were scattered everywhere round this fatal place. The blood of the Crow and the Blackfeet mingled together in this common pool, for many of our warriors fell in this terrible strife.

All was silent within a few minutes after we had gained an entrance. Victims who were making away with their bowels ripped open were instantly felled with the battle-axe and stilled in death. . . . Upwards of forty Crows were killed, and double the number wounded. There were engaged on the side of the Crows about twenty white men, and only one was wounded, though nearly all scaled the wall with the Indians.

Our spoils were one hundred and sixty scalps, and an immense quantity of guns and ammunition, a large amount of dried meats, with arrows, lances, knives, in great abundance.[3]

Jim Beckwith was now "the Medicine Calf," head chief in the land of Absaroka.

"I was on the pinnacle of my fame."[4]

JIM TIRES OF ABSAROKA

Circa 1834

IN 1833 Jim went to Fort Bonneville on the upper Green for the summer rendezvous. Perhaps he went as a free trapper, or he may have gone as representative of the American Fur Company. For beyond his boasting, he was in fact on their payroll for most of the years he lived in Absaroka, and he made repeated trips to Fort Cass on company business.

The end of the mountain fairs was near. Cutthroat competition, Indian debauchery with liquor, a ruthless depletion of the beaver, and changing fashions were writing finis to the most romantic and dangerous era of western American history. The inexorable drive of civilization had thrown a cordon of towns and forts and laws around the mountain fastnesses, and that last stand of pure, uninhibited freedom would soon succumb to a choking influx of missionaries and immigrants unlimited.

And Jim Beckwith felt the strangling shadow. Then too, he was becoming tired of the incessant bloodshed of Indian wars; tired of the wailing, tired of faces painted for defeats in "battles" too trivial to remember, tired of mutilated hands with fingers chopped off for the death of every relative, tired even of the plurality of wives, who had become something of a bore.

But just as it took Jim some time to renounce civilization, so now he was only vaguely uneasy, and repudiation of the Crows was not to come yet.

As the fame of the mountain fairs spread throughout the world, many people attended them who had nothing to do with the fur business. Big game hunters, tuberculosis sufferers, artists, and scientists came to see the most exciting shows ever staged in North America.

This summer of 1833 Dr. Benjamin Harrison, son of the war hero and President, was in the mountains for reasons of health. And Sir William Drummond Stewart, of Murthy Castle, Scotland, led the first of his suspiciously large "hunting parties" which filtered into the lands between 42 and 49 degrees north during the very years England and the United States were contesting for the Oregon country.

The Rocky Mountain Fur Company, which included Thomas Fitzpatrick, Milton E. Sublette, Jim Bridger, Henry Fraeb, and Jean Baptiste Gervais, had taken over from the Smith-Jackson-Sublette combine, and it had not had a good year thus far in 1833.[1] The Astor-Chouteau interests had more than 150 men in the mountains with more capital, more liquor, and perhaps less ethics.

Hoping to put off monopoly by Astor-Chouteau, Fitzpatrick made an agreement with his latest competitor, a combination of Robert Campbell and William Sublette backed by Ashley money. Campbell was bringing supplies to Fitzpatrick, and Sublette was building Fort William almost on the doorstep of Fort Union at the mouth of the Yellowstone. This location was economically untenable and was almost immediately abandoned, and a new Fort William was put up at the mouth of the Laramie.

Jim Beckwith had nothing to do with any of these decisions. But he told his own version of the several changes in order to make himself the prime mover and hero of a dastardly attack on Fitzpatrick which in truth did take place.

On a trip to the Crows, Fitzpatrick was robbed of 100 horses, all his goods, some pelts, and even his personal clothes and watch. It is almost certain that the attack, although committed by Indians, was ordered by McKenzie of the Astor-Chouteau Company and that Jim, Tullock, and S. P. Winter, all Company employees, used their own methods to incite the Indians to do the dirty work.

McKenzie gleefully reported to Pierre Chouteau at Fort Union on December 10, 1833, "That party can consequently make no hunt this fall." Instead Jim and Winter collected all the choice pelts the Crows had harvested.[2]

But Jim had to exculpate his actions, at least to himself, and so his story of the attack says he was camped peacefully on the Big Horn when he received an invitation to visit Fitzpatrick nearby. Since he could not leave his own duties just then, he suggested that Fitzpatrick come to see him, which he did, setting up camp near the Crow site.

Later Jim visited Fitzpatrick and met Sir William Drummond Stewart, with whom he was not too impressed, considering him somewhat priggish. Fitzpatrick returned Jim's call, and the two had a long, friendly chat about old times when the mountain rendezvous were young. In the course of the evening, Fitzpatrick admitted that he knew certain of Jim's Indians had been killed; but he neglected to admit that his men had been involved. After Fitzpatrick returned to his tent, Jim was asked by one of his Crows what action should be taken toward Fitzpatrick's men. Jim said to treat them as guests.

Nevertheless, next morning Fitzpatrick was brought to Jim as a prisoner. He said at once that he believed all his men had been killed by the Crows and insinuated that Jim would now kill him. On the contrary, said Jim, he would try to save Fitzpatrick as well as any of his men still alive.

Suiting action to promise, Jim sprang to horse and dashed pell-mell to the rescue of the men in the clutches of his angry Crows. Soon Fitzpatrick's men were seen fleeing from the screeching Indians.

"Come to me," shouted Jim, and, since no other action appeared to offer any hope of escape, they obeyed. Over the protests of the scalping party, Jim ordered each white trapper to mount behind a Crow, knowing that tribal law made the warrior responsible for the life of his hostage.

"I will get behind no d——d rascal," said Sir William Drummond Stewart.

Dr. Harrison reminded him they were scarcely in a position to quibble over the manner of their salvation.

Jim then quieted the Crows, collected and returned Fitzpatrick's goods and horses, and told him to ride hard for three days before camping, promising that the Crows would not pursue him that far.

"Instead of following my advice, he camped the following afternoon. Within an hour . . . almost all his horses were taken, not leaving him enough to pack his goods. . . . However, I was satisfied I had done my duty."[3]

Jim Beckwith knew how to twist details to soften the fact that he had robbed Fitzpatrick.

The Blackfeet were a troublesome and unrepentant people, and by 1835 it was apparent that Fort Cass could not be maintained at a profit because of their repeated raids. It was abandoned, and a new post, Fort Van Buren, was built near the mouth of the Tongue.

Jim had nothing to do with this move, either, although he took credit for it, perhaps to offset the effects of certain horse raids and battles in which he had lost more than he had gained. By 1835 these misfortunes had caused a notable diminution in his position among the Crows, and with some fifteen or twenty braves he started on a tour which, quite aside from any bombast about prestige, was a journey of mark.

At least once Jim had visited Bayou Salade, the Tongue River Valley, Clark's Fork of the Yellowstone, the Rosebud, the Laramie Forks, the Mussel Shell, the Assiniboine, the Green, the Big Horn, the Wind, the Sweetwater; and he had gone to the Mandans and crossed and recrossed the mountains more times than he could remember.

But all these journeys were minor in comparison with the one he now undertook to bolster his sagging status.

Down on the headwaters of the Arkansas lived the Arapahoes, rich in horses and far enough away from the Crows that they had no need to fear very serious reprisals.

Jim was off to the Arapahoes. To repeat or even summarize his versions of nighttime raids, hairbreadth escapes, and feats of strength and daring would be to compound boredom. But his itinerary, an item about which he never lied and seldom even exaggerated, deserves repetition.

For more than a year he tramped: from Absaroka to the Arapahoes, 300 miles or more; north to the Snakes nearly twice as far; another 400 miles to the Flatheads and the Kootenais; 900 more to the Mussel Shell, the Assiniboine, and the flanks of Absaroka, and westward across the mountains for winter forage; 500 or 600 miles to recross to spring grass, and up to the Assiniboine again; then into Piegan land in western Montana and back to Absaroka, another 500 miles. With only a short rest Jim went south 800 miles to the Comanches on a horse raid, and returned to Absaroka via the Arkansas, Bayou Salade, the Laramie, and the Sweetwater. The grand total was almost 5,000 miles as the crow flies, and 1,000 more by trail.

Jim Beckwith had camped, trapped, rode, and fought over more of the vast Rocky Mountain realm than probably any other one man. Even Kit Carson, Smith, or Fitzpatrick could lay claim to no more thorough knowledge of the mountains. There was hardly a pass, a beaver pond, a mountain meadow that Jim did not know, either from personal contact or through his Crows. To argue geography with him was to show one's ignorance of both geography and the mulatto.

But, as we said, the end of the mountain fur trade was nearing. Both gross and net business profits were declining, and it was only human to lay the blame on those nearest at hand. And so Jim got a letter from a Mr. Halsey, a longtime employee of the Astor-Chouteau Company and currently in charge at Fort Union, which said in part, "For ——'s sake, do keep your d——d Indians at home, so that other tribes may have a chance to work a little, and the company may drive a more profitable business"[4]—and please report to Fort Union. Jim obeyed, but he was unhappy and increasingly restless. Life had ceased to be a thrill. To kill was no novelty. To scalp was no pleasure. To steal horses was no challenge. Even Crow women and Black Panther, son of the little-girl wife of so many years ago, held no great interest. Life in Absaroka was out of tune:

What had I done? ... it seemed as if I had slumbered away the last twelve years. . . . What had been my career? . . . I had visited the Indian territory to gratify a youthful thirst for adventure; I had narrowly escaped starvation in a service in which I had no interest; I had travelled the fastnesses of the Rocky Mountains in summer heats and winter frosts; I had encountered savage beasts and wild men, until my deliverance was a prevailing miracle. By the mere badinage of a fellow-trapper I had been adopted among the savages. . . . I had accompanied them in their mutual slaughters, and dyed my hand with crimson with the blood of victims who had never injured me; I had distinguished myself in my barbarian seclusion, and had risen to supreme command in the nation I had devoted myself to. And what had I to show for so much wasted energy, and such a catalogue of ruthless deeds?

I resolved to go home and see my friends, and deliver myself from my present vagabond life. The attachments I had formed during my savage chieftainship still retained some hold upon my affections, and it was barely possible I might return to them, and end my days among my trusty braves. There at least was fidelity, and, when my soul should depart for the spirit land their rude faith would prompt them to paint my bones, and treasure them until I should visit them from my ever-flowering hunting ground and demand them from their hands.[5]

The Sparrowhawk people were gathered to hear Jim's decision, and he eased his departure by promising to return when the grass was green. Admonishing the Crows to remain peaceful and trap well, he stepped aboard the last company boat for St. Louis before ice would close the Upper Missouri.

". . . my only wealth consisted of an order upon the company for seven thousand eight hundred dollars."[6]

Since Jim rarely told the truth concerning numbers, this sum may be questioned. Indeed, it would be interesting to know whether his propensity for error in figures was a part of his general love of exaggeration or whether he had no concept of numbers as such.

The Astor-Chouteau boat stopped many times on the way downriver. When it tied up at the Arikara towns, there was a brawl between Jim, with three of his companions, and two sons of "old Garro," doubtless Joseph Garreau, long a resident trader-trapper-interpreter on the mid-Missouri. Just when the fight was becoming interesting, the elder Garreau grabbed a club and flailed mightily against his own half-breed sons and their Ree friends—all the while giving them a tongue-lashing for daring to threaten bodily harm to white men.

And on this note of mild adventure, Jim Beckwith coasted into St. Louis more than a decade after he had last seen its quayside hovels and plantation mansions.

38

PINE LEAF

ONE more phase of Jim's life with the Crows warrants cursory consideration: his loves with Absaroka women. He admits to many "marriages" but says little about any particular woman except for the "little innocent" child bride, who eventually bore him Black Panther, and Pine Leaf, the Crow amazon, who was almost certainly pure fiction, but fiction with a true Beckwith coloring.

His story goes that as a girl Pine Leaf swore she would never marry until she had personally killed 100 enemy warriors to avenge the death of her twin brother. When she reached adulthood, she eschewed feminine life, became equal to any Crow warrior, went on war parties and had a good start on her 100 scalps when her lithe figure caught Jim's wandering eye.

She replied, "You have too many already." But she agreed to come to him when the pine needles turned yellow. It was some time before Jim remembered that pine needles never turn yellow. He accepted the teasing but kept up his suit, and she made a new promise—she would come when he found a red-haired Indian.

It is all rather fun. She knows how to tease, to be a woman, and wield a mighty battle-ax. She kills Jim's captives, the sooner to reach her 100 scalps; she saves his life when an arrow fells his horse; when Jim rides a Blackfoot down, Pine Leaf pins him to the ground with her lance, slashes off his scalp, and says with a smile, "Ride on, I have him safe now";[1] and she is along on the day Johnson Gardner tosses the writhing villains into the fire to avenge Ed Rose and Hugh Glass.

But the years pass, and the pine needles never turn yellow, and Jim has found no red-haired Indian, and the virgin Pine Leaf still sends the hot blood racing through mulatto veins; and he vows he will never marry again until she comes to him.

Then, time runs out, and Jim is strolling the dusty streets of St.

Louis, alone and more than a little downhearted. Eliza got tired of waiting and has married another; his old friends are gone; new slaves tend new plantations and sweep new back porches; his brothers and sisters have moved or been sold to new masters in other parts of the Missouri-Mississippi world. Only two sisters* remain to welcome him home, and there is really very little to say. They would not understand the war and rapine, the blood and thieving, the lust and loves of the mountains, so Jim touches but lightly on the years just gone.

General Ashley welcomes him cordially, but their worlds are too far apart—Jim is still a mulatto ex-slave, and General Ashley is a member of Congress from Missouri. It is with genuine relief that Jim receives a dispatch from Tullock urging him to return to Fort Van Buren to quiet his braves, who believe he has been killed by his white brothers and are determined to avenge his death by wiping out the Fort. In the nick of time Jim rescues his friends and greets Pine Leaf, Little Wife, and Black Panther, their son.

Now Pine Leaf stands before her people.

Warriors, I am now about to make a great sacrifice for my people. For many winters I have been on the war path with you; I shall tread that path no more. . . .

I said I would kill one hundred foes before I would marry any living man. I have more than kept my word. . . . I have fought my last battle, and hurled my last lance; I am a warrior no more.

Today the Medicine Calf has returned . . . angry at the follies of his people, and they fear he will again leave them. . . . I therefore bestow myself upon him; perhaps he will be content with me, and will leave us no more. Warriors, farewell!

"She then approached me," said Jim; "she placed her hand under my chin, and lifted my head forcibly up."

"Look at me," she said. "I know your heart is crying for the follies of the people. But let it cry no more. . . . And now, my friend, I am yours after you have so long been seeking me . . . our lodge shall be a happy one. . . ."

"This was my last marriage in the Crow nation."[2]

Jim led his warriors on a raid for old times' sake. On returning he

---

* But Jim later referred to a "brother's house"; see Chapter 40.

told them he must again leave them because they had called him away from St. Louis before his business there was complete. He promised to be gone no more than four seasons.

"Pine Leaf inquired if I would certainly come back. I assured her that, if life was preserved to me, I would. I had been married but five weeks when I left, and I have never seen her since.

"I was tired of savage life under any aspect."[3]

With the recitation of this sentimental bit, Jim Beckwith returned to civilization.

39

BECKWITH FIGHTS THE
SEMINOLES

1833–1838

WERE the saga of Jim Beckwith to be told in the classic pattern, it would close with his departure from Pine Leaf (assuming that she existed at all) and his renunciation of Absaroka. After that date, his story becomes increasingly indefinite and his professed deeds more difficult to check—and less interesting.

After his departure from the Crows, he remained in St. Louis only until he became aware of United States Army activities against the Seminoles. These were the years of the Second Seminole War, and Beckwith says he took part in the most famous fight of the war, the Battle of Okeechobee, and there is no valid reason to believe he did not. An examination of his version of the engagement against those of recent biographers of Zachary Taylor and historians of the war shows only such differences of opinion and detail as may well be expected from eyewitnesses.

And so, excepting the exaggerations of his personal heroics, perhaps we should accept Jim's story, supplementing it as necessary from modern authorities.

In 1833 four chiefs purporting to represent several groups of Florida Indians, mulattoes, and escaped Negro slaves signed the Treaty of Fort Gibson, in which they promised to vacate central Florida to the white man. When the treaty was repudiated on the ground that the chiefs had no right to commit their people without tribal consent, the War Department sent Brevet Brigadier General Duncan L. Clinch with ten companies of regulars to enforce the agreement.

The dissentients, headed by the Seminoles, resisted, and shortly

St. Louis, 1848. *State Historical Society of Missouri, Columbia.*

Jim Beckwith's Seminole War theater.

thereafter their famous chief, Osceola, took general command of their forces. Osceola was another of the half-breeds who at one time or another were dominant figures on the American frontier. His father was a white man named Powell. His mother, the daughter of an escaped Negress slave,[1] had been thrown into jail for some fancied offense, and when Osceola objected, he too was seized. Pretending submission, he obtained his release, and then rallied his allies and set about making the white man pay for his insolence.

Three days after Christmas, 1835, Osceola met Major Francis Langhorne Dade in a pitched battle northeast of Tampa Bay on the east side of the Withlacoochee River, and killed 107 of Dade's 110 officers and men. The "Dade massacre" became a battle cry, and the War Department was in a tizzy to avenge the loss of face.

Generals Clinch, Winfield Scott, and Edmund P. Gaines (the latter two such deadly personal enemies they refused to cooperate in any way) were all unable to disassociate their battle plans from the Army rule books, with the result that Osceola, who had never heard of the rules, fought them to a standstill on his swamplands. The generals were replaced by Colonel Thomas Sidney Jesup.

Jesup, being something less of a robot than his predecessors, had sufficient success against the tribal leaders Osceola, Jumper, Alligator, and Micanopy that the last-named three came into Fort Brooke at the head of Tampa Bay and promised obedience to the government.

Osceola and Sam Jones, another native leader, hinted they too might surrender. Jesup relaxed his pressure, and the wily Indians used the breathing spell to plant corn, round up their cattle and horses, recruit more adherents, and prepare to resume the conflict.

In the meantime, Jesup violated a flag of truce and seized Osceola, Micanopy, and 200 others.

The United States Army code of honor did not apply to Indians.

Up at St. Louis, Jim Beckwith found himself a stranger in his old city, and was wandering restlessly about wondering what to do next when the Army (St. Louis was western headquarters for most Army business) posted a call for volunteers to serve in Florida. Two or more companies of mounted muleteers, scouts, spies, and common soldiers were to be recruited.

In later years Jim claimed that his old employer, William L. Sublette, told General Gaines about the very special abilities of Jim Beckwith, and the General promised a captaincy and "renown" in return for his knowledge of Indian ways. Jim pretended aversion to further bloodshed, but boasted that it was he who raised most of one of the two companies.

And he may have induced a considerable number of footloose adventurers to join the volunteers. Jim Beckwith could weave a mighty spell, and it takes no great strain on the imagination to see him lounging against a horse trough down on the fringe of the segregated district, holding forth on the fun and glory of scalping Indians.

As for his being an officer, it is inconceivable that a mulatto would have been allowed to command a white company during those years of bitter slavery controversy.

Nine days after his arrival in St. Louis, Jim was aboard ship heading for New Orleans and Tampa Bay. During the latter leg of the trip, he pictured himself the hero in a supposed shipwreck.

Colonel Zachary Taylor did indeed land in Tampa Bay en route from New Orleans in the autumn of 1837, accompanied by 1,000 or more men and their heavy baggage; but he mentioned neither shipwreck nor Jim. However, Jim did not claim he was with Taylor. Instead he insinuated that before Taylor arrived, he was carrying dispatches between Fort Brooke and Colonel Jesup's headquarters at Picolata on the St. John's River, about 150 air miles from Tampa Bay; and that following or during this duty he trained mules at Fort Brooke. After all of this, he said, he was assigned to Taylor's command.

At this juncture we may properly return to the indisputable record.

Taylor planned to set up a chain of small posts and use each of them as a base for the next to pursue the Seminoles into their swamps until they could neither maneuver nor retreat. He would then attack and annihilate. Accordingly, he built Fort Fraser, forty miles east of Fort Brooke, and placed Lieutenant Colonel William S. Foster in charge. When this post was ready, Taylor, with the 1st Infantry and eighty wagons commanded by Lieutenant Colonel William Davenport, left Fort Brooke, passed Fort Fraser, and moved twenty-five miles eastward to the Kissimmee River, arriving November 27, 1837. His pontoniers threw a bridge across the stream, his carpenters fashioned Fort Gardiner, and Taylor himself settled down to await the Indian surrenders in which Colonel Jesup so firmly believed.

When they failed to materialize after two weeks, Taylor moved. Seizing a civilian hostage here and a lone warrior there, he compelled them, by what means we should very much like to know, to divulge the whereabouts of chiefs Jumper, Alligator, Sam Jones, Wild Cat, and Micanopy, who had escaped captivity.

Late in December Jumper did surrender, and sometime after the next midnight, Taylor pounced upon Alligator's camp. It was deserted. But he picked up the rumor that the chief was about to surrender, and arranged for a rendezvous several miles farther down the Kissimee River.

At this point Jim Beckwith was having a mildly joyous time. His life was in almost no danger; he had no responsibilities; he needed to maintain no status; and he could play cat and mouse with the Seminoles as much or as little as he pleased, and his officers would overlook.

To Colonel Zachary Taylor and his brother, Captain Joseph P. Taylor, as well as their associate officers, it was not nearly so amusing. For the first time in his life, Zachary Taylor had the responsibility of more than 1,000 officers and men, 727 regulars and 340 volunteers like Jim, men who might do anything or nothing under fire.

The volunteers were commanded by Colonel Richard Gentry and Major Alexander G. Morgan. There were now only twenty miles between the troops and Lake Okeechobee in the cypress swamps, where Sam Jones, Wild Cat, and Alligator lay waiting on a knoll covered with lush palmettos.

When Alligator failed to meet his rendezvous, Taylor erected Fort Bassinger to house his sick and extra supplies. He then crossed the Kissimmee and entered the swamp on the northeast shoulder of Lake Okeechobee with 834 officers and men.

It was a grueling experience for both regulars and volunteers. Even Jim Beckwith had had no acquaintance with this sort of travel. Saw grass cut deep and painfully; bruised feet sank into murky water above which swarmed millions of mosquitoes and in which the deadly water moccasins lurked.

And the enemy was nowhere in sight.

Jim knew what to expect and look for—he had fought Indians all his adult life—but Taylor and his brother officers, some little more than boys, were never to learn the finer points of Indian warfare. They never ceased to be thrown slightly off balance when the enemy crawled into trees, hugged flat along the brown boles, and poured fatal fire from behind the broad fanlike leaves.

The Battle of Okeechobee began shortly after noon on Christmas

Day, 1837. Sam Jones lay quietly on Taylor's left with almost 200 warriors; Alligator held the center with more than 100 Indians and ex-slaves; Wild Cat supported the right with nearly 100 breeds and half-breeds.

But they could not be seen. The palmetto screen was much too effective. And under these conditions, Taylor ordered Gentry and Morgan to lead the volunteers in a head-on attack.

How Jim Beckwith must have shuddered. He would not have attacked a dozen squaws in that manner.

Every Seminole laid his sights on a volunteer and waited. Waited until they were within sixty feet. Twenty volunteers fell; Gentry died with a bullet through his head; Jim said he was surrounded; the Missouri volunteers broke; Captain Taylor begged them to reform their lines, and Colonel Zachary Taylor rushed in the regulars.

Four hours later the Seminoles gave way, but Captain Van Swearingen, Lieutenants Brooke and Center, and Lieutenant Colonel Thompson were dead. In fact, every officer but one was either dead or wounded, and in the swamp at Okeechobee lay an additional hundred volunteers and regulars.

Jim Beckwith for once did little boasting and gave no lurid details beyond saying that the retreating Indians scalped a sergeant major and a private while they were still alive. He thought Army casualties were less than Taylor admitted, but agreed that the enemy left ten dead on the field.

The day after Christmas the Colonel buried his dead, made litters for the wounded, reassigned his forces to the several small posts, and returned toward Tampa Bay.

And became Brigadier General Zachary Taylor.[2]

"The action was a severe one. . . . it continued from half-past twelve until after three P.M. . . . We suffered much, having twenty six killed and one hundred and twelve wounded . . . ," said Taylor in his official report.[3]

"I could not see that O-ke-cho-be was much of a victory; indeed I shrewdly suspected that the enemy had the advantage; but it was called a victory by the soldiers, and they were the best qualified to decide," said Jim.[4]

After the battle Jim resumed carrying dispatches: Fort Brooke, Fort Bassinger, Charlotte Harbor, Fort Dade—all very routine and very, very dull. A scant year after his enlistment, he was back in

St. Louis—whether by permission or as a deserter is unknown. A week later he signed with the Vasquez-Sublette Company as a trader among the Cheyennes, Arapahoes, and Sioux on the headwaters of the Arkansas and Platte.*

Jim had journeyed almost full circle. Absaroka was just beyond the northern hills.

---

* It was Andrew Sublette who was in partnership with Louis Vasquez on the Platte. The partnership may have had some working relationship with Bent–St. Vrain. (See Robert Newell, *Memoranda: Travles in the territory of Missourie; travle to the Kayuse War; together with a report on the Indians south of the Columbia River*, ed. Dorothy O. Johansen, Portland, Ore., Champoeg Press, 1959, p. 58.)

40

OLD JIM

1840–1866

INDIAN storekeeping was a stale, flat life, and at the end of two seasons, about 1840, Jim turned up in the company of the Bent brothers, Charles and William. In partnership with the St. Vrains, Céran, and Marcelin, the Bents had entered the Upper Arkansas and Santa Fe trade as early as 1824, and by 1834 had built Bent's Fort on the north bank of the Arkansas eight miles downstream from the present La Junta, Colorado.

The post was supported by trade from lesser ones scattered among the southern Cheyennes and Arapahoes, and Jim said he was assigned to the Laramie Forks on the North Platte where his duties were only less boring than they had been with Vasquez and Sublette. True, some renegade caused enough trouble to compel Jim to exchange posts with another Bent employee until the trouble blew over but he was soon weary of even this much respectability, and he quit the Bent–St. Vrain Company.

The next several years of his life are impossible to verify. Jim told stories of going into business in New Mexico, making many journeys to Santa Fe, and revisiting the northern tribes; of a new marriage to a Spanish girl, participation at the Alamo before he joined Bent and St. Vrain, and heroics in the Bear Flag revolt; of being under suspicion as a horse thief (a not unlikely charge); of leaving California to avoid involvement in the Mexican War, while at the same time boasting of joining Kearny in the march from Missouri to Santa Fe to take that city without a shot; of serving Kearny on innumerable dispatch missions through dangerous Indian country; of constant trips over the Missouri–New Mexico–California route; of weeks of

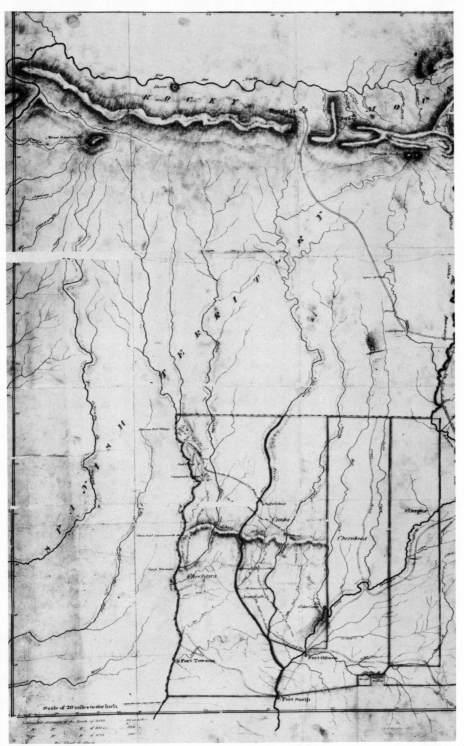

The Santa Fe–Fort Leavenworth and Red River routes as patrolled by the
Dragoons, 1833–1835. Map by Lieutenant E. Steen, 1835. *The National
Archives, Record Group #77, Q 14.*

Bent's Fort, an early undated engraving. *U.S. Signal Corps, Photo 111-sc-89567, The National Archives.*

The old palace of the governors, Santa Fe. *Museum of New Mexico, Santa Fe.*

idleness, chicken-stealing for fun, and horse-raiding for profit; and of bold rescues of Indian friends and the greenhorn military.

Very little of it is subject to verification. However, under date of July 9, 1842, John C. Frémont confirms that Jim was then employed by "Bent and St. Vrain's Company," and was being accompanied by a Spanish girl from Taos when Frémont found "two white men and a mulatto, named Jim Beckwith . . . in search of a band of horses that had gone off from a camp some miles above,"[1] near Bijou's Fork of the Platte.*

Jim was assuredly living somewhere in the West between the 1830's and the Civil War, and it would be absurd to assume he took no part in the great events of those years. As the fur trade declined, the mountain men changed jobs and locale. They became "guides, hunters, packers for the Frémont expedition of 1842–43. Others turn up as employees of Santa Fe traders, or as émigrés seeking a place for themselves in the confusion of revolt-ridden California."[2]

It is certain that Jim was residing on a ranch near Marysville on the Feather River, California, in 1855; apparently he was operating an immigrant stop on the route from Salt Lake to the Stockton–Sacramento Valley area via Beckwith Pass, which he had discovered on one of his wanderings.

But Indian trade and the immigrant inn business were equally stifling, and the years were catching up. He was "old Jim" now, and the great days were about gone. Although he was helpless to reverse time, he surrendered to his restlessness, sold out his Feather River holdings, and went once more to St. Louis.

But "I could find no St. Louis. I got lost in the streets and had to get a guide to lead me to my brother's house."[3]

In St. Louis Jim visited old Louis Vasquez, and was hired by him and his nephew, A. P. Vasquez, to accompany their merchandise train just leaving for the Vasquez store in Denver. They arrived in November of 1859.[4]

The Denver of 1859 was a shambling, whiskey-drinking, brawling mountain town of 1,000 souls more or less housed in some 300 pine log buildings with three-legged stools, pole bedsteads, and rough board tables as their invoice of furniture. An adobe hearth fronted a

---

* LeRoy R. Hafen and W. J. Ghent place Beckwith and two others "with their Indian and Mexican wives" at the site of Pueblo in 1842 (*Broken Hand*, Denver, Old West Publishing Co., 1931, p. 205).

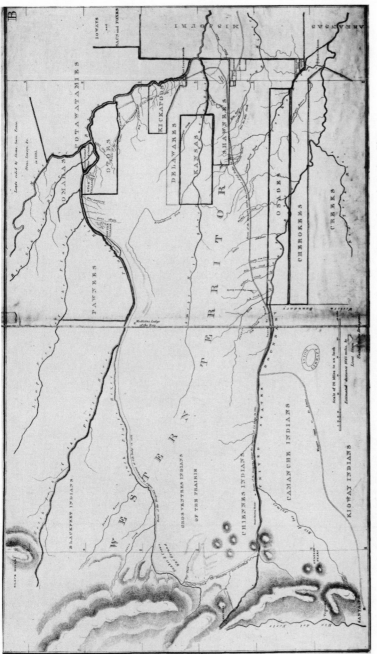

John C. Fremont's map of 1842–1844. The curious legend embracing the Sierra Nevada–Rockies and the Columbia–Colorado axes reads in part, "The Great Basin:... surrounded by lofty mountains, almost unknown but believed to be filled with rivers and lakes which have no communication with the sea, deserts and oases never... explored... savage tribes which no traveller has seen or described." In contradiction, the Spaniards and trapper-traders had visited parts of the area long before Fremont. *The National Archives, Record Group #77.*

Auraria and Pike's Peak, 1859. The A. P. Vasquez and Company store sign does not show. *Denver Public Library Western Collection.*

Larimer Street, Denver, at the time Jim Beckwith lived there, circa 1860–1870. *Denver Public Library Western Collection. Photo by W. G. Chamberlain.*

Wagon Train on Market Street, Denver, 1866, six years after Jim Beckwith left the city. *Denver Public Library Western Collection.*

mud-daubed fireplace, which poked its smoking chimney through a grass- and earth-covered pole roof to accent the new town.

Six years later, 5,000 ladies and gentlemen lived in a brick and stone city; paid $12,000 for valuable lots; visited a library with good books, pictures, and rich carpets; and enjoyed a piano concert while sipping after-dinner wine of excellent vintage.[5]

Three days after Jim's arrival in Denver, the following appeared in the *Rocky Mountain News:* *

Just arrived for A. P. Vasquez & Co., their Winter Supply of Goods, consisting in part of Nails, from 4 pennies up to 10s, Window Glass and

* According to W. H. H. Larimer, the first issue of the *News,* with William N. Byers as editor, came from the press April 23, 1859 (*Reminiscences of W. H. H. Larimer,* Pittsburgh, 1918, p. 143).

Glass Dishes, a large assortment of Queensware [no longer any necessity of eating out of tin], containing rare and curious pieces, new in this country; Groceries, Candles, Champaign and Catawba Wines [in lieu of strychnine whiskey]; Dried and preserved Fruits, Pickles, Sugar and Fresh Flour. In their selection, the outward person was not forgotten, a lot of Good Warm, Winter Clothing forms a part of their stock. Three Hundred Deer Skins, all of which they would exchange for the glittering ore, or coin would be taken sooner than miss a sale. A. P. Vasquez & Co., Auraria,* Nov. 28, 1859.

What a descent from the days of Absaroka!—standing behind a dingy plank counter, being obsequious, wearing civilized clothes; no knife flashing from a thong belt, no scalp dances, no full-breasted wives with fresh bear grease in their hair to warm his sleep. Indeed, Jim was getting old.

But, Jim Beckwith never went unnoticed. One day a stage with almost $50,000 in gold dust was readying to leave for the Missouri:

A motley crowd awaits the departure. Here is a well-formed elderly man, with a devil-may-care expression, but a face full of character and wonderful perceptive faculties; long black hair, complexion like a Mexican, and eyes like an Indian. It is James P. Beckwourth, the half-breed, so long a chief among the Crow tribe, and the most famous Indian fighter of his generation. His body is scarred from wounds. . . . But he is the very pink of courtesy, and specially devoted to a comely young wife whom he invariably dignifies with the title of "Lady Beckwourth."†[6]

Sometimes the Cheyennes and Arapahoes came to buy and talk over the old days; once Jim fed several of them who were hungry, and registered a tribal complaint for them with the Indian agent; and once, too, he publicly and therefore bravely sided with a group of his friends who were set upon by a gang of white ruffians on the streets of Denver.

But with it all, by 1860 storekeeping palled as had all the rest of civilization, and when Vasquez asked him to manage a farm a few

---

* Auraria and Denver, rival townsites, were on opposite sides of Cherry Creek where it empties into the South Platte.

† Probably Elizabeth Lettbetter, daughter of the town's leading laundress, who did her best to make Jim happy but failed and dropped from his life without further record.

miles above Denver, he accepted. But a year later he was squatting on his own small holding just south of the town, doing a bit of placer mining, trapping a few beaver, and being waited on by Sue, Indian wife number—unknown.

Said W. H. H. Larimer, remembering his military service and business ventures in the Denver area:

Jim Beckwith was another frontiersman with whom I became acquainted in those days. Beckwith was a negro. I called on Jim and his bride in their cabin on the banks of the Platte River, a few miles up the river from Denver, in 1860. He had invited me there to eat 'possum with them. Jim had passed through many adventurous experiences, of which perhaps none was more thrilling or dangerous than that of his sixteenth year. It was at the "Massacre of the Alamo" that tragic event in the history of our southwest. It is said that only seventeen escaped the Alamo that fateful Sunday morning.

Mrs. Dickinson, (wife of Captain Dickinson) with her baby born in the Alamo, and known as the "Babe of the Alamo", succeeded in making her way to safety, and the daughter was still living in Austin, Texas, 1892. . . . The negro, a 16-year old valet to Colonel Travis, who went out behind Mrs. Dickinson on the horse, became afterward the chief of the Crow tribe of Indians in the Crow nation, and was known throughout all the western country by the name of Beckwith.

For a number of years he left the tribe and went to a place on Clear Creek near the present site of Denver. It was here that he married a colored woman and built him a house but afterwards returned to his old tribe, and remained until his death, about 1883. His widow Candelaria, at the extremely advanced age of 107 years, in 1892 still lived in her little adobe house in Mexican San Antonio.[7]

Now, Jim Beckwith probably was no more a hero at the Alamo on March 6, 1836, than he was in a hundred other tales, but he *just could have been*. Most assuredly Colonel William B. Travis was in command that morning; certainly Mrs. Dickinson did escape with her infant girl and a Negro servant; and there is enough unverified time between Jim's renunciation of Absaroka and his almost positive service in the Seminole War to permit him to dash off to San Antonio, attach himself to Colonel Travis, and help Mrs. Dickinson escape.

Some errors in the story are obvious, others probable. Jim went to the Crows before the Alamo, not after; he was nearer forty than six-teen that tragic morning; few historians will accept his number of escapees; and the presently known facts do not indicate he spent his last years with the Crows, although he may have died among them—but if so, it was long before 1883.

As for Candelaria—who knows? Perhaps she was the Spanish girl authenticated by Frémont.

Fragments of fact do appear here and there. Once Jim Bridger wrote to Beckwith, probably about a gold strike in Montana; once Beckwith believed he might receive a commission from the Union when the Civil War touched the fringes of the West; often a dozen tepees cluttered his dooryard while the only friends he ever held fast came to visit; and in August of 1864, he was tried and acquitted of the murder of one Nigger Bill. Self-defense, said the jury, and the *Rocky Mountain News* reported the decision in a scant eight lines of type.

Jim Beckwith was now sixty-six by his count of the years. And if it was fitting that he who, just perhaps, was the greatest Indian fighter of them all should once more hear the death chants and see the tawny bodies writhe, it is regrettable that it should have been in association with one of the half-dozen most dastardly and execrable actions ever perpetrated by the United States Army.

By late in November of 1864, the passions and hates of the Civil War had spread westward, where the Indian, understanding little of the events east of the Mississippi, had nevertheless become a prime target for those whose frenzy fed on blood. The red man must be exterminated. And make no mistake about it—the racists and the military, with certain notable exceptions, were quite as willing to wipe the Indians from the face of the earth as their counterparts were willing to annihilate the Jews a scant eight decades later.

Twenty years before, John M. Chivington from Warren County, Ohio, had "got religion" and joined the Methodist church. He was a big, uncouth, profane man, harboring most of the evil tenets of racism and irresponsible militarism and practicing little of the Christianity which he so loudly professed.

After trying his fortune as a carpenter, he moved west and entered the ministry, in which occupation his warped mind found no conflict with his basic drives—love of a uniform and hate for the Indian. He rationalized the latter by boasting that he was pro-Union, antislave, and antirebel, be they red or white.

Chivington had taken part in the Kansas border troubles, following which he served two years as a missionary to the Wyandots and then a time as interpreter-guide for the Methodist bishops traveling about the West.

He moved to Denver shortly after the Fort Sumter clash and became presiding elder for the church in western Kansas and Colorado. He preached to the soldiers at the barracks, and they saw in this blood-thirsty elder a man they could trust, one who would never damn their profession or rebuke their sins. They asked him to become their chaplain. But John Chivington wanted blood, and the Army wanted ruthless men. He was made a major, then a colonel.

All during the Civil War, the struggle to force the Indians onto reservations had gone on. Treaties were made and broken with such regularity by both reds and whites that it was impossible for the few honest Indian agents to do more than keep the raids and revenge killings from bursting into full-scale wars.

In April of 1864 a white man complained that the Cheyennes or Arapahoes had stolen certain of his horses. Without much verification, the Army sent a young lieutenant and forty privates to recover the animals. The outcome was so inconclusive that the military seized the opportunity to send a Major Downing to administer proper punishment. He surrounded a sleeping village, killed and wounded more than fifty Cheyennes, and burned their lodges. The Indians sued for peace and were referred to the governor of Colorado, who promised them Army protection while he formulated an official answer.

Relying on military honesty, some 500 Cheyennes and Arapahoes encamped near Fort Lyon to await word from the governor.[8]

In the meantime, on the night of November 28, 1864, Colonel Chivington with 750 men and artillery moved stealthily along the west side of Big Sandy Creek in southeastern Colorado. It had been five days since Jim Beckwith had led Chivington and his men out of their barracks 200 trail miles north and west. It was cold, but there was no snow.

Forty years ago Jim would have found his duties as guide and scout purely routine. Tonight he was "old Jim"; his legs ached, his feet stumbled, and his eyes strained to see the track. Did the stars shed less light than they had when he was young? Was he really that old? It was no use. He could not see the trail this late November night.

Sighing silently, he turned his task over to the half-breed Jack

Smith.* Near daybreak Smith, presumably trying to stay a massacre, told an officer that the Cheyennes had been warned and had escaped. There were too many wolf-dog barks echoing across the frozen prairie, he said.

Find the Indians or be shot was Chivington's answer.

Jack Smith had little choice.

More than 100 Cheyenne and Arapaho lodges were just stirring as the dawn and Chivington topped the last rise of ground before the sleepy camp. A squaw mistook the tramp of cavalry for buffalo, but since those great beasts were not wont to carry banners or flash sabers in the sun, a principal chief ran up the Stars and Stripes and the white flag of surrender.

Chivington attacked.

Half-failing to believe the Army perfidy blasting through their tepee walls, the Cheyennes and Arapahoes attempted a confused defense.

Jack Smith's father, trading with the Cheyennes, streaked toward American lines, ran into a crossfire, and returned to the Indians. Outgunned and outnumbered, they tried to escape. Three-quarters of a mile upstream where the banks were high and narrow, they turned at bay.

A naked three-year-old boy scrambled wildly up the bank while a mounted soldier fired and missed.

"Let me try the ———, I can hit him," said another. A third trooper dismounted and fired.[9]

Officers lent their superior weapons to the sharpshooters to pick off those clutching at life up the steep banks. For four hours the Indians fought and died and clawed and crawled upstream. By noon the sport had become tiresome to the military, and two howitzers were brought up. At evening time the soldiers returned to the Cheyenne camp to loot, scalp, and mutilate.

Jack Smith, half-breed interpreter-guide, was shot.

Chivington made no effort to control the brutality. It was blood —raw, cruel, and savage. He loved it.

Three hundred lay dead: 150 warriors who had trusted a white

---

* John (Jack) Smith was the son of a John Smith and a Cheyenne girl. Smith, Sr., was an Indian trader and a close friend of Jack Jones (McGaa), who was one of the original members of the Denver Town Company. At one time the Smith and Jones families lived together in a small house during the early days of Denver. (See Larimer, *op. cit.*, p. 171.)

man's word, 150 women and children whose sin was a red-brown hide.

And Jim Beckwith was ashamed. His savage Crows had met the Cheyennes many times. But it had not been like this.

"Jim's final meeting with the Cheyenne was a great victory but he could take no pleasure in it. . . . Among such savages as the Crows the massacre of squaws and children had not been approved," wrote Bernard DeVoto.[10]

Washington made frantic efforts to hush up the disgrace, but a Congressional investigation brought out most of the sorry facts. The military denied there was a flag of truce and insisted they had attacked a hostile war party—conveniently overlooking the fact that no American Indian ever took his women and children on a war party.

Representative Loughridge made the accusation that "Some of the few captured children, after they had been carried many miles by the troops, were taken from the wagons and their brains dashed out." The military denied this atrocity too, but the denial was very much weakened when Lieutenant Cannon admitted that he knew of one child who had been "thrown into a feed box . . . and after being carried some distance, left on the ground to perish." * [11]

One more episode is vouchsafed Jim Beckwith. Not quite two years after the Chivington massacre, he signed a note for $93.70 in favor of Seth Ward, Fort Laramie. The note was never redeemed. Late in the summer of 1866, Colonel H. B. Carrington employed Jim Bridger, Henry Williams, and Jim Beckwith to visit the Crows on a conciliatory mission necessitated, at least in part, by Indian resentment against the Sand Creek Chivington massacre.

Jim never returned.†

His life ended, as had those of so many of the great interpreter-guides, with a legend. The legend begins by saying that his visit to

---

* Adverse publicity was the most severe punishment the military received. After the Civil War, Chivington moved to Ohio, tried newspaper work and politics, and failed in both. The Sand Creek massacre was not forgiven, and Chivington never repented.

† There is an apparent discrepancy here, for under the dateline of Fort Philip Kearny, December 9, 1866, Mrs. Margaret Carrington, wife of Colonel Carrington, says, "Lieutenant Bingham and Sergeant Bowers were buried today. Lieutenant Grummond conducted the Masonic services, assisted by Mr. Weston, Mr. Saunders, Mr. Beckwourth and others, while Chaplain White conducted the religious portion" (Margaret Carrington, *Ab-sa-ra-ka, Home of the Crows*, Chicago, Lakeside Press, 1950, pp. 225–226).

Absaroka was greeted with wide rejoicing. Throughout all the years, the Sparrowhawk People had kept track of the Enemy of Horses, Medicine Calf, Bloody Arm. They had no reproach for his wanderings, for they too knew the wild call of another day and another land. For many nights the celebrations continued, and for as many nights old Jim was entreated to resume his duties as Bloody Arm. But Jim had had a surfeit of blood and war, and prepared to return to Denver.

The Crows intended otherwise. Jim Beckwith had been mighty medicine. Under him Absaroka had attained heights beyond their dreams: more buffalo killed, more horses stolen, more scalps flying from the lodge poles, more miles of domain unchallenged by a foe. And so the Crows called the great warriors together, and a farewell feast of dog was prepared. The braves sat down in the order of their rank to count coups for a last time; the pipes were smoked, the speeches made, the steaming bowls passed.

Jim Beckwith ate, and died of poison, and remained forever in Absaroka[12] with "his precious amulet, a perforated bullet and two oblong beads, around his neck."[13]

The geography of the West as it was known at the close of the fur trade era.
The National Archives, Record Group #77.

EPILOGUE

A MERE two centuries separates the Age of Discovery from the Age of Space which engages the attention of the twentieth century. The voyageurs, the interpreter-guides, and the mountain men have given way to migrant laborers, scientists, and astronauts. Mandan towns and buffalo hunts have been diluted to nightclubs and pigeon shoots, and the grumbler complains that he would prefer the rhythm of the scalp dance to the blood of race riots.

The long roll of history must judge the comparative values of two eras so diverse as these. Each must plead its case before the backdrop of human experience. If the interpreter-guides could seldom read or write, neither did they depend on a consensus before daring to act. If the mountain men knew nothing of aerodynamics or metallurgical stresses, neither did they cringe before the hardships of their time. They maintained outsize egos and nourished them with a healthy respect for the imponderables of their world.

If the end of the mountain fur trade may be said to have closed the major exploration of North America, the dust from immigrant wagons and the roar of the freeways may be said to express the heart of a restless people—a people who invaded a frontier which contradicted all previous human experience. Millions have left old homes to seek new lands in peace or by war, but they sought to join or conquer an already organized society. The aqueducts, the forums, and the legions of Rome met the invading barbarians; the temples and the Zend-Avesta would have given pause to Alexander the Great; a society with courts and an organized economy challenged the invading Moors. Only on the New World frontier did man thrust his might against an unorganized wilderness. Excepting the restricted realms of the Aztecs, the Incas, and the Chibchas, here were no temples to desecrate, no courts to defy, no towns to burn, no domestic animals (save the half-wild dog) to relieve the drudgery of mass transportation. Here were no sources where food, shelter, or clothes could be bought or even stolen. No apothecary shops offered surcease from the aches of fevers and the stings of poisonous snakes. In fact, there were none of the attributes our forefathers had a right to expect when they set aside the ordered society of their European world and dared a new one.

Only in America could a Hernando de Soto wade into the swamps wearing velvets and slashed silks, pink on pink, confident that he would soon sleep on the golden bed of Ed Dorado instead of dying in the mud of the Mississippi. Only on this frontier could a Francisco Vásquez de Coronado tramp for a thousand miles and see nothing but the mirage of tomorrow. Only here could a Francisco de Orellana sail the mightiest river on the globe and hear no sound but the chattering of his ancestral simians.

If Matonabbee helped prove there is no Strait of Anian across this continent without in the least glimpsing the significance of his act; if the interpreter-guides and the mountain men gorged and starved, abstained and sinned, and explored and counted coups with no thought of the social implications of their lives, so too do their descendants in the Age of Space tear down the ancient concepts of a Happy Hunting Ground and the river Styx without in the least knowing where the new paths lead.

It is the heritage of an unquiet people, but a people who need not blush for that unrest; for they have offered and given more than any civilization since the days of Greece and Rome. Nor need they fabricate excuses for those giants who helped make it all possible—the breeds and half-breeds, men with fallible flesh and earthy minds, but giants cast from giant molds for all of that.

SOURCE NOTES

Prologue

1. Robert E. Pinkerton, *Hudson's Bay Company,* New York, Henry Holt & Co., 1931, pp. 230 ff. Pinkerton's interpretation of frontier and fur company history is sometimes in dispute. Nevertheless, he represents one school of opinion and is cited in this volume as such.

2. W. J. Ghent, *The Road to Oregon,* New York, Tudor Publishing Co., 1934, pp. 2–3.

3. Clarence A. Vandiveer, *The Fur Trade and Early Western Exploration,* Cleveland, Arthur H. Clark Co., 1929, p. 267.

4. Alexander Ross, *Adventures of the First Settlers on the Oregon or Columbia River,* London, Smith, Elder & Co., 1849, p. 173.

5. T. D. Bonner, *The Life and Adventures of James P. Beckwourth,* New York, Alfred A. Knopf, 1931, p. 144.

6. Elliot Coues, *New Light on the Early History of the Greater Northwest,* 3 vols., New York, Francis P. Harper, 1897, I, 416.

7. David Thompson, *David Thompson's Narrative of His Explorations in Western America, 1784–1812,* ed. J. B. Tyrrell, Toronto, Champlain Society, 1916, p. 107.

8. Pinkerton, *op. cit.,* p. 231.

9. Ross, *op. cit.,* p. 12.

10. *Ibid.,* pp. 176ff.

11. Evan Jones, *The Minnesota, Forgotten River,* New York, Holt, Rinehart & Winston, 1962, p. 23.

12. Hiram Martin Chittenden, *The American Fur Trade of the Far West,* 3 vols., New York, Francis P. Harper, 1902, I, 57n.

13. Andrew Graham, "Extract from a Letter of Andrew Graham, Master at York Fort, to the Governor and Committee of the Hudson's Bay Company, Dated York Fort, August 26, 1772," in W. S. Wallace, ed., *Documents Relating to the North West Company,* Toronto, Champlain Society, 1934, p. 43.

14. Pinkerton, *op. cit.,* p. 236.

15. Coues, *op. cit.,* I, 426, 426n.

16. George A. Custer, *My Life on the Plains,* Chicago, R. R. Donnelley & Sons, 1952, pp. 233–234.

17. William H. Prescott, *History of the Conquest of Mexico,* 2 vols., London, George Routledge & Sons, 1843, I, 245. See also Bernal Diaz del Castillo, *The Bernal Diaz Chronicles,* ed. Albert Idell, New York, Doubleday & Co., 1956, pp. 245 ff.

18. Hector Charles Cameron, *Sir Joseph Banks,* London, Batchworth Press, 1952, p. 26n.

19. Custer, *op. cit.,* pp. 255–256.

20. Thompson, *op. cit.,* pp. 230 ff.

21. Leroy R. Hafen and W. J. Ghent, *Broken Hand,* Denver, Old West Publishing Company, 1931, pp. 280–281. See also H. R. Lemly, "Among the Arrapahoes," *Harper's Magazine,* March, 1880, p. 494; and H. G. Nickerson, *Indian Depredations in Sweetwater County,* ed. R. C. Morris, Cheyenne, Wyoming Historical Society Collections, 1897, I, 182.

Chapter 1. The Search for the Strait of Anian

1. C. C. A. Gosch, *Danish Arctic Expeditions, 1605–1620,* London, Hakluyt Society, 1897, pp. 33, 34n.

2. *Ibid.,* p. 47.

3. *Ibid.,* p. 48.

4. *Ibid.,* pp. 48–49.

5. The full details of the winter on the Churchill River will be found in Jens Munk, *Navigatio Septentrionalis,* Copenhagen, Henry Waldkirch, 1624.

Chapter 2. The Hudson's Bay Company

1. Hector Charles Cameron, *Sir Joseph Banks,* London, Batchworth Press, 1952, p. xix.

2. Robert E. Pinkerton, *Hudson's Bay Company,* New York, Henry Holt & Co., .1931, p. 57.

3. *Ibid.,* pp. 54–55.

4. *Ibid.,* p. 64.

5. James Isham, *James Isham's Observations on Hudson's Bay, 1743, and Notes and Observations on a Book Entitled 'A Voyage to Hudsons Bay in the Dobbs Galley, 1749,'* ed. E. E. Rich, Toronto, Champlain Society, 1949, p. xlix.

6. *Ibid.,* p. lxii.

7. Henry Ellis, *A Voyage to Hudson's Bay, by the Dobbs Galley and California, in Years 1746 and 1747. For Discovering a Northwest Passage,* London, H. Whitridge, 1748, p. 258.

8. Isham, *op. cit.,* p. xcv.

Chapter 3. Matonabbee and Samuel Hearne

1. Samuel Hearne, *A Journey from Prince of Wales's Fort in Hudson's Bay to the Northern Ocean in the Years 1769, 1770, 1771, and 1772,* ed. J. B. Tyrrell, Toronto, Champlain Society, 1911, pp. 325–326, 329.

2. *Ibid.,* p. 312.

3. *Ibid.,* p. 59.

4. *Ibid.,* p. 102.

Chapter 4. The Third Coppermine Expedition

1. Beckles Willson, *The Great Company,* New York, Dodd, Mead & Co., 1906, p. 305.

2. Samuel Hearne, *A Journey from Prince of Wales's Fort in Hudson's Bay to the Northern Ocean in the Years 1769, 1770, 1771, and 1772,* ed. J. B. Tyrrell, Toronto, Champlain Society, 1911, p. 110.

3. *Ibid.,* pp. 111–112.

4. *Ibid.,* p. 112.

5. *Ibid.,* p. 118.

6. *Ibid.,* p. 305.

7. *Ibid.,* p. 306.

8. *Ibid.,* p. 307.

Chapter 5. Matonabbee and His Wives

1. John M. Cooper, *Analytical and Critical Bibliography of the Tribes of Tierra Del Fuego and Adjacent Territory,* Washington, D.C., Smithsonian Institution, Bureau of American Ethnology, 1917, p. 63:171. See also Ales Hrdlicka, *Physiological and Medical Observations,* Washington, D.C., Smithsonian Institution, Bureau of American Ethnology, 1908, pp. 34:163 ff.

2. James Isham, *James Isham's Observations on Hudson's Bay, 1743, and Notes and Observations on a Book Entitled 'A Voyage to Hudsons Bay in the Dobbs Galley, 1749,'* ed. E. E. Rich, Toronto, Champlain Society, 1949, pp. 79–80, 95.

3. Samuel Hearne, *A Journey from Prince of Wales's Fort in Hudson's Bay to the Northern Ocean in the Years 1769, 1770, 1771, and 1772,* ed. J. B. Tyrrell, Toronto, Champlain Society, 1911, p. 129.

4. Canadian Board on Geographical Names, Ottawa; 1958 letter to the author.

5. Hearne, *op. cit.,* p. 143.

6. *Ibid.,* p. 140.

7. *Ibid.,* p. 141.

Chapter 6. The Coppermine River

1. Samuel Hearne, *A Journey from Prince of Wales's Fort in Hudson's Bay to the Northern Ocean in the Years 1769, 1770, 1771, and 1772,* ed. J. B. Tyrrell, Toronto, Champlain Society, 1911, pp. 149–150.

2. *Ibid.,* p. 172.

Chapter 7. But There Is No Anian

1. Samuel Hearne, *A Journey from Prince of Wales's Fort in Hudson's Bay to the Northern Ocean in the Years 1769, 1770, 1771, and 1772,* ed. J. B. Tyrrell, Toronto, Champlain Society, 1911, pp. 175–176.

2. *Ibid.,* p. 178.

3. *Ibid.,* p. 179.

4. *Ibid.,* p. 180.

5. *Ibid.,* p. 182.

6. *Ibid.,* p. 295.

7. *Ibid.,* p. 194.

8. J. B. Tyrrell, *The Coppermine Country,* Toronto, Champlain Society, 1912, p. 29.

9. Hearne, *op. cit.,* p. 206.

Chapter 8. The Return to the Churchill

1. Samuel Hearne, *A Journey from Prince of Wales's Fort in Hudson's*

Bay to the Northern Ocean in the Years 1769, 1770, 1771, and 1772, ed. J. B. Tyrrell, Toronto, Champlain Society, 1911, p. 234.

2. *Ibid.,* pp. 263–264.

3. *Ibid.,* p. 283.

4. *Ibid.,* p. 289.

5. *Ibid.,* p. 295.

Chapter 9. Suicide

1. David Thompson, *David Thompson's Narrative of His Explorations in Western America, 1784–1812,* ed. J. B. Tyrrell, Toronto, Champlain Society, 1916, pp. 9–11.

2. Beckles Willson, *The Great Company,* New York, Dodd, Mead & Co., 1906, p. 323.

3. Thompson, *op. cit.,* p. 11.

4. Robert E. Pinkerton, *Hudson's Bay Company,* New York, Henry Holt & Co., 1931, p. 109.

5. New-York Historical Society records say that Albert Gallatin, Colonial patriot and public official, met La Pérouse at Machias, Maine, and that the latter told Gallatin he had made publication of Hearne's journal a condition of his release. See Edward Weber Allen, *The Vanishing Frenchman. The Mysterious Disappearance of Laperouse,* Rutland, Charles E. Tuttle Co., 1959, pp. 153–155.

6. Samuel Hearne, *A Journey from Prince of Wales's Fort in Hudson's Bay to the Northern Ocean in the Years 1769, 1770, 1771, and 1772,* ed. J. B. Tyrrell, Toronto, Champlain Society, 1911, p. 334.

Chapter 10. Extra-Expeditionary Pursuits

1. Meriwether Lewis and William Clark, *Original Journals of the Lewis and Clark Expedition, 1804–1806,* ed. Reuben Gold Thwaites, 8 vols., New York, Dodd, Mead & Co., 1904–1905, IV, 298.

2. *Ibid.*, I, 18.

3. *Ibid.*, I, 4.

4. *Ibid.*, I, 20–21.

5. *Ibid.*, I, 9–10.

6. *Ibid.*, I, 62.

7. *Ibid.*, I, 85.

8. *Ibid.*, I, 190–193.

9. David Thompson, *David Thompson's Narrative of His Explorations in Western America, 1784–1812,* ed. J. B. Tyrrell, Toronto, Champlain Society, 1916, pp. 225–228.

10. *Ibid.*, p. 235.

11. *Ibid.*, p. 234.

12. Lewis and Clark, *op. cit.*, I, 189, 195.

13. *Ibid.*, I, 245.

14. Thompson, *op. cit.*, p. 235.

15. Patrick Gass, *Gass's Journal of the Lewis and Clark Expedition,* ed. James Kendall Hosmer, Chicago, A. C. McClurg & Co., 1904, p. 72.

16. Lewis and Clark, *op. cit.*, I, 279.

17. *Ibid.*, I, 227.

18. *Ibid.*, III, 123.

19. *Ibid.*, III, 125, 209.

20. Gass, *op. cit.*, p. 176.

21. Lewis and Clark, *op. cit.*, III, 240; IV, 16.

Chapter 11. René Jusseaume

1. Bernard DeVoto, Introduction, in T. D. Bonner, *The Life and Adventures of James P. Beckwourth,* New York, Alfred A. Knopf, 1931, p. xxvii.

2. Gordon Charles Davidson, *The North West Company,* Berkeley, University of California Press, 1918, p. 93.

3. Quoted in Elliot Coues, *New Light on the Early History of the Greater Northwest,* 3 vols., New York, Francis P. Harper, 1897, I, 333.

4. David Thompson, *David Thompson's Narrative of His Explorations in Western America, 1784–1812,* ed. J. B. Tyrrell, Toronto, Champlain Society, 1916, p. lxxiv.

5. Meriwether Lewis and John Ordway, *The Journals of Captain Meriwether Lewis and Sergeant John Ordway,* ed. Milo M. Quaife, Madison, Wisconsin Historical Society, 1916, pp. 21–23.

6. Thompson, *op. cit.,* p. 209.

7. Coues, *op. cit.,* I, 333, 401.

8. Meriwether Lewis and William Clark, *Original Journals of the Lewis and Clark Expedition, 1804–1806,* ed. Reuben Gold Thwaites, 8 vols., New York, Dodd, Mead & Co., 1904–1905, I, 233.

9. Thompson, *op. cit.,* p. 212.

10. *Ibid.,* p. 212.

11. *Ibid.,* p. 209.

12. *Ibid.,* p. 216.

13. *Ibid.,* p. 226.

14. Jusseaume to Jefferson, St. Louis, December 3, 1807; Thomas Jefferson Papers, Bixby Collection, Missouri Historical Society, St. Louis.

15. Instrument of indenture, René Jusseaume to Meriwether Lewis, St. Louis, May 13, 1809; Meriwether Lewis Collection, Missouri Historical Society, St. Louis.

Chapter 12. George Drouillard

1. For a recent characterization, see M. O. Skarsten, *George Drouillard, Hunter and Interpreter for Lewis and Clark and Fur Trader, 1807–1810,* Glendale, Arthur H. Clark Co., 1964, pp. 17 ff.

2. Hiram Martin Chittenden, *The American Fur Trade of the Far West,* 3 vols., New York, Francis P. Harper, 1902, I, 146.

3. Della Gould Emmons, *Sacajawea of the Shoshones,* Portland, Ore., Binfords & Mort, 1943, p. 164. Mrs. Emmons is a highly respected curator of the Washington State Historical Society and a recognized historian who has used the novel as the vehicle for her research on the Bird Woman.

4. Lewis to Clark, December 17, 1803; Clark Papers, Vooris Collection, Missouri Historical Society, St. Louis. See also Skarsten, *op. cit.,* Chap. 2.

5. Meriwether Lewis and William Clark, *Original Journals of the Lewis and Clark Expedition, 1804–1806,* ed. Reuben Gold Thwaites, 8 vols., New York, Dodd, Mead & Co., 1904–1905, I, 46.

6. *Ibid.,* I, 48.

7. *Ibid.,* I, 56–57.

8. *Ibid.,* I, 100 ff.

9. Olin D. Wheeler, *The Trail of Lewis and Clark,* 2 vols., New York, G. P. Putnam's Sons, 1926, I, 157.

10. Burton Harris, *John Colter,* New York, Charles Scribner's Sons, 1952, pp. 28–29.

11. Lewis and Clark, *op. cit.,* III, 339.

12. Harris, *op. cit.,* p. 80.

Chapter 13. George Drouillard and Manuel Lisa

1. Notarized statement of Ante. Dubreuil before Thomas Riddick,

Justice of the Peace, St. Louis, August 5, 1808; Missouri Historical Society, St. Louis.

2. M. O. Skarsten, *George Drouillard, Hunter and Interpreter for Lewis and Clark and Fur Trader, 1807–1810,* Glendale, Arthur H. Clark Co., 1964, pp. 252 ff.

3. Hiram Martin Chittenden, *The American Fur Trade of the Far West,* 3 vols., New York, Francis P. Harper, 1902, I, 119.

4. Burton Harris, *John Colter,* New York, Charles Scribner's Sons, 1952, pp. 88 ff.; see also W. J. Ghent, *The Early Far West,* New York, Tudor Publishing Co., 1936, pp. 118–119.

5. Harris, *op. cit.,* p. 89; Skarsten, *op. cit.,* pp. 260–270, 339.

6. Chittenden, *op. cit.,* I, 119 ff.

7. Skarsten, *op. cit.,* Chap. 24.

8. Olin D. Wheeler, *The Trail of Lewis and Clark,* 2 vols., New York, G. P. Putnam's Sons, 1926, I, 110–111.

9. Ghent, *op. cit.,* p. 120.

10. For a vivid description of this ailment, see Skarsten, *op. cit.,* pp. 287–289.

11. Harris, *op. cit.,* p. 149.

12. Chittenden, *op. cit.,* I, 146.

Chapter 14. Toussaint Charbonneau

1. Grace Raymond Hebard, *Sacajawea,* Glendale, Arthur H. Clark Co., 1933, pp. 115, 237; Patrick Gass, *Gass's Journal of the Lewis and Clark Expedition,* ed. James Kendall Hosmer, Chicago, A. C. McClurg & Co., 1904, p. xxxvi.

2. Olin D. Wheeler, *The Trail of Lewis and Clark,* 2 vols., New York, G. P. Putnam's Sons, 1926, I, 131.

3. Della Gould Emmons, *Sacajawea of the Shoshones,* Portland, Ore., Binfords & Mort, 1943, pp. 69–71.

4. David Thompson, *David Thompson's Narrative of His Explorations in Western America, 1784–1812,* ed. J. B. Tyrrell, Toronto, Champlain Society, 1916, p. 244n.

5. *Ibid.,* p. 234.

6. Emmons, *loc. cit.*

7. Meriwether Lewis and John Ordway, *The Journals of Captain Meriwether Lewis and Sergeant John Ordway,* ed. Milo M. Quaife, Madison, Wisconsin Historical Society, 1916, p. 196n.

8. Emmons, *op. cit.,* p. 71.

9. Meriwether Lewis and William Clark, *Original Journals of the Lewis and Clark Expedition, 1804–1806,* ed. Reuben Gold Thwaites, 8 vols., New York, Dodd, Mead & Co., 1904–1905, I, 217.

10. *Ibid.,* I, 229n; Hebard, *op. cit.,* p. 133.

11. W. J. Ghent, *The Early Far West,* New York, Tudor Publishing Co., 1936, p. 106.

12. Hebard, *op. cit.,* pp. 49n, 95.

13. *Ibid.,* p. 49n.

14. Lewis and Clark, *op. cit.,* VII, 111.

15. Hebard, *op. cit.,* p. 31n.

16. Lewis and Clark, *op. cit.,* I, 219.

17. Hebard, *op. cit.,* p. 49n; Stanley Vestal, *The Missouri,* New York, Farrar & Rinehart, 1945, p. 248.

18. Lewis and Clark, *op. cit.,* I, 275.

19. *Ibid.,* I, 285.

20. Lewis and Ordway, *op. cit.,* p. 196.

21. Lewis and Clark, *op. cit.,* II, 15–16.

Chapter 15. Across the Continent

1. Meriwether Lewis and William Clark, *Original Journals of the Lewis and Clark Expedition, 1804–1806,* ed. Reuben Gold Thwaites, 8 vols., New York, Dodd, Mead & Co., 1904–1905, II, 34.

2. Grace Raymond Hebard, *Sacajawea,* Glendale, Arthur H. Clark Co., 1933, p. 235.

3. For a discussion of these divergent views regarding Sacajawea's later life, see *ibid.;* W. J. Ghent, *The Road to Oregon,* New York, Tudor Publishing Co., 1934; John C. Luttig, *Journal of a Fur Trading Expedition on the Upper Missouri, 1812–1813,* ed. Stella M. Drumm, St. Louis, Missouri Historical Society, 1920.

4. Luttig, *op. cit.,* p. 138.

5. Lewis and Clark, *op. cit.,* II, 163.

6. *Ibid.,* II, 161–169.

7. *Ibid.,* VII, 108.

8. Meriwether Lewis and John Ordway, *The Journals of Captain Meriwether Lewis and Sergeant John Ordway,* ed. Milo M. Quaife, Madison, Wisconsin Historical Society, 1916, p. 239.

9. Lewis and Clark, *op. cit.,* II, 207.

10. *Ibid.,* II, 335.

11. *Ibid.,* II, 356.

12. *Ibid.,* III, 28; Stanley Vestal, *The Missouri,* New York, Farrar & Rinehart, 1945, p. 253.

13. Lewis and Clark, *op. cit.,* III, 291.

14. *Ibid.,* V, 319.

15. *Ibid.,* V, 327.

16. *Ibid.,* VII, 329–330.

17. Hebard, *op. cit.,* p. 89.

Chapter 16.   Charbonneau and the War of 1812

1. John C. Luttig, *Journal of a Fur Trading Expedition on the Upper Missouri, 1812–1813,* ed. Stella M. Drumm, St. Louis, Missouri Historical Society, 1920, p. 78.

2. *Ibid.,* p. 83.

3. *Ibid.,* pp. 84–85.

4. *Ibid.,* p. 106.

5. *Ibid.,* p. 128.

Chapter 17.   Charbonneau Goes to Santa Fe

1. Jules de Mun, *The Journals of Jules de Mun,* St. Louis, Missouri Historical Society, 1927, V, 175.

2. John C. Luttig, *Journal of a Fur Trading Expedition on the Upper Missouri, 1812–1813,* ed. Stella M. Drumm, St. Louis, Missouri Historical Society, 1920, p. 138.

3. Charbonneau's affidavit is reproduced in U.S. Congress, *American State Papers, Documents, Legislative and Executive,* 38 vols., Washington, D.C., Gales & Seaton, 1832–1861, IV, 210.

4. Dale E. Morgan, *Jedediah Smith and the Opening of the West,* Indianapolis, Bobbs-Merrill Co., 1953, p. 160.

5. De Mun, *op. cit.,* pp. 175–176.

6.   *Ibid.*, p. 180.

Chapter 18.   Charbonneau, Major Long, and Prince Paul

1.   Edwin James, *Edwin James's Account of an Expedition from Pitts-burgh to the Rocky Mountains,* Vol. XIV of Reuben Gold Thwaites, ed., *Early Western Travels,* Cleveland, Arthur H. Clark Co., 1905, p. 187.

2. *Ibid.*, pp. 204 ff.

3. *Ibid.*, p. 14.

4. Grace Raymond Hebard, *Sacajawea,* Glendale, Arthur H. Clark Co., 1933, pp. 94 ff.; John C. Luttig, *Journal of a Fur Trading Expedition on the Upper Missouri, 1812–1813,* ed. Stella M. Drumm, St. Louis, Missouri Historical Society, 1920, pp. 137–140.

5. Hebard, *op. cit.,* pp. 148–154.

6. *Ibid.*, pp. 150 ff.

7. Maximilian, Prince of Wied, *Travels in the Interior of North Amer-ica,* Vols. XXII–XXIV of Reuben Gold Thwaites, ed., *Early Western Travels,* Cleveland, Arthur H. Clark Co., 1906, XXIII, 203.

8. Charles L. Camp, *James Clyman, American Frontiersman,* San Francisco, California Historical Society, 1928, p. 38n.

9. Dale E. Morgan, *Jedediah Smith and the Opening of the West,* Indianapolis, Bobbs-Merrill Co., 1953, p. 375.

10. *Ibid.*, p. 385.

11. Hebard, *op. cit.,* p. 211.

Chapter 19.   Charbonneau and Maximilian, Prince of Wied

1. Dale E. Morgan, *Jedediah Smith and the Opening of the West,* Indianapolis, Bobbs-Merrill Co., 1953, pp. 78–79, 444.

2. Leavenworth to the Arikaras, August 14, 1823; South Dakota Historical Collections, *Official Correspondence of the Leavenworth Expedition into South Dakota for the Conquest of the Ree Indians in 1823,* Aberdeen, State Historical Society, News Printing Co., 1902, p. 193.

3. John C. Luttig, *Journal of a Fur Trading Expedition on the Upper Missouri, 1812–1813,* ed. Stella M. Drumm, St. Louis, Missouri Historical Society, 1920, p. 156.

4. Maximilian, Prince of Wied, *Travels in the Interior of North America,* Vols. XXII–XXIV of Reuben Gold Thwaites, ed., *Early Western Travels,* Cleveland, Arthur H. Clark Co., 1906, XXIII, 236n.

5. W. J. Ghent, *The Road to Oregon,* New York, Tudor Publishing Co., 1934, p. 13.

6. Grace Raymond Hebard, *Sacajawea,* Glendale, Arthur H. Clark Co., 1933, p. 97; Luttig, *op. cit.,* p. 137.

7. Maximilian, *op. cit.,* XXII, 345.

8. *Ibid.,* XXIII, 230.

9. *Ibid.,* XXII, 351.

10. See William Marshall Anderson, *A Horseback Ride to the Rocky Mountains in 1834,* Manuscript Collection, Huntington Library, San Marino, Calif.

11. Hebard, *op. cit.,* p. 105.

12. Hiram Martin Chittenden, *The American Fur Trade of the Far West,* 3 vols., New York, Francis P. Harper, 1902, I, 350; Maximilian, *op. cit.,* XXIII, 218.

13. Maximilian, *op. cit.,* XXIII. 221.

14. *Ibid.,* XXIII, 255n.

15. *Ibid.,* XXIII, 343.

16. *Ibid.,* XXIII, 282–283.

17. *Ibid.,* XXIV, 20.

Chapter 20. Toussaint Charbonneau Grows Old

1. Bernard DeVoto, *Across the Wide Missouri,* New York, Houghton Mifflin Co., 1947, p. 272.

2. Carl Russell Fish, *The Rise of the Common Man,* New York, Macmillan Co., 1927, p. 294.

3. DeVoto, *op. cit.,* p. 283.

4. Charles Larpenteur, *Forty Years a Fur Trader,* Chicago, R. R. Donnelley & Sons, 1933, pp. 117–119.

5. DeVoto, *op. cit.,* p. 134.

6. John C. Luttig, *Journal of a Fur Trading Expedition on the Upper Missouri, 1812–1813,* ed. Stella M. Drumm, St. Louis, Missouri Historical Society, 1920, p. 139.

7. DeVoto, *op. cit.,* p. 134.

Chapter 21. Pierre Dorion, Sr.

1. See Tesson to Delassus, August 4 through October 10, 1799; Pierre Chouteau Collection, Missouri Historical Society, St. Louis.

2. *Ibid.,* August 18, September 4, and September 18, 1799.

3. Washington Irving, *Astoria,* New York, Century Co., 1909, p. 202.

4. Meriwether Lewis and John Ordway, *The Journals of Captain Meriwether Lewis and Sergeant John Ordway,* ed. Milo M. Quaife, Madison, Wisconsin Historical Society, 1916, p. 85.

5. Meriwether Lewis and William Clark, *Original Journals of the Lewis and Clark Expedition, 1804–1806,* ed. Reuben Gold Thwaites, 8 vols., New York, Dodd, Mead & Co., 1904–1905, I, 129 ff.

6. Olin D. Wheeler, *The Trail of Lewis and Clark,* 2 vols., New York, G. P. Putnam's Sons, 1926, I, 93; W. J. Ghent, *The Early Far West,* New York, Tudor Publishing Co., 1936, p. 116.

7. William Clark, Indian agent at St. Louis, to General Henry Dearborn, Secretary of War, May 18, 1807; War Department Records, National Archives, Washington, D.C. Copy with the Missouri Historical Society, St. Louis.

8. *Ibid.*

9. Wheeler, *op. cit.*, I, 93–94.

10. Hiram Martin Chittenden, *The American Fur Trade of the Far West,* 2 vols., Stanford, Academic Reprints, 1954, I, 123.

11. *Ibid.*, I, 123.

12. Maximilian, Prince of Wied, *Travels in the Interior of North America,* Vols. XXII–XXIV of Reuben Gold Thwaites, ed., *Early Western Travels,* Cleveland, Arthur H. Clark Co., 1906, XXII, 318n.

Chapter 22.   Pierre Dorion, Jr., and Wilson Price Hunt

1. For a concise review of the beginnings of the Astorians, see W. J. Ghent, *The Early Far West,* New York, Tudor Publishing Co., 1936, Chap. 4.

2. Henry Marie Brackenridge, *Brackenridge's Journal of a Voyage up the Missouri River in 1811,* in Vol. VI of Reuben Gold Thwaites, ed., *Early Western Travels,* Cleveland, Arthur H. Clark Co., 1904, pp. 33–34.

3. Ghent, *op. cit.*, pp. 137–138.

4. John Bradbury, *Travels in the Interior of America,* London, Smith & Galway, 1817, pp. 102–103.

5. Brackenridge, *op. cit.*, pp. 106–107.

6. Bradbury, *op. cit.*, p. 103.

7. *Ibid.*, p. 103.

8. Brackenridge, *op. cit.*, p. 107.

9. *Ibid.*, pp. 107–108.

10. Bradbury, *loc. cit.*

Chapter 23. Lisa and Hunt Reach an Agreement

1. John Bradbury, *Travels in the Interior of America,* London, Smith & Galway, 1817, p. 113.

2. *Ibid.,* p. 137.

3. *Ibid.,* p. 145.

4. *Ibid.,* p. 125.

5. *Ibid.,* p. 131.

Chapter 24. Disaster

1. Washington Irving, *Astoria,* New York, Century Co., 1909, p. 163.

2. *Ibid.,* pp. 336–338.

3. *Ibid.,* p. 218.

4. Hiram Martin Chittenden, *The American Fur Trade of the Far West,* 3 vols., New York, Francis P. Harper, 1902, I, 206 ff.

5. Robert Stuart, *The Discovery of the Oregon Trail. Robert Stuart's Narratives,* ed. Philip Ashton Rollins, New York, Charles Scribner's Sons, 1935, p. 152.

6. *Ibid.,* p. 157.

7. See Barry J. Neilson, "Madame Dorion of the Astorians," *Oregon Historical Society Quarterly,* September, 1929, pp. 272–278.

Chapter 25. Baptiste Dorion

1. Robert Newell, *Memoranda: Travles in the territory of Missourie; travle to the Kayuse War; together with a report on the Indians south*

of the Columbia River, ed. Dorothy O. Johansen, Portland, Ore., Champoeg Press, 1959, p. 115.

2. W. H. Gray, *A History of Oregon,* Portland, Harris & Holman, 1870, p. 313.

3. John K. Townsend, *Narrative of a Journey Across the Rocky Mountains to the Columbia River,* Vol. XXI of Reuben Gold Thwaites, ed., *Early Western Travels,* Cleveland, Arthur H. Clark Co., 1905, p. 347.

4. Nard Jones, *The Great Command,* Boston, Little, Brown & Co., 1959, p. 162.

5. For a pro-White version of this quarrel, see W. J. Ghent, *The Early Far West,* New York, Tudor Publishing Co., 1936, pp. 319 ff.; and his *Road to Oregon,* New York, Tudor Publishing Co., 1934, pp. 58 ff.

6. Francis Fuller Victor, *Early Indian Wars of Oregon,* Salem, F. C. Baker, State Printer, 1894, pp. 44 ff.

7. "Dr. John McLoughlin to Sir George Simpson, March 20, 1844," Introduction by Katherine B. Judson, *Oregon Historical Society Quarterly,* September, 1916, p. 232.

8. Victor, *op. cit.,* p. 45.

9. Gray, *op. cit.,* pp. 312–313.

10. Jones, *op. cit.,* p. 271.

11. Newell, *op. cit.,* p. 153.

12. Ray H. Glassley, *Pacific Northwest Indian Wars,* Portland, Ore., Binfords & Mort, 1953, p. 10.

13. Newell, *op. cit.,* p. 124.

14. Jones, *op. cit.,* pp. 269 ff.

15. Gray, *op. cit.,* pp. 312–313.

16. "Dr. John McLoughlin to Sir George Simpson," *loc. cit.*

17. Victor, *op. cit.,* pp. 200 ff.

18. Barry J. Neilson, "Madame Dorion of the Astorians," *Oregon Historical Society Quarterly,* September, 1929, p. 275; see also *Dictionary of American Biography,* ed. Allen Johnson and Dumas Malone, New York, Charles Scribner's Sons, 1930, V, 379–380.

19. S. D. Durban and Francis Dupre, "Cayuse War," *Oregon Spectator,* July 27, 1848, p. 4.

20. Victor, *op. cit.,* p. 210.

21. Durban and Dupre, *op. cit.,* p. 2, and "Cayuse War," *Oregon Spectator,* April 6, 1848, p. 4; July 27, 1848, p. 2.

22. Newell, *op. cit.,* p. 99.

23. H. S. Lyman, "Reminiscences of Hugh Cosgrove," *Oregon Historical Society Quarterly,* September, 1900, pp. 266–267.

24. *Ibid.,* pp. 266–267.

Chapter 26. Ed Rose

1. Lyle Saxon, *Fabulous New Orleans,* New York, D. Appleton-Century Co., 1937, p. 108.

2. Marquis James, *Andrew Jackson, the Border Captain,* New York, Garden City Publishing Co., 1940, p. 337.

3. Otto A. Rothert, *The Outlaws of Cave-in-Rock,* Cleveland, Arthur H. Clark Co., 1924, pp. 172–199, 265n.

4. *Ibid.,* p. 199.

5. Charles L. Camp, *James Clyman, American Frontiersman,* San Francisco, California Historical Society, 1928, p. 40.

Chapter 27. Ed Rose Becomes a Mountain Man

1. Hiram Martin Chittenden, *The American Fur Trade of the Far West,* 3 vols., New York, Francis P. Harper, 1902, II, 654 ff; Clarence A. Van-

diveer, *The Fur Trade and Early Western Exploration,* Cleveland, Arthur H. Clark Co., 1929, p. 167; and Harrison Clifford Dale, *The Ashley-Smith Explorations and the Discovery of a Central Route to the Pacific,* Cleveland, Arthur H. Clark Co., 1918, p. 35n.

2. Burton Harris, *John Colter,* New York, Charles Scribner's Sons, 1952, p. 63.

3. Washington Irving, *The Adventures of Captain Bonneville,* New York, Society of English and French Literature, n.d., p. 133.

4. LeRoy R. Hafen and W. J. Ghent, *Broken Hand,* Denver, Old West Publishing Co., 1931, p. 31.

5. *Ibid.,* p. 31. See also W. J. Ghent, *The Early Far West,* New York, Tudor Publishing Co., 1936, p. 118; Charles L. Camp, *James Clyman, American Frontiersman,* San Francisco, California Historical Society, 1928, p. 40; Dale, *op. cit.,* p. 26; Chittenden, *op cit.,* II, 714 ff.; and Harris, *op. cit.,* pp. 72 ff.; 118 ff.

6. Horace S. Lyman, *History of Oregon,* 4 vols., New York, North Pacific Publishing Society, 1903, II, 279.

7. Robert Stuart, *The Discovery of the Oregon Trail. Robert Stuart's Narratives,* ed. Philip Ashton Rollins, New York, Charles Scribner's Sons, 1935, p. 285.

8. John C. Luttig, *Journal of a Fur Trading Expedition on the Upper Missouri, 1812–1813,* ed. Stella M. Drumm, St. Louis, Missouri Historical Society, 1920, p. 77.

9. *Ibid.,* p. 105.

10. Camp, *op. cit.,* pp. 41 ff.

Chapter 28. The Arikara-Ashley Fight

1. James Clyman, *James Clyman, Frontiersman, 1792–1881,* Portland, Ore., Champoeg Press, 1960, p. 14.

2. *Ibid.,* p. 14.

3. Dale E. Morgan, *Jedediah Smith and the Opening of the West,* Indianapolis, Bobbs-Merrill Co., 1953, p. 51.

4. *Ibid.,* p. 52.

5. Charles L. Camp, *James Clyman, American Frontiersman,* San Francisco, California Historical Society, 1928, p. 15.

6. Hiram Martin Chittenden, *The American Fur Trade of the Far West,* 2 vols., Stanford, Academic Reprints, 1954, I, 267.

7. *Ibid.,* I, 267.

8. Camp, *op. cit.,* pp. 16–18.

9. *Ibid.,* p. 18.

10. Morgan, *op. cit.,* pp. 65–66.

11. South Dakota Historical Collections, *Official Correspondence of the Leavenworth Expedition into South Dakota for the Conquest of the Ree Indians in 1823,* Aberdeen, State Historical Society, News Printing Co., 1902, p. 186.

Chapter 29. The Missouri Legion

1. South Dakota Historical Collections, *Official Correspondence of the Leavenworth Expedition into South Dakota for the Conquest of the Ree Indians in 1823,* Aberdeen, State Historical Society, News Printing Co., 1902, p. 212.

2. *Ibid.,* p. 189.

3. *Ibid.,* p. 193.

4. *Ibid.,* p. 215.

5. *Ibid.,* pp. 224–225.

6. *Ibid.,* pp. 225–226.

7. *Ibid.,* p. 228.

8. Charles L. Camp, *James Clyman, American Frontiersman,* San Francisco, California Historical Society, 1928, p. 21.

9. South Dakota Historical Collections, *op. cit.,* pp. 228–231.

10. *Ibid.,* p. 231.

11. *Ibid.,* p. 240.

12. *Ibid.,* p. 238.

13. *Ibid.,* p. 194.

Chapter 30. Ed Rose, Crow Chief

1. Dale E. Morgan, *Jedediah Smith and the Opening of the West,* Indianapolis, Bobbs-Merrill Co., 1953, p. 385.

2. Charles L. Camp, *James Clyman, American Frontiersman,* San Francisco, California Historical Society, 1928, p. 25.

3. *Ibid.,* p. 26.

4. *Ibid.,* p. 27.

5. Morgan, *op. cit.,* p. 89.

Chapter 31. The Last Decade

1. T. D. Bonner, *The Life and Adventures of James P. Beckwourth,* New York, Alfred A. Knopf, 1931, p. 379.

2. Washington Irving, *The Adventures of Captain Bonneville,* New York, Society of English and French Literature, n.d., p. 134.

3. Zenas Leonard, *Narrative of the Adventures of Zenas Leonard,* Chicago, R. R. Donnelley & Sons, 1934, p. 84.

4. *Ibid.,* p. 228.

5. Dale E. Morgan, *Jedediah Smith and the Opening of the West,* Indianapolis, Bobbs-Merrill Co., 1953, p. 319; and South Dakota Historical Collections, *Official Correspondence of the Leavenworth Expedi-*

tion into South Dakota for the Conquest of the Ree Indians in 1823, Aberdeen, State Historical Society, News Printing Co., 1902, p. 255.

6. Leonard, *op. cit.,* pp. 241–243.

7. Francis Parkman, *The Oregon Trail,* New York, Doubleday & Co., 1946, Chap. 10.

8. W. J. Ghent, *The Road to Oregon,* New York, Tudor Publishing Co., 1934, p. viii.

9. Morgan, *op. cit.,* p. 319.

10. Irving, *op. cit.,* p. 134.

Chapter 32. James P. Beckwourth

1. Judges 15 : 4–5.

2. Hiram Martin Chittenden, *The American Fur Trade of the Far West,* 2 vols., Stanford, Academic Reprints, 1954, II, 690.

3. Francis Parkman, *The Oregon Trail,* New York, Doubleday & Co., 1946, p. 106.

4. Bernard DeVoto, Introduction, in T. D. Bonner, *The Life and Adventures of James P. Beckwourth,* New York, Alfred A. Knopf, 1931, p. xxvi.

5. *Ibid.,* p. xxiv.

6. *Ibid.,* p. xxv.

7. Bonner, *op. cit.,* p. 5.

8. *Rocky Mountain News* (Denver), December 1, 1859.

Chapter 33. Beckwith Joins Ashley

1. Harrison Clifford Dale, *The Ashley-Smith Explorations and the*

Discovery of a Central Route to the Pacific, Cleveland, Arthur H. Clark Co., 1918, p. 115n.

2. For this itinerary, we are indebted to W. J. Ghent, *The Early Far West,* New York, Tudor Publishing Co., 1936, pp. 211–212.

3. Dale, *op. cit.,* p. 92.

4. *Ibid.,* p. 216.

5. *Ibid.,* p. 112; Bernard DeVoto, Introduction, in T. D. Bonner, *The Life and Adventures of James P. Beckwourth,* New York, Alfred A. Knopf, 1931, p. xxxii.

6. Bonner, *op. cit.,* p. 373; DeVoto, *loc. cit.*

7. Dale, *op. cit.,* pp. 90–92.

8. *Ibid.,* pp. 92, 116n.

9. Bonner, *op. cit.,* pp. 11–17.

10. Dale, *op. cit.,* pp. 90–92.

11. Bonner, *op. cit.,* p. 21.

12. *Ibid.,* p. 21.

13. Dale E. Morgan, *Jedediah Smith and the Opening of the West,* Indianapolis, Bobbs-Merrill Co., 1953, pp. 159, 160.

14. *Ibid.,* p. 161.

Chapter 34. The First Mountain Fair

1. W. J. Ghent, *The Early Far West,* New York, Tudor Publishing Co., 1936, p. 213.

2. For this segment of Ashley's trail, we are indebted to DeVoto's interpretation as expressed in T. D. Bonner, *The Life and Adventures of James P. Beckwourth,* New York, Alfred A. Knopf, 1931, p. 377.

3. Dale E. Morgan, *Jedediah Smith and the Opening of the West,* Indianapolis, Bobbs-Merrill Co., 1953, p. 165.

4. Bonner, *op. cit.,* pp. 35–36.

5. *Ibid.,* p. 37.

6. Morgan, *op. cit.,* pp. 166, 171.

7. Bonner, *op. cit.,* pp. 34, 36.

8. Morgan, *op. cit.,* p. 407.

9. Ghent, *op. cit.,* pp. 214–215.

10. Gordon Speck, *Northwest Explorations,* Portland, Ore., Binfords & Mort, 1954, pp. 348–349.

11. Morgan, *op. cit.,* p. 73.

12. Bonner, *op cit.,* pp. 48–49.

13. *Ibid.,* p. 53.

14. *Ibid.,* p. 56.

15. *Ibid.,* p. 57.

16. *Ibid.,* pp. 18, 380; Morgan, *op. cit.,* pp. 408–409.

17. For this itinerary, we have accepted Bonner, *op. cit.,* pp. 60, 380, and Morgan, *op. cit.,* p. 177.

18. Morgan, *loc. cit.*

Chapter 35. Jim Beckwith Becomes a Crow

1. T. D. Bonner, *The Life and Adventures of James P. Beckwourth,* New York, Alfred A. Knopf, 1931, p. 61.

2. Dale E. Morgan, *Jedediah Smith and the Opening of the West,* Indianapolis, Bobbs-Merrill Co., 1953, p. 181.

3. Bonner, *op. cit.*, p. 64.

4. Morgan, *op. cit.*, p. 228.

5. Bonner, *op. cit.*, pp. 72–73.

6. Morgan, *op. cit.*, p. 291.

7. Bonner, *op. cit.*, p. 75.

8. *Ibid.*, p. 66.

9. *Ibid.*, pp. 66–69.

10. *Ibid.*, pp. 97–98.

11. Morgan, *op. cit.*, pp. 305–306.

12. Bonner, *op. cit.*, p. 94.

13. *Ibid.*, pp. 90 ff.

Chapter 36. Absaroka, Home of the Crows

1. T. D. Bonner, *The Life and Adventures of James P. Beckwourth,* New York, Alfred A. Knopf, 1931, p. 112.

2. *Ibid.*, p. 169.

3. *Ibid.*, pp. 125–128.

4. *Ibid.*, p. 180.

Chapter 37. Jim Tires of Absaroka

1. W. J. Ghent, *The Early Far West,* New York, Tudor Publishing Co., 1936, p. 255.

2. For an accepted version of this theft, see Hiram Martin Chittenden,

The American Fur Trade of the Far West, 3 vols., New York, Francis P. Harper, 1902, I, 300 ff.

3. T. D. Bonner, *The Life and Adventures of James P. Beckwourth,* New York, Alfred A. Knopf, 1931, pp. 181–187.

4. *Ibid.,* p. 245.

5. *Ibid.,* pp. 252–253.

6. *Ibid.,* p. 257.

Chapter 38. Pine Leaf

1. T. D. Bonner, *The Life and Adventures of James P. Beckwourth,* New York, Alfred A. Knopf, 1931, pp. 140–141.

2. *Ibid.,* pp. 273–275.

3. *Ibid.,* p. 276.

Chapter 39. Beckwith Fights the Seminoles

1. J. S. Bassett, *A Short History of the United States,* New York, Macmillan Co., 1921, p. 467.

2. For this interpretation of the battle, we are indebted to Holman Hamilton, *Zachary Taylor, Soldier of the Republic,* 2 vols., Indianapolis, Bobbs-Merrill Co., 1941, I, 122–135.

3. *Ibid.,* I, 133.

4. T. D. Bonner, *The Life and Adventures of James P. Beckwourth,* New York, Alfred A. Knopf, 1931, p. 284.

Chapter 40. Old Jim

1. John C. Frémont, *Narratives of Explorations and Adventure,* New York, Longmans, Green & Co., 1956, pp. 119–121.

2. Robert Newell, *Memoranda: Travles in the territory of Missourie; travle to the Kayuse War; together with a report on the Indians south of the Columbia River,* ed. Dorothy O. Johansen, Portland, Ore., Champoeg Press, 1959, p. 21.

3. *Rocky Mountain News* (Denver), December 1, 1859.

4. LeRoy R. Hafen, "The Last Years of James P. Beckwourth," *Colorado Magazine,* August, 1928, pp. 134–135.

5. Albert D. Richardson, *Beyond the Mississippi,* Hartford, American Publishing Co., 1867, p. 186.

6. *Ibid.,* p. 299.

7. W. H. H. Larimer, *Reminiscences of W. H. H. Larimer,* Pittsburgh, 1918, pp. 208–209.

8. J. S. Bassett, *A Short History of the United States,* New York, Macmillan Co., 1921, p. 684.

9. J. P. Dunn, Jr., *Massacres of the Mountains: A History of the Indian Wars of the Far West,* New York, Archer House, 1958, p. 344.

10. Bernard DeVoto, Introduction, in T. D. Bonner, *The Life and Adventures of James P. Beckwourth,* New York, Alfred A. Knopf, 1931, p. xxxix.

11. Dunn, *op. cit.,* p. 374.

12. Hafen, *op. cit.,* pp. 138 ff.

13. Robert Glass Cleland, *This Reckless Breed of Men,* New York, Alfred A. Knopf, 1950, p. 345.

A SELECTED BIBLIOGRAPHY

ASBURY, HERBERT. *The French Quarter.* New York: Garden City Publishing Co., 1938.

BANCROFT, HUBERT HOWE. *Works.* 39 vols. San Francisco: A. L. Bancroft Co., 1871–1890.

BARKER, BURT BROWN. *The McLoughlin Empire and Its Rulers.* Glendale: Arthur H. Clark Co., 1959.

BASSETT, J. S. *A Short History of the United States.* New York: Macmillan Co., 1921.

BAUMER, W. H. *Not All Warriors.* New York: Smith & Durrell, 1941.

BECHDOLT, FREDERICK RITCHIE. *Giants of the Old West.* New York: Century Co., 1930.

BLACKER, IRWIN R. *The Old West in Fact.* New York: Ivan Obolensky, 1962.

BONNER, T. D. *The Life and Adventures of James P. Beckwourth.* New York: Alfred A. Knopf, 1931.

BRACKENRIDGE, HENRY MARIE. *Brackenridge's Journal of a Voyage up the Missouri River in 1811.* In Vol. VI of Reuben Gold Thwaites, ed., *Early Western Travels, q.v.* below. Cleveland: Arthur H. Clark Co., 1904.

————. *Views of Louisiana.* Baltimore: Schaeffer & Maund, 1817.

BRADBURY, JOHN. *Travels in the Interior of America.* London: Smith & Galway, 1817.

CAMERON, HECTOR CHARLES. *Sir Joseph Banks.* London: Batchworth Press, 1952.

CAMP, CHARLES L. *James Clyman, American Frontiersman.* San Francisco: California Historical Society, 1928.

CARRINGTON, MARGARET I. *Absaraka, Home of the Crows.* Chicago: R. R. Donnelley & Sons, 1950.

CHASE, DON MARQUIS. *Jedediah Strong Smith.* Crescent City, Calif.: Del Norte Triplicate Press, 1958.

CHITTENDEN, HIRAM MARTIN. *The American Fur Trade of the Far West.* 3 vols. New York: Francis P. Harper, 1902.

————. *The American Fur Trade of the Far West.* 2 vols. Stanford: Academic Reprints, 1954.

CLARK, WILLIAM. Papers. Voorhis Collection. Missouri Historical Society, St. Louis.

CLELAND, ROBERT GLASS. *This Reckless Breed of Men.* New York: Alfred A. Knopf, 1950.

CLUNY, ALEXANDER. *The American Traveller.* London, 1769; New York, 1770.

CLYMAN, JAMES. *James Clyman, Frontiersman, 1792–1881.* Portland, Ore., Champoeg Press, 1960.

COLNETT, JAMES. *The Journals of Captain James Colnett Aboard the* Argonaut *from April 26, 1789, to November 3, 1791.* Ed. F. W. Howay. Toronto: Champlain Society, 1940.

COOK, JAMES. *Journals of Captain James Cook on His Voyages of Discovery.* Ed. J. C. Beaglehole. Cambridge, Eng.: Hakluyt Society, 1955.

————. *Voyages of Captain James Cook.* London: Richard Phillips, 1809.

————. *The Voyages of Captain Cook Around the World.* Ed. Christopher Lloyd. London: Cresset Press, 1949.

COUES, ELLIOT. *History of the Expedition Under the Command of Lewis and Clark.* 4 vols. New York: Francis P. Harper, 1893.

————. *New Light on the Early History of the Greater Northwest.* 3 vols. New York: Francis P. Harper, 1897.

CROUSE, NELLIS. *The Search for the Northwest Passage.* New York: Columbia University Press, 1934.

CUSTER, GEORGE A. *My Life on the Plains.* Chicago: R. R. Donnelley & Sons, 1952.

DALE, HARRISON CLIFFORD. *The Ashley-Smith Explorations and the Discovery of a Central Route to the Pacific.* Cleveland: Arthur H. Clark Co., 1918.

DANIELS, JONATHAN. *The Devil's Backbone: The Story of the Natchez Trace.* New York: McGraw-Hill Book Co., 1962.

DAVIDSON, GORDON CHARLES. *The North West Company.* Berkeley: University of California Press, 1918.

DEVOTO, BERNARD. *Across the Wide Missouri.* New York: Houghton Mifflin Co., 1947.

DRAGE, T. S. *An Account of a Voyage for the Discovery of a Northwest Passage by Hudson's Streights to the Western and Southern Ocean of America.* London, 1748–1749.

DUNN, J. P., JR. *Massacres of the Mountains. A History of the Indian Wars of the Far West.* New York: Archer House, 1958.

DURBAN, S. D., and Francis Dupre. "Cayuse War," *Oregon Spectator* (Oregon City), April 6 and July 27, 1848.

ELLIS, HENRY. *A Voyage to Hudson's Bay, by the* Dobbs Galley *and* California, *in Years 1746 and 1747. For Discovering a North West Passage.* London: H. Whitridge, 1748.

EVANS, OLIVER WENDELL. *New Orleans.* New York: Macmillan Co., 1959.

FOXE, LUKE, and THOMAS JAMES. *The Voyages of Captain Luke Foxe* and Captain Thomas James in Search of a Northwest Passage in *1631–1632.* London: Hakluyt Society, 1894.

FRANCHERE, GABRIEL. *Franchere's Voyage to the Northwest Coast, 1811–1814.* In Vol. VI of Reuben Gold Thwaites, ed., *Early Western Travels, q.v.* below. Cleveland: Arthur H. Clark Co., 1904.

————. *A Voyage to the Northwest Coast of America.* Chicago: R. R. Donnelley & Sons, 1954.

FRANKLIN, SIR JOHN. *Narrative of a Journey to the Shores of the Polar Sea.* London: J. Murray, 1823.

FREMONT, JOHN C. *Narratives of Explorations and Adventures.* New York: Longmans, Green & Co., 1956.

FROST, D. M. *Notes on General Ashley, the Overland Trail, South Pass.* Worcester, Mass.: American Antiquarian Society, 1945.

GASS, PATRICK. *Gass's Journal of the Lewis and Clark Expedition.* Ed. James Kendall Hosmer. Chicago: A. C. McClurg & Co., 1904.

_____. *A Journal of the Voyages and Travels of a Corps of Discovery Under the Command of Captain Lewis and Captain Clarke, 1804, 1805 & 1806.* Pittsburgh: David M'Keehan, 1808.

GHENT, W. J. *The Early Far West.* New York: Tudor Publishing Co., 1936.

_____. *The Road to Oregon,* New York: Tudor Publishing Co., 1934.

GOSCH, C. C. A. *Danish Arctic Expeditions, 1605–1620.* London: Hakluyt Society, 1897.

GREGG, JOSIAH. *Commerce of the Prairies.* Norman: University of Oklahoma Press, 1954.

HAFEN, LEROY R. "The Last Years of James P. Beckwourth," *Colorado Magazine,* August, 1928.

_____. "Mountain Men," *Colorado Magazine,* September, 1933.

HAFEN, LEROY R., and W. J. GHENT. *Broken Hand.* Denver: Old West Publishing Co., 1931.

HAKLUYT, RICHARD. *Voyagers' Tales and Voyages in Search of the North-West Passage.* London: Cassell & Co., 1892.

HAMILTON, HOLMAN. *Zachary Taylor, Soldier of the Republic.* 2 vols. Indianapolis: Bobbs-Merrill Co., 1941.

HARRIS, BURTON. *John Colter.* New York: Charles Scribner's Sons, 1952.

HAWORTH, PAUL LELAND. *Trailmakers of the Northwest.* New York: Harcourt, Brace & Co., 1921.

HEARNE, SAMUEL. *A Journey from Prince of Wales's Fort in Hudson's Bay to the Northern Ocean in the Years 1769, 1770, 1771, and 1772.* London: A. Strahan and T. Cadwell, 1795.

_____.*A Journey from Prince of Wales's Fort, in Hudson's Bay, to the Northern Ocean. Undertaken by Order of the Hudson's Bay Company. For the Discovery of Coppermines, a North West Passage, in the Years 1769, 1770, 1771, & 1772.* Dublin: P. Byrne and J. Rice, 1796.

_____.*A Journey from Prince of Wales's Fort in Hudson's Bay to the Northern Ocean in the Years 1769, 1770, 1771, and 1772.* Ed. J. B. Tyrrell. Toronto: Champlain Society, 1911.

HEBARD, GRACE RAYMOND. *Sacajawea.* Glendale: Arthur H. Clark Co., 1933.

HOIG, STAN. *The Sand Creek Massacre.* Norman: University of Oklahoma Press, 1961.

HOLMES, REUBEN. "The Five Scalps," *Weekly Reveille* (St. Louis), July 17, 1848.

IRVING, WASHINGTON. *Astoria*. New York: Century Co., 1909.

ISHAM, JAMES. *James Isham's observations on Hudson's Bay, 1743, and Notes and Observations on a book entitled 'A voyage to Hudson's Bay in the Dobbs Galley, 1749.'* Ed. E. E. Rich. Toronto: Champlain Society, 1949.

JAMES, EDWIN. *Edwin James's Account of an Expedition from Pittsburgh to the Rocky Mountains*. Vol. XIV of Reuben Gold Thwaites, ed., *Early Western Travels, q.v.* below. Cleveland: Arthur H. Clark Co., 1905.

JEFFERSON, THOMAS. *The Writings of Thomas Jefferson: Being His Autobiography, Correspondence, Reports, Messages, Addresses, and Other Writings, Official and Private*. 9 vols. Ed. H. A. Washington. Washington, D.C.: Taylor & Maury, 1853–1854.

_____. *The Complete Jefferson*. New York: Duell, Sloan & Pearce, 1943.

JEFFREYS, THOMAS. *The Great Probability of a Northwest Passage*. London, 1768.

JONES, EVAN. *The Minnesota, Forgotten River*. New York: Holt, Rinehart & Winston, 1962.

JONES, NARD. *The Great Command*. Boston: Little, Brown & Co., 1959.

KEARNY, STEPHEN WATTS. *Journal of Stephen Watts Kearny*. Ed. V. Matt Porter. St. Louis: Missouri Historical Society Collections, 1911.

KIRWAN, L. P. *A History of Polar Exploration*. New York: W. W. Norton & Co., 1959.

KNIGHT, JAMES. *The Founding of Churchill*. Ed. James F. Kenny. Toronto: J. M. Dent & Sons, 1932.

LARPENTEUR, CHARLES. *Forty Years a Fur Trader*. Chicago: R. R. Donnelley & Sons, 1933.

LATROBE, BENJAMIN H. B. *Impressions Respecting New Orleans*. New York: Columbia University Press, 1951.

LEMLY, H. R. "Among the Arrapahoes," *Harpers Magazine,* March, 1880.

LEONARD, ZENAS. *Narrative of the Adventures of Zenas Leonard*. Chicago: R. R. Donnelley & Sons, 1934.

LEWIS, MERIWETHER, and WILLIAM CLARK. *Original Journals of the Lewis and Clark Expedition, 1804–1806*. Ed. Reuben Gold Thwaites. 8 vols. New York: Dodd, Mead & Co., 1904–1905.

LEWIS, MERIWETHER, and JOHN ORDWAY. *The Journals of Captain Meriwether Lewis and Sergeant John Ordway*. Ed. Milo M. Quaife. Madison: Wisconsin Historical Society, 1916.

LORD, WALTER. *A Time to Stand*. New York: Harper & Row, Publishers, 1961.

LUTTIG, JOHN C. *Journal of a Fur Trading Expedition on the Upper Missouri, 1812–1813*. Ed. Stella M. Drumm. St. Louis: Missouri Historical Society, 1920.

LYMAN, HORACE S. *History of Oregon*. 4 vols. New York: North Pacific Publishing Society, 1903.

MacLeod, William Christie. *The American Indian Frontier.* New York: Alfred A. Knopf, 1928.

Madariaga, Salvador de. *Hernan Cortes.* New York: Macmillan Co., 1941.

Maximilian, Prince of Wied. *Travels in the Interior of North America.* Vols. XXII–XXIV of Reuben Gold Thwaites, ed., *Early Western Travels, q.v.* below. Cleveland: Arthur H. Clark Co., 1906.

Merk, Frederick. *Fur Trade and Empire.* Cambridge, Mass.: Harvard University Press, 1931.

Mirsky, Jeannette. *To the Arctic.* New York: Alfred A. Knopf, 1948.

Morgan, Dale E. *Jedediah Smith and the Opening of the West.* Indianapolis: Bobbs-Merrill Co., 1953.

Motte, Jacob Rhett. *Journey into Wilderness.* Ed. J. F. Sunderman. Gainesville: University of Florida Press, 1953.

Nevins, Allan. *Frémont, The West's Greatest Adventurer.* 2 vols. New York: Harper & Brothers, 1928.

Ogden, Peter Skene. *Snake Country Journals.* London: Hudson's Bay Record Society, 1950.

Oglesby, Richard Edward. *Manuel Lisa and the Opening of the Missouri Fur Trade.* Norman: University of Oklahoma Press, 1963.

Paxson, Frederick Logan. *Last American Frontier.* New York: Macmillan Co., 1928.

Pennant, Thomas. *Arctic Zoology.* London: Robert Faulder, 1792.

Phillips, Paul Chrisler. *The Fur Trade.* Norman: University of Oklahoma Press, 1961.

Pike, Warburton. *The Barren Grounds of Northern Canada.* New York: Macmillan Co., 1892.

Pinkerton, Robert E. *Hudson's Bay Company.* New York: Henry Holt & Co., 1931.

Powell, E. Alexander. *Gentlemen Rovers.* New York: Charles Scribner's Sons, 1913.

Prescott, William H. *History of the Conquest of Mexico.* 2 vols. London: George Routledge & Sons, 1843.

Reed, Charles B. *Masters of the Wilderness.* Chicago: Chicago Historical Society, 1909.

Rich, E. E. *The Hudson's Bay Company, 1670–1870.* 3 vols. New York: Macmillan Co., 1961.

Riesenberg, Felix, Jr. *The Golden Road.* New York: McGraw-Hill Book Co., 1962.

Ross, Alexander. *Adventures of the First Settlers on the Oregon or Columbia River.* London: Smith, Elder & Co., 1849.

Saxon, Lyle. *Fabulous New Orleans.* New York: D. Appleton-Century Co., 1937.

Seton, Ernest Thompson. "The Arctic Prairies." *Scribner's Magazine,* November and December, 1910, and January and February, 1911.

SKARSTEN, M. O. *George Drouillard, Hunter and Interpreter for Lewis and Clark and Fur Trader, 1807–1810.* Glendale: Arthur H. Clark Co., 1964.

SOLIS-COHEN, B. "An American Search for the Northwest Passage," *The Beaver* (Winnipeg), 1943.

SOUTH DAKOTA HISTORICAL COLLECTIONS. *Official Correspondence of the Leavenworth Expedition into South Dakota for the Conquest of the Ree Indians in 1823.* Aberdeen: State Historical Society, News Printing Co., 1902.

SPECK, GORDON. *Northwest Explorations.* Ed. L. K. Phillips. Portland, Ore.: Binfords & Mort, 1954.

————. *Samuel Hearne and the Northwest Passage.* Caldwell: Caxton Printers, 1963.

STEFANSSON, VILHJALMUR. *Great Adventures and Explorations.* New York: Dial Press, 1947.

————. *Unsolved Mysteries of the Arctic.* New York: Macmillan Co., 1939.

STRONG, EMORY M. *Stone Age on the Columbia River.* Portland, Ore.: Binfords & Mort, 1959.

STUART, ROBERT. *The Discovery of the Oregon Trail. Robert Stuart's Narratives.* Ed. Philip Ashton Rollins. New York: Charles Scribner's Sons, 1935.

SWAINE, CHARLES. *An Account of a Voyage for the Discovery of a Northwest Passage.* London, 1768.

TABEAU, PIERRE ANTOINE. *Tabeau's Narrative of Loisel's Expedition to the Upper Missouri.* Ed. A. H. Abel. Norman: University of Oklahoma Press, 1939.

THOMPSON, DAVID. *David Thompson's Narrative of His Explorations in Western America, 1784–1812.* Ed. J. B. Tyrrell. Toronto: Champlain Society, 1916.

THWAITES, REUBEN GOLD, ed. *Early Western Travels, 1748–1846.* 32 vols. Cleveland: Arthur H. Clark Co., 1904–1907. Vols. VI (Brackenridge and Franchere), XIV (James), XXI (Townsend), and XXII-XXIV (Maximilian, Prince of Wied), *q.v.* above and below.

TINKLE, LON. *Massacre of the Alamo.* New York: McGraw-Hill Book Co., 1958.

TOWNSEND, JOHN K. *Narrative of a Journey Across the Rocky Mountains to the Columbia River.* In Vol. XXI of Reuben Gold Thwaites, ed., *Early Western Travels, q.v.* above. Cleveland: Arthur H. Clark Co., 1905.

TYRRELL, J. B. *The Coppermine Country.* Toronto: Champlain Society, 1912.

————. ed. *Documents Relating to the Early History of Hudson Bay.* Toronto: Champlain Society, 1931.

UMFREVILLE, EDWARD. *The Present State of the Hudson's Bay Company.* London: C. Stalker, 1790.

U.S. NATIONAL PARK SERVICE. *Soldier and Brave.* New York: Harper & Row, Publishers, 1963.

VANDIVEER, CLARENCE A. *The Fur Trade and Early Western Exploration.* Cleveland: Arthur H. Clark Co., 1929.

VESTAL, STANLEY. *Jim Bridger, Mountain Man.* New York: Morrow & Co., 1946.

————. *King of the Fur Traders.* Boston: Houghton Mifflin Co., 1940.

————. *The Missouri.* New York: Farrar & Rinehart, 1945.

VICTOR, FRANCIS FULLER. *Early Indian Wars of Oregon.* Salem: F. C. Baker, State Printer, 1894.

VINTON, STALLO. *John Colter, Discoverer of Yellowstone Park.* New York: Edward Eberstadt, 1926.

WAGNER, HENRY RAUP. *Apocryphal Voyages to the Northwest Coast of America.* Worcester, Mass.: American Antiquarian Society, 1932.

————. *The Rise of Hernando Cortes.* Los Angeles: Cortes Society, 1944.

WALLACE, W. STEWART. *The Pedlars from Quebec.* Toronto: Ryerson Press, 1954.

WHEELER, OLIN D. *The Trail of Lewis and Clark.* 2 vols. New York: G. P. Putnam's Sons, 1926.

WILLSON, BECKLES. *The Great Company.* New York: Dodd, Mead & Co., 1906.

INDEX

Boldface figures refer to illustrations

DATE DUE